Lost Chords and Christian Soldiers

IAN BRADLEY

Lost Chords and Christian Soldiers

The Sacred Music of Sir Arthur Sullivan

scm press

© Ian Bradley 2013

Published in 2013 by SCM Press
Editorial office
3rd Floor
Invicta House
108–114 Golden Lane,
London
EC1Y 0TG

SCM Press is an imprint of Hymns Ancient & Modern Ltd
(a registered charity)
13A Hellesdon Park Road
Norwich NR6 5DR, UK

www.scmpress.co.uk

British Library Cataloguing in Publication data

A catalogue record for this book is available
from the British Library

978-0-334-04421-5

Typeset by Regent Typesetting, London
Printed and bound by
CPI Group (UK) Ltd, Croydon

Contents

My sacred music is that on which I base my reputation as a composer. These works are the offspring of my liveliest fancy, the children of my greatest strength, the products of my most earnest thought and most incessant toil.

Preface and Acknowledgements

This is the first book-length study of the church and sacred music of Arthur Sullivan, justifiably described by an early twentieth-century musical historian who was not very keen on him as 'probably the most widely popular English composer who has ever lived'.[1] It is extraordinary that this part of Sullivan's output has never before been subjected to serious and comprehensive study. It encompasses two oratorios, a sacred cantata, three Te Deums, 61 original hymn tunes and 75 hymn tune arrangements, 26 sacred part-songs and ballads, 19 anthems and several other liturgical pieces. Among these works are ST GERTRUDE, written to accompany 'Onward, Christian Soldiers' and still one of the best known and loved of all hymn tunes, NOEL, the melody to which the popular Christmas carol 'It came upon the midnight clear' is universally sung in Britain and 'The Lost Chord', the best-selling sacred parlour ballad of all time.

Sullivan himself wanted to be chiefly remembered for his sacred music. He is not, of course, nor is he ever likely to be. The comic operas that he wrote with Gilbert will always be his most enduring legacy. However, his sacred work deserves to be much better known and appreciated. During his lifetime and for much of the century following his death, it was dismissed and, indeed, vilified by many of his fellow musicians and by critics as shallow, sentimental, secular and second-rate. Over the last two or three decades awareness and appreciation of the work Sullivan did without Gilbert has grown considerably. This is partly a consequence of the wider move away from the anti-Victorianism which afflicted so much academic and critical thought throughout most of the twentieth century. It is also more directly a result of the tireless advocacy and activities of the Sir Arthur Sullivan Society, which have brought many of his long and unjustly neglected works to public attention through performances, recordings and new editions.

This book is offered as a contribution to this process of rehabilitation and increasing public awareness. It is not a technical musicological study. Rather it attempts to locate Sullivan's church and sacred music in the context of its time, to explore the motives and the faith that led him to engage substantially in this area of composition and to assess its theological and spiritual impact and legacy. It offers a radical reassessment of the composer's own religious faith on the basis of a careful reading of his letters and diaries and an analysis of the texts that he chose to set and the way that he set them. It places his work in the context of Victorian sentimentalism, liberal Christianity and fervent patriotism and charts its popular and critical reception during his lifetime and through the twentieth century. If it leads some readers to discover Sullivan's sacred works for the first time and others, already familiar with them, to ponder more deeply their significance and influence, then it will have done its job.

Like most other devotees of Sullivan that I know, I was first drawn to him as a pre-teenager through the magical melodies of the Savoy operas. While my contemporaries clamoured to buy the latest Beatles' single, I saved my pocket money to collect the complete Ace of Clubs D'Oyly Carte collection. I saw my first Savoy opera at the age of 11, and Gilbert and Sullivan has been one of the main and most consistent passions of my life ever since. I have performed it over five decades, attended hundreds of performances, written three books and contributed to numerous radio and television programmes about it. Over the last 20 or so years, while retaining my love for the Savoy operas, I have also become increasingly interested in and captivated by Sullivan's rich corpus of church and sacred music, thanks in no small part to my involvement in the Sir Arthur Sullivan Society, and this has fuelled the research which finds fruit in this volume.

I should probably begin my acknowledgements with a nod to the Norwegian psychotherapist with whom I fell into conversation in May 2004 while walking across the island of Iona to St Columba's Bay. As we tramped over the rough boggy ground speaking mostly of spiritual matters but also of my passion for Sullivan's music, she suddenly stopped, turned to me and said in an intense and serious voice: 'I believe you are the reincarnation of Arthur Sullivan.' It was an uncanny experience. As a Christian, and indeed as a Presbyterian minister, albeit of the most liberal rather than the most bigoted and persecuting type, I do not believe in reincarnation, and I do not for one moment think that I somehow embody the soul of Sullivan come to earth again. I certainly possess none of his musical gifts. However, I do feel a strong affinity and empathy towards him and a mission to explain, promote and defend his work in the face of the torrent of criticism and abuse to which it has been and still is subjected. I have no recollection of the name of my walking companion and have had no further contact with her since that memorable early summer day. She deserves a word of thanks, however, for recognizing my fascination for and sense of closeness to Sullivan, both of which have been driving factors in the researching and writing of this book.

Much more lasting and substantial is my indebtedness to fellow members of the Sir Arthur Sullivan Society, who have been my companions and increasingly my friends in the exploration and enjoyment of Sullivan's sacred music over the last 20 years. I first encountered the Society when I was invited to speak at its conference in Cliff College, Calver, Derbyshire in 1992 on the subject of Sullivan's hymn tunes. I have missed few subsequent conferences and festivals and was deeply touched when I was nominated to be one of the Society's vice presidents in 2001. I have met nothing but kindness and generosity from the Society's officials and members, who have helped me with references, book loans and helpful comments in a wholly generous and selfless way, characteristic of Sullivan himself. I am particularly grateful to John Balls, Arthur Barrett, Vincent Daniels, David Eden, Robin Gordon-Powell, William Parry, David Stone, Ray Walker, Roger Wilde, Robin Wilson and Martin Yates.

Stephen Turnbull, the tireless and impressively knowledgeable secretary of the Sullivan Society, deserves my special thanks not just for many helpful suggestions and comments but also for reading carefully through the draft typescript of this book and pointing out mistakes. He has saved me from several howlers. In respect of any errors that remain, I can only plead like Pooh Bah for mercy and echo the words of Richard Shadbolt to Sir Richard Cholmondeley, 'My lord, 'twas I – to rashly judge forbear!'

I am also indebted to David Owen Norris, whose analysis of and enthusiasm for Sullivan's songs have been an inspiration and who has warmly embraced my advocacy of Sullivan as the possible composer of ST CLEMENT and supported it with musicological evidence. Scott Hayes, Sullivan's great-great nephew, and Katie Treherne, his great-great-great niece, have generously shared with me family letters and reminiscences. Peter Aitkenhead, Assistant Librarian at the Library and Museum of Freemasonry, assisted me in my research on Sullivan's freemasonry. I have benefited from Richard Cockaday's work in identifying and publishing Sullivan's hymn tunes. My good friend, Stephen Shipley, whom I fear I will never quite convince of the merits of Sullivan's sacred music, has helped me with sources and generous hospitality.

The staff of the Beinecke Library at Yale University made microfiche copies of Sullivan's diaries available to me, and Maria Molestina of the Pierpont Morgan library has been helpful in securing me access to his letters there. I would also like to record my special thanks to Dr Natalie Watson of SCM Press for her faith in this book, which in some senses forms a natural successor to my two earlier books for this publisher, *Abide With Me: The World of Victorian Hymns* (1997) and *You've Got To Have a Dream: The Message of the Musical* (2004).

Successive student members of the St Andrews University Gilbert and Sullivan Society, of which I have been honorary Life President since 2004, have been a constant joy and inspiration to me and it has been a delight to perform with them Sullivan's hymns, anthems, sacred part-songs and his oratorio *The Prodigal Son* as well as those equally spiritual numbers in the Savoy operas. In the words of one of our favourite and most full-throated choruses: 'Hail, flowing fount of sentiment! All Hail, All Hail, Divine Emollient!'

Things Are Seldom What They Seem: Changing Views of Sullivan's Sacred Music

My sacred music is that on which I base my reputation as a composer. These works are the offspring of my liveliest fancy, the children of my greatest strength, the products of my most earnest thought and most incessant toil.[1]

The above statement by Arthur Sullivan in an interview with the *San Francisco Chronicle* published on 22 July 1885 ill accords with his reputation as a lightweight dilettante, who prostituted his talents and his art for the undemanding but lucrative genres of comic opera and parlour ballads. It is, however, consistent with the view prevailing among his own descendants. Some years ago, I met his great-great niece at a graduation garden party in St Andrews, where I regularly lead student members of the University Gilbert and Sullivan Society in impromptu singing. I invited her over to listen to our somewhat raucous rendering of choruses from the Savoy operas composed by her illustrious ancestor. She politely declined saying, 'We were always told in the family that it was his sacred music that meant more to him.'

Perhaps the most moving testimony to the high regard in which Sullivan held sacred music comes in a conversation recorded while he was rehearsing Bach's B Minor Mass for the 1886 Leeds Festival. Despite being laid low with the kidney complaint that gave him excruciating pain for much of his life, he took infinite trouble over this work, which had hitherto been regarded in Britain as almost impossible to perform, and wrote an organ part specially for it. On one occasion during the rehearsal period, Fred Spark, the festival secretary, found Sullivan lying on his couch scarcely able to raise himself on his elbow. Speaking of the Sanctus, his whole demeanour changed, and he became quite animated, describing it as the grandest piece of music extant and declaring: 'I would willingly give up all I have ever written if I could produce one piece like that.'[2]

It is striking and surely significant that Sullivan's first and last compositions were settings of a biblical and a liturgical text respectively. At the
age of eight, he wrote an anthem setting the opening verses of Psalm 137,
'By the waters of Babylon', the manuscript of which is now lost. His first
published work, written when he was 13, was a sacred song, 'O Israel',
based on verses from the book of Hosea. His last finished composition
was the *Boer War Te Deum*, written when his strength was ebbing fast.
He devoted much of the last six months of his life to this sacred piece, con-
centrating on it to the detriment of his operetta *The Emerald Isle*, which
remained unfinished at his death.

So in a real sense, church music was Sullivan's first and last love. He
was schooled in it, first as a young boy at Sandhurst parish church, then
as a chorister in the Chapel Royal, where he loved singing anthems and
liturgical items, and subsequently as an organist in two London churches.
George Martin, organist of St Paul's Cathedral, who had commissioned
the *Boer War Te Deum*, wrote to *The Times* following Sullivan's untimely
death at the age of 58 in November 1900:

> Thus the lad who received most of his early musical education in the
> church, and who afterwards won such phenomenal popularity, not only
> where the English language is spoken, but in other countries, devoted
> his last effort to his Queen, to his Church and to his Country.[3]

This particular trinity was well chosen. Queen and country were undoubtedly close to Sullivan's heart – he was an unashamed monarchist and
patriot – but so also was the Church in which he had been reared and
for which he wrote so much glorious music. His obituary in the *Musical
Times* ended with a paean of praise to his work for the church, which it
described as being 'distinguished by a happy and original beauty hardly
surpassed by the greatest masters':

> His early upbringing in the school of English church music was of the
> greatest value to him in after years. His anthems are characterised by
> pure melody and dignified harmony. The same may be said, even in a
> more marked degree, of his hymn tunes, which are sung by worshippers
> of all denominations wherever the English language is spoken.[4]

Fulsome as it was, this tribute was considered insufficient and a subsequent issue of the *Musical Times* carried a substantial article on 'Sir
Arthur Sullivan as a church musician', prompted by concern that 'in the
many biographical notices of Arthur Sullivan that have recently appeared,

comparatively little attention has been paid to the church-musician side of his genius' and by the fact 'that the gifted composer returned to his first love – church music – in the last completed composition he has left'.[5]

Sullivan's earliest biographers agreed with these verdicts and portrayed church music as his first and greatest love. Noting how much he enjoyed the choir which he led at St Michael's Chester Square, his nephew Herbert, to whom he was effectively a second father, and his collaborator Newman Flower wrote:

> His later composing of church music proved how full was his understanding of religious thought in music. He once said that his music was really intended for the Church. Lying somewhere in his brain was an inexhaustible store of melody upon which he drew to express religion as no contemporary composer could express it, except perhaps Stainer and Gounod.[6]

Sullivan's church and sacred music compositions included two oratorios, a sacred cantata, three Te Deums, 61 original hymn tunes and 75 hymn tune arrangements, 26 sacred part-songs and ballads, 19 anthems and several other liturgical pieces. It is not, however, as a composer of religious music that he is now remembered. Rather, he is indelibly and almost exclusively associated with the Savoy operas on which he collaborated with W. S. Gilbert. His recent biographers have portrayed him as an essentially secular figure, without strong religious commitment or interests, and as a libertine pursuing a hedonistic lifestyle. His sacred music, when it is noticed at all, is castigated either for its vulgarity or its forced and dull religiosity. Sullivan's genius is seen to lie in his comic operas rather than in his anthems and oratorios. It has to be said that this was also the view of some of his more candid friends and contemporaries. Ethel Smyth, the most prominent female composer in late nineteenth- and early twentieth-century Britain, famously disappointed him by saying that she regarded *The Mikado* rather than *The Golden Legend* as his true masterpiece (page 140).[7]

Many of his biographers and critics are agreed in seeing Sullivan's collaboration with Gilbert, which first began with *Thespis* in 1871 and really got going when Richard D'Oyly Carte brought them together for *Trial by Jury* in 1875, as marking a turning point in the composer's career away from sacred music. For some it was a happy release which allowed his true talents to flourish. Writing in 1926, A. H. Godwin argued that Sullivan was in danger of 'drooping into a sentimental ecclesiastical composer, a pot-boiler of anthems and syrupy hymns', until Gilbert rescued him and 'focused his vision on the brighter, if not precisely the higher, things'.[8] Others took a rather different view of the composer's change of direction. The reviewer for the London weekly *Figaro*, commenting on the first night of *The Sorcerer* in 1877, expressed his disappointment 'at the downward art course that Sullivan appears to be drifting into'. Another review, in *The World*, remarked: 'It was hoped that he would soar with Mendelssohn, whereas he is, it seems, content to sink with Offenbach.' [9]

The most caustic comments about Sullivan's prostitution of his art through his involvement with musical theatre came from those associated with the so-called English Musical Renaissance. Joseph Bennett, who as chief music critic for the *Daily Telegraph* coined this phrase in a review of Hubert Parry's First Symphony, believed that Sullivan's abandonment of serious music, in fact, pre-dated his first meeting with Gilbert and was driven by social ambition and a craving for popularity. He wrote that as early as 1867 'Sullivan, who was already on the side of the angels as far as that position is assured to a church organist, drifted across to the butterflies, became a friend of Royalty, and a darling of the drawing-rooms.'[10] This view has been echoed by several biographers. Hesketh Pearson, for example, wrote that:

> Naturally lazy and genial, he was born for the salon, and the only criticism ever passed on him was that he had lavished on the salon (some said the Savoy) the gifts that were meant for mankind (some said oratorio) ... Apart from Sullivan's innate gift for composing light music, one of the causes of his early experiments in comic opera may have been his desire to give the dukes and princes on his visiting list the kind of entertainment they could understand and enjoy; for no sooner had he been acclaimed by grave critics as the chief hope of religious music in England than he started trifling with a giddier muse.[11]

The two leading composers associated with the English Musical Renaissance were agreed that Sullivan's collaboration with Gilbert signalled his departure from serious music-making into a world of populist drivel. Hubert Parry wrote after seeing *The Sorcerer*, 'I thought it the poorest flippant fooling I ever sat through ... it is cheap and second-rate altogether.' His biographer, Jeremy Dibble, comments 'rarely thereafter did Sullivan's music ever strike a note of sympathy with him'.[12] Charles Villiers Stanford just about brought himself to praise Sullivan's 1886 cantata *The Golden Legend*, for which Joseph Bennett supplied the libretto, but could not forbear from pointing out that having showed so much promise in his early sacred work, he had then squandered most of his life 'on a class of composition distinctly below the level of his abilities'. He continued in even more damning vein:

> It is natural, nay more, it is right that in the Paradise of Music, as in other Paradises, there should be more rejoicing over Sullivan's great and legitimate success, than over the works of the ninety and nine just composers who have remained uninfluenced (perhaps because untempted) by consideration of profit and popularity.[13]

It was almost certainly the machinations of the leading lights of the Musical Renaissance movement that led to the unceremonious ousting of Sullivan from his role as musical director of the Leeds Festival after 18 very successful years and his replacement by Stanford.[14] The mutterings against him reached a crescendo in the aftermath of his death when John Fuller Maitland, music critic of *The Times* and chief standard bearer for the English Musical Renaissance, penned an obituary castigating him for displaying 'the spirit of compromise' and 'deference to the taste of the multitude'. Maitland felt that Sullivan's sacred work in particular showed a fatal lowering of standards, the oratorios being 'lamentable examples of uninspired and really uncongenial work'.[15] Edward Elgar, a staunch defender of Sullivan who acknowledged a considerable musical debt to him, described this spiteful obituary as 'foul' and representing 'the shady side of musical criticism'.[16]

Several factors lay behind these attacks. In Fuller Maitland's case snobbishness undoubtedly played a part. He eulogized Parry and Stanford because they were upper-middle-class Oxford graduates. Sullivan, like Elgar, came from lowlier stock and was consequently despised. In the case of his fellow composers, as Stanford's remarks above show all too clearly, the sour grapes of envy and jealousy undoubtedly contributed considerably to the sullying of Sullivan's reputation. He made a great deal of money out of his comic operas and his parlour songs and was taken up by high society because of them. Sullivan's treatment at the hands of his critics and contemporaries is very similar to that meted out in our own day to Andrew Lloyd Webber, who is similarly accused of vulgarity, commercialism and prostituting his art. There are striking similarities in the lives, personalities and talents of these two composers. Both were schooled in the tradition of Anglican church music which they continued to love and cherish throughout their lives. Both grew up as the sons of accomplished musicians who made relatively little money and were themselves determined to profit from their music-making. Both were supremely gifted melodists and parodists who made their mark in the glittering world of musical theatre and escaped from the confines of their bourgeois upbringing to indulge their love of high society and high living. It was inevitable that their considerable fame and fortune would bring criticism from other more 'serious' and less successful musicians and composers that they had squandered their talents in vulgar populism.

Attacks on Sullivan continued for much of the twentieth century but changed somewhat in their focus. Criticism of him for spending too much time on theatrical froth and not fulfilling his serious youthful potential gave way to denigration of his sacred and church music for being dull, affected, insincere, vulgarly populist and over-sentimental. The tone was set by Ernest Walker, another enthusiast for the English Musical Renaissance, in his influential *History of Music in England* published in 1907. While acknowledging that 'Sullivan was, beyond all question, the most widely popular English composer of the nineteenth century' and that 'the comic operas written to the libretti of W. S. Gilbert made his reputation and form indeed his chief title to fame', he went on to pour scorn on his more serious works:

> We can never recollect without shame that the composer who stood for contemporary English music in the eyes of the world could put his name to disgraceful rubbish like 'The lost chord' or 'The sailor's grave' or, in what purported to be serious artistic work, sink to the abysmally cheap sentimentality of the opening tune of the *In Memoriam* overture or the 'O pure in heart' chorus in *The Golden Legend*; and indeed there is a pitiful amount of this kind of thing. The sacred cantata *The Martyr of Antioch* ... alternates between dullness and vulgarity, and sometimes attains both at once; while the more ambitious oratorio *The Light of the World* has hardly enough vitality even to be vulgar.[17]

The most sustained assault on Sullivan's church music came from the eminent twentieth-century hymnologist, Erik Routley. He did nothing to disguise his contempt, noting that 'none of Sullivan's church music anywhere rises above the second-rate', seeing it as distinguished by 'a shameless secularism' and identifying its predominant characteristic as 'dreariness'.[18] Routley attacked Sullivan from various angles, not all of them consistent. Writing in 1942, he saw Sullivan, as have many other critics, as being fundamentally too lightweight to write sacred music:

> Sullivan's genius was not in the least religious; it was too light for the graver themes. We can imagine the relief with which he escaped from his early occupation with church music, in which he was not at home,

into that wholly congenial field of light opera in which, along with his twin genius, W. S. Gilbert, he was to achieve his artistic immortality.[19]

Routley later developed a rather different and even contradictory thesis, arguing that Sullivan desperately wanted to write for the Church, but that he was inhibited and imprisoned by what he felt church music should be. In an article in 1949, he suggested that it was Sullivan's 'consuming desire' to write church music that destroyed his partnership with Gilbert. It led him to 'repudiate the best music he ever wrote', the Savoy operas, and to believe that in order to write for the Church, he had to unlearn everything he had done in his stage music and cultivate a kind of dreary dullness. 'To realize his vocation, he had to wrench himself out of the Savoy style into what he conceived to be a church style.' This went against all his natural instincts but it was what he thought the Church wanted. His genius, according to Routley, was for melody. In the Savoy operas that genius flowered, but it was something he felt that he must sacrifice when he wrote for the Church:

> Melody, having associations with the stage, must be severely limited. 'Religious' music was not melodic, but in the style of *The Lost Chord*, meditative. Religion needed from him not the boldness which melodic shape always carries, but the submission which a flat melody with shifting harmonies suggested to him.[20]

So there was a huge disparity within Sullivan's compositions: 'At the Savoy Theatre, artistic perfection; in church, halting technique and consistent ineffectiveness.' In Routley's view, Sullivan was a prisoner of Victorian attitudes – he found himself imprisoned and trapped in the dreary and the maudlin in his sacred music, because this was what he felt that the Church demanded. As a result everything that he wrote for the Church was artificial and mannered, meditative rather than melodic.

> The medieval synthesis between drama and the church would have saved him; the Victorian confusion compassed his musical and spiritual ruin ... In the middle ages a man could perform juggling tricks to the glory of God and the satisfaction of the church; in 1880 it was essential for such a man to dress himself correctly and sing very solemnly and warily in the key of F major.[21]

Other musicologists writing in the mid twentieth century echoed these themes. Gervase Hughes, in the first and so far the only book devoted to the study of Sullivan's music, published in 1959, launched attack after attack on his church and sacred compositions. Having dismissed the anthems, hymn tunes and part-songs as 'trifles' of no worth, he turned on the oratorios:

> It is in vain that we search the pages of *The Prodigal Son* for any sign of initiative; one of the first choruses is a setting of the words 'Let us eat and drink, for tomorrow we die', and as we wade through the rest of the work, half-submerged in a bog of conventional clichés, this strikes us as having been sound advice. *The Light of the World* is not much better.

The choruses in *The Golden Legend* were criticized for being 'in his worst Moody-and-Sankey tradition', the *Festival Te Deum* castigated for its brassy vulgarity and more than once Hughes delivered his damning verdict that Sullivan's entire corpus of oratorios, sacred cantatas and liturgical works should be allowed to 'rest in peace'.[22]

The assault on Sullivan's sacred music continued unabated in the 1960s and 1970s. In the context of a general attack on the Victorian hymn tune in 1967, Arthur Hutchings singled out Sullivan for his self-conscious and contrived religiosity:

> It is not in the deeply religious Dykes that one finds revolting sanctimosity but in the charmingly worldly Sullivan ... If he had not felt the need to be a different Sullivan on Sundays, he might have contributed something enduring to church music ... Sullivan's church music is best forgotten; from it we can but illustrate only the nadir of sanctimonious vulgarity.[23]

Kenneth Long, writing in 1972 about the history of English church music, pursued the same theme:

> It is sad that his creative life was torn between two irreconcilable ideals. On the one hand his genius expressed itself naturally in the way most congenial to it – the operettas: on the other, feeling somehow that such frivolities were unworthy of a musician and unbecoming in a gentleman, he yearned to excel in 'serious' music, especially sacred music. It is not surprising then that many of his sacred pieces seem merely an extension of the operettas; indeed, if Katisha were to make a dramatic entry (assisted by the Chorus) in several of his anthems, the effect would in no way seem incongruous. Actually it would improve most of them.

Long further dug in the knife by observing that 'Sullivan was one of those people (they still abound) who thought that so long as the words were sacred – or at least vaguely religious – their aura automatically makes the music itself sacred.'[24]

More recent musicologists, notably Nicholas Temperley, Nigel Burton and Richard Silverman, whose comments will be found at relevant points in this book, have been considerably kinder about Sullivan's sacred music. His recent biographers, however, including those fundamentally sympathetic to and admiring of him, have still tended to be dismissive about this aspect of his work. David Eden, for example, feels that Sullivan's exposure to the Anglican church music tradition as a boy inhibited his natural spontaneity and lyricism: 'Sullivan must have learned very early with Alexander Pope that dullness is sacred in a sound divine.' Eden also pursues another theme common to critics of Sullivan's sacred music, writing that 'As soon as he began to receive income from the theatre Sullivan virtually ceased to compose songs and church music.'[25] The implication here is that, far from having a vocation and natural bent towards church music, as Routley suggested, Sullivan simply took it up as hack work and ditched it as soon as he was able to earn money from more congenial compositions.

Underlying all these criticisms is a conviction that Sullivan's personality was essentially worldly and not in the least spiritual. However much he might want to write sacred music, it was somehow alien to his natural inclinations and that was why it was artificial and contrived. The hugely popular film *Topsy-Turvy* has encouraged the idea that Sullivan's natural and preferred milieu was the brothel rather than the church organ loft. Yet this seems to me a fundamentally false and flawed distinction. The fact was that he was at home in both environments. He had a deeply spiritual side to his character as well as an undeniably worldly one. It is instructive to explore the context of the interview to the *San Francisco Chronicle* that stands at the top of this chapter. He gave it during a visit that he made to California to see his closest relatives, the family of his beloved late brother, Fred. The day before his arrival in San Francisco, he was playing the organ at the Mormon Tabernacle in Salt Lake City, where the choir sang *The Lost Chord* and his setting of the hymn tune ST ANN. After giving the newspaper interview he went on a tour of what he gleefully called 'the vilest dens' of San Francisco's Chinatown. These activities bring out three central themes in Sullivan's life and character: his devotion and generosity to his family, his love of church music and his taste for rather racy and louche experiences. William Parry rightly points to other occasions when these different aspects of his personality are juxtaposed:

Sullivan's life is peppered with vignettes in which inner seriousness and spirituality and outer joie de vivre are delightfully juxtaposed. In the 1890s we find Sullivan providing the church music for the Queen at Cimiez while he was on one of his pleasure trips to the South of France; his diary for 1883 finds him grappling with a new church anthem for Novello at the same time as he was grappling with a mystery lady in the shrubbery; and it is particularly charming to find that, when late in life Sullivan took up racehorse ownership, one of his horses should be named after Cranmer, that great leader of the English Reformation. These are only trivial indications of the way in which the sacred and the secular could jostle together, but they should help us to remember that it was absolutely possible for Sullivan to lead a life in which a personal spirituality could co-exist with utter exuberance. We should not misunderstand that outward personality to mean that Sullivan was hypocritical, or that the inner religious feeling, while largely unexpressed, was not strongly felt.[26]

Was Sullivan a person of faith and religious feeling? This question is clearly crucial for assessing and understanding his church and sacred music, and it is one on which I have changed my own position significantly during the research and writing of this book. Nearly all of those writing about Sullivan's sacred music over the last 30 years, including those like myself who have been sympathetic and supportive towards it, have seen him as an essentially secular figure without any real Christian faith. We have taken our cue from what Arthur Jacobs wrote in his 1984 biography of Sullivan:

> His religion hardly went beyond a superficial conformity to the Church of England: neither on the threshold of death nor earlier in his mature years is there evidence of 'spiritual' guidance sought or offered. A strong family piety together with a deep commitment to friendship and to his art – these purely human values were, perhaps, enough.[27]

Jacobs described Sullivan as 'a conventional Anglican' in his biography, clearly implying by this term very little in the way of religious belief or commitment, as indicated in his further remarks on this subject in a radio interview in 1992:

> Sullivan conformed to the normal practice of someone who was brought up in the Chapel Royal and in a conventional home. He would have considered it to be very odd not to have been able as someone who

mixed in royal and official circles to take part in official church celebrations and so on. He set biblical texts. But there is no evidence that he
had any personal fervour. It is rather odd that even towards the end of
his life and even when he knew he was dying or about to die he did not
seek what we would call spiritual or church consolation.[28]

In my own first published work on Sullivan's hymn tunes in 1992, I
wrote of 'his own fundamental lack of religious belief and spiritual sensitivity' and suggested that 'in so far as he had a guiding philosophy it was
that of hedonism'.[29] David Eden wrote in similar terms in his penetrating
talk on Sullivan's Christianity at the Sullivan Society Conference in Ely
in 1995:

> I think we can conclude with some safety that he was a person for
> whom the inner life of Christianity had little if any meaning. There is no
> suggestion that he ever experienced the pain of separation from God, or
> felt that the burden of his sins had been lifted by the atonement. On the
> contrary he lived an almost completely secular life. His real religion was
> probably sun worship. ... if he had a cathedral at all it was probably the
> casino at Monte Carlo.[30]

I now feel that these remarks and judgements, not least my own, have
been inaccurate and misleading. Two factors have led me to change my
mind on Sullivan's religious position: sustained exploration and study of
his church and sacred music over the last 20 years in terms of its motivation, inspiration and context; and the experience of reading through his
diaries and letters. Observations and conclusions on the first of these factors permeate this book. The evidence of his faith from his letters and
diaries is more tentative and impressionistic, but it is there. His letters to
his family almost always concluded with the words 'God bless you.' They
do not read like a formulaic valediction but rather as considered, heartfelt and sincere. In a letter to his mother on her birthday in November
1857, he writes that he and his brother have been ruminating on what to
say to her and have settled on the words 'May God bless you and keep
you.'[31] In the face of death, his diaries and letters express the essence of
Christian hope and invoke the blessing of God in a way that is more than
perfunctory. When his beloved father died in September 1866, he noted
that what he found particularly hard was 'never to hear his cheery voice
saying, "God bless you, my boy"' and went on to reflect that 'although he
is gone for ever, perhaps he can look upon me and see all I do; and please
God I will try and never do anything that will make him turn away his

head and regret that he left me alone here'.[32] Following the death of his friend and mentor, George Smart, a few months later, Sullivan ended his letter of condolence to his widow: 'With *Him*, in whom I sought comfort lately in my own great trouble, You will I know find peace and happiness.'[33] His diary entries following the death of his beloved mother in May 1882 include the reflection 'I was alone in the room, alone that is with dear Mother's lifeless body. Her soul had gone to God' and the simple and moving affirmation 'God bless you, and take you to eternal rest.'[34] Perhaps most revealing of his Christian faith and hope is the letter that he wrote to his young nephews and nieces on the death of his sister-in-law Charlotte in 1885:

> Now, in your prayers night and morning, pray that your dear mother may have joined your father in God's eternal Rest, and that you all may lead such lives on earth, that hereafter you may be taken to where our hope is they are.[35]

This is surely more than just the conventional family piety that Jacobs suggests represented Sullivan's religion. These and other statements in his letters and diaries suggest a simple, trusting religious faith. They certainly do not display Sullivan as a fervent born-again card-carrying Evangelical Christian, and they do betray more than a hint of the Pelagian belief in salvation by good works that has long been seen as the besetting sin or heresy of the British. They are, however, emphatically not the utterances of a man of wholly secular or worldly inclination and without religious faith or spiritual sensibilities.

It is noticeable that these sentiments are expressed considerably more often in the first three decades of his life than in his more mature years. They are not wholly absent from the letters and diary entries that he wrote in his forties and fifties. His only surviving letter to his great love Fanny Ronalds, written in 1885, when he was 43, ends 'God bless you all', a blessing encompassing her parents as well as herself. His diary entries for 1892 include a heartfelt thanks to God for the completion of his comic opera *Haddon Hall* and a poignant reflection on the last day of the year: 'Saw New Year in; hoped and prayed that it might be a happier one for me than this last, half of which was lost through my illness.'[36] For the most part, however, he seems to have had less recourse to such prayers and blessings as he got older. Could it be that he gradually lost the simple faith of his childhood and moved into adult agnosticism in later life? There is no direct evidence for this. The reason why there are more expressions of religious belief in the diaries and letters of his earlier years may simply be because this was the period which saw two of the events which affected him most deeply in his life: the death of his father, which occurred when he himself was just 24, and the death of his brother which happened when he was 34. It is significant that these deaths directly inspired two of Sullivan's most spiritually charged compositions, the overture *In Memoriam* and the sacred song *The Lost Chord*. If these are the products of family piety, they are surely even more expressions of deep and profound spiritual yearning.

If Christian faith and hope played a rather larger role in Sullivan's life and outlook than has hitherto been acknowledged, then it remains accurate, I think, to see him primarily as a spiritual rather than a religious person. David Eden illuminates this well:

> It seems to me that there is in Sullivan both as a man and as a composer a quality one can only call spiritual. This quality is not Christian in the sense that it is not concerned with the dark night of the soul or the mystery of the incarnation. Nor is it pagan, as we currently use the term to mean orgiastic or violent. In terms of the Christian tradition it is prelapsarian. There is in Sullivan a beautiful quality of innocence and joy which belongs to childhood, or the time in the garden before Adam and Eve became acquainted with sin.[37]

This essentially spiritual quality of innocence and joy came out in Sullivan's appearance, his life and character. It was written all over his face, which was described by an American journalist in 1879 as one 'of wonderful nobility and sensitiveness, in which the slightest emotion plays with unmistakable meaning, with eyes which only the Germanic adjective of "soulful" would fitly describe'.[38] It was certainly and self-evidently there in his personality. Eden writes that 'everyone who encountered Sullivan noticed his lack of affectation and his modesty'.[39] They also noticed his extraordinary kindness and generosity. Edward Dicey, a journalist on the *Daily Telegraph* and *Observer*, who became a close friend and eventually served as his executor, wrote that 'no man I have ever known had so perfect a genius for kindness' and listed many specific examples of this trait in respect of friends, servants, casual acquaintances and members of D'Oyly Carte's opera company.[40] Scott Hayes, Arthur Sullivan's great-great nephew, has uncovered and chronicled the extraordinary generosity that he showed to his nephews and nieces after both their father and their mother died.[41] Henry Lytton, who first joined a D'Oyly Carte tour in 1884 and went on to be the company's leading patter man, described Sullivan as 'a warm-hearted Irishman, he was always ready to do a good turn for anyone'.[42] Even Stanford was obliged to acknowledge him as 'that genial composer'.[43] This generosity of character went with a fundamentally cheerful disposition and a love of life but it went further than this, having a spiritual quality, springing from a sense of belonging to a benign universe presided over by a gracious and forgiving God. David Eden characterizes it as a prelapsarian outlook, although it could equally well be described, I think, in rather less technical theological terms as benevolent deism or even more simply as liberal Christianity.

Perhaps Sullivan's involvement in Freemasonry gives us a clue to his religious beliefs and spiritual sensibilities. For the most part his biographers have ignored or dismissed this aspect of his life, suggesting that if it had any significance it was simply as a means of improving his social standing and advancing in society. After briefly alluding to his Freemasonry, Arthur Jacobs writes: 'membership of the order may have strengthened his social advancement at a time when the Royal Princes and other notables lent their name to it'.[44] It is certainly true that many well-connected and eminent Victorians were Freemasons, not least those involved in music and theatre. However, the record of his involvement with the Craft suggests that it was more than just a token or perfunctory matter for him.

Sullivan was initiated in the Lodge of Harmony, No. 255, Richmond, Surrey on the same day (11 April 1865) as his friend and fellow composer, Frederic Clay, who four years later first introduced him to W. S. Gilbert. Gilbert himself became a Freemason in 1871. Sullivan went on to progress through the Holy Royal Arch, one of the highest degrees and described as 'the perfection and completion of all Freemasonry', being exalted in Friends in Council Chapter No. 1383, London in July 1877, five months after Gilbert had taken the same step.[45] Both men joined the Rose Croix Chapter, the eighteenth degree within the Ancient and Accepted Rite for England and Wales, membership of which was open only to master Masons of at least one year's standing who professed the Christian faith and went through a series of mystical experiences expressing the figurative passage of humanity through the darkest vale, accompanied and sustained by the three theological virtues, before finally being received into the abode of light. Gilbert was perfected in Bayard Chapter Rose Croix, No. 71, London, in 1876, and Sullivan followed in 1878. In 1887, he was appointed Grand Organist by the United Grand Lodge of England, although he appears to have performed only once in this capacity at a special Grand Lodge held in the Albert Hall on 13 June 1887 in celebration of Queen Victoria's Golden Jubilee. In 1896, he joined Studholme Lodge, No. 1591, London. He also gave his name to the Arthur Sullivan Lodge No. 2156 in Manchester, which was consecrated in 1886.

It is surely significant that Sullivan involved himself in the rituals necessary for attaining the higher degrees 'beyond the Craft'. The standard work on these degrees points out that 'they are a vital means of teaching lessons in the value of such virtues as Honesty, Charity, Industry, Fidelity, Humility and such like'.[46] The three great principles of Freemasonry – brotherly love, charity directed both to one's own family and to the community as a whole, and the pursuit of truth – were all close to Sullivan's heart. I find myself echoing Meinhard Saremba's comment that 'Probably Sullivan's warm-hearted and generous personality contributed to an identification with some of the freemasons' ideals.'[47] I think one might go rather further and suggest that Sullivan's spiritual yearnings were also touched by Freemasonry, with its belief in a supreme being (without too much concern about the finer points of interpretation), its strong moral and ethical values and its romantic and chivalric connotations.

It is perhaps worth noting that at least two of Sullivan's songs were taken up and sung at Masonic gatherings. The library of the United Grand Lodge of England contains a copy of 'I care not if the cup I hold' from his comic opera *The Rose of Persia* with a note that it was used by Unity Chapter No. 1868, Oldham, 'although the song is not masonic'. 'Take a pair of sparkling eyes' from *The Gondoliers* appeared in a song book published by the same Oldham chapter in 1893. 'Onward, Christian soldiers' set to ST GERTRUDE and 'Courage, brother, do not stumble' set to COURAGE BROTHER continue to have a prominent place in Masonic hymnals.

A final footnote to Sullivan's involvement in Freemasonry is provided in his obituary in the *Masonic Illustrated*, written by Arthur Lawrence, himself a Mason and the author of the first biography of the composer, published in 1899. While acknowledging that 'he had but little time to spare for the work of our Craft', it went on to suggest that 'there can have been few men who have approached more closely to the great ideals of the Fraternity' and to give a catalogue of Sullivan's qualities of character, which echo similar comments by many who knew or came across him:

He was, indeed, honest – in that high sense of the word as Carlyle uses it – in all things sincere, and unswerving in his fidelity. In the building up of his life and character, one felt that each stone was well and truly laid on the other; his nature was without eccentricity or extravagance; with him, genius was sane; he had a keen aversion to anything morbid ...

His benevolence was large and unfailing, and in his charity there was no self-advertisement. Apart from the pecuniary aid which he gave to individuals and charities, he possessed in rare measure that benevolence which is not less valuable, and is more difficult of attainment. He had an unfailing courtesy, which was of the manner that makes the man, and his keen and untiring sympathies were ever on the alert. His was a sunny disposition, and not the least of his qualities was the equability – the serenity of his temperament – which enabled him to display the best principles of an active philosophy in all the chances of life.[48]

Later in this obituary, Lawrence mentioned a conversation where the subject of death had come up and in which Sullivan had simply said, 'Death has absolutely no terrors for me.' Perhaps this says something about his own faith. As previously noted, Arthur Jacobs took it as a sign of Sullivan's lack of religious faith that even when wracked with pain and on the threshold of death, there is no evidence that he sought spiritual guidance. Yet could it in fact be rather that he faced both illness and death with equanimity, sharing with Samuel that 'sweet unmurmuring faith, obedient and resigned to thee in life and death' about which James Drummond Burns wrote in the hymn 'Hushed was the evening hymn' that he set so beautifully and sensitively? Sullivan's letters suggest that, like many of his contemporaries, he believed in heaven as a place of eternal rest where family and friends would be reunited. This simple and sentimental belief was perhaps enough to sustain him. Did he also, perhaps, share something of the stoical approach to death outlined by Colonel Fairfax in his song 'Is life a boon?' from *The Yeomen of the Guard*, the opening lines of which Gilbert chose to have inscribed on his memorial in the Embankment gardens? Meinhard Saremba has written of a recent conversation with a Swiss conductor who knew nothing of Sullivan's religious beliefs but was moved to ask if he had been a Freemason because of the attitudes to life and death revealed in *The Yeomen of the Guard*, especially in Fairfax's song.[49]

Arthur Sullivan was certainly not deeply pious or fervently evangelical. He was not a weekly churchgoer although his diaries show that he did attend church on considerably more than an occasional basis. He could, however, be deeply moved by religious services, as shown by his description of a visit to Cologne Cathedral which he made with Mrs David Beach Grant and her two children in the summer of 1875:

We went into the cathedral and heard a pretty children's service. It is a blazing hot day, the first they have had here, and the cathedral was so peaceful and cool it did one good and took me out of this world for a time. When the service began, the organ struck up, and then in the far distance the boys' voices were heard singing a little motet, and they came nearer and nearer singing all the while. The result was I burst out crying, as I always do at children's voices. I have no doubt the music was weak, and the boys' voices execrable, but the whole thing moved me and did me good. The priest, after the service, which was a sort of little litany, gave a short address. It seemed earnest and simple, but as the very young folks didn't understand a word I brought them out.[50]

That letter tells us something about Sullivan's faith. It shows how deeply it was based on music and also points to its simplicity and sentimentality. Sullivan was moved to tears by the sound of children singing church music of the kind that he himself had sung and loved as a child. He also appreciated the earnestness and simplicity of the priest's homily. Typically, although he would like to have stayed to hear it all, he thought of others and brought the children out. Indeed, the whole trip of which this day was a part underlined his kindness. He had originally been due to accompany the Grants only as far as Cologne, but Mrs Grant fainted on the journey, and as none of the party spoke German, he re-routed his ticket and baggage and accompanied them to their destination, the spa town of Kissingen, where she was to take the waters.

Ultimately Sullivan's faith is revealed and expressed most in his music. It is displayed in the way that he set Norman MacLeod's hymn 'Courage, brother', which is also about simple, uncomplicated, trusting faith, so that its central message 'Trust in God' is repeated not just once but twice and so rings out three times as a penetrating refrain. It is displayed in the calm sense of reassurance found in his first published song, 'O Israel' and the theme of God's forgiving, gracious mercy and embrace of the repentant sinner which permeates his oratorio *The Prodigal Son*. As part of its expression of a simple trusting hope-filled faith, Sullivan's sacred music looks forward to heaven as a place where all tears will be wiped away (the aria 'The Lord is risen' from *The Light of the World*) and where we shall at last hear the great 'Amen' that links all perplexed meaning into one perfect peace ('The Lost Chord'). The faith that is revealed though his music is perhaps above all sentimental in terms of being based on and appealing to feelings and emotions rather than intellectual arguments or dogmatic propositions. In the same interview that was quoted at the beginning of this chapter, he gave his opinion that 'Music should speak to the heart, and not to the head.' In that, as in so much else, he was both representing and responding to the zeitgeist of his age.

2

Are You in Sentimental Mood?
The Religious, Cultural and
Musical Context

Arthur Sullivan's life was lived entirely within the reign of Queen Victoria. He was born five years after she came to the throne and died just two months before she did. His world was entirely and quintessentially Victorian. He imbibed, reflected, benefited from and indeed himself helped to shape Victorian values.

In social and economic terms, the Victorian age was broadly one of stability and rising prosperity. Although the aristocracy still clung on to political power, despite successive Reform Acts which widened the franchise, and many in the working classes enjoyed higher living standards despite persistent pockets of rural and urban poverty, the chief beneficiaries of these trends were the bourgeoisie. It was the booming professional and mercantile middle classes who gave Victorian Britain its distinctive tone, morality and cultural tastes. They also made Sullivan a rich man, providing the audiences for his Savoy operas, cantatas and oratorios and buying sheet music editions of his sacred songs and hymns.

To a considerable extent the temper of the age was moulded by the character of the monarch herself. Victoria both exemplified and influenced the outlook of the country over which she reigned in a way that has not been true of any other British monarch. She was venerated by many of her subjects in a quasi-religious way, not least by Sullivan who was an ultra-royalist, devoted to the Queen and on close terms with several members of the Royal Family, most especially Victoria's second son, Prince Alfred, Duke of Edinburgh. Victoria embodied and expressed what came to be seen as the characteristic values of the age through her staunch Protestant faith, her family piety – she largely invented the whole notion of the Royal Family – her philanthropic and charitable endeavour, her lively interest and middle-brow taste in music and literature, her strong sentimental streak and her fundamentally conservative disposition. Like her Lutheran husband Albert, she epitomized those Germanic values of solid, dedicated, unshowy respectability, formality and devotion to duty which originated with her Hanoverian ancestors and have continued to characterize her Windsor successors.

The Queen's religious bent was reflected to a considerable extent among her subjects. In so far as Victorian Britain had a dominant spiritual ethos, it was that of respectable and reserved Protestantism. Seen from the perspective of the early twenty-first century, it was indeed an age of faith, not least in terms of churchgoing. Around 58% of the population of England and Wales were at church on the Sunday in 1851 when a national religious census was taken. They were evenly divided in their attendance between the Church of England and other mainly Nonconformist denominations. In Wales, Nonconformists predominated and in Scotland, church attenders, who made up 60.7% of the population in the 1851 census, were fairly evenly split between the three main Presbyterian denominations. In Ireland, where Sullivan's own family roots lay, there was a huge Roman Catholic majority. In absolute terms, the number of churchgoers increased through much of Victoria's reign, with Nonconformist churches and Roman Catholics gaining ground, the latter largely through Irish immigration. As a proportion of the population as a whole, however, they declined, with an extensive survey in 1881 suggesting average church attendance across the country of just under 40%. The closing decade of the reign saw churchgoing start to decline in both absolute and proportionate terms.[1]

The great majority of those who did not go regularly to church were exposed to the principles and precepts of Christianity through Sunday school attendance, their education in public and private schools and the influence of a popular culture that was saturated in biblical stories and images. In his recent book on the nineteenth-century crisis of faith, Giles St Aubyn rightly observes that 'the Victorians were the most Biblically literate people known in British history'.[2] Another recent study by Timothy Larsen, appropriately entitled *A People of One Book*, demonstrates the extent to which the Victorians' tendency to read their own experiences through a biblical lens and express their thoughts and emotions in scriptural language extended to agnostics and even militant atheists.[3] This shared scriptural heritage and common grounding in the Christian story helps to explain the popularity of sacred cantatas and oratorios like Sullivan's *The Prodigal Son* and *The Light of the World*.

Among all but the most determined secularists and freethinkers, there was a broad recognition of the Christian character of the nation, something which the Queen herself strongly encouraged. The Church of England enjoyed a dominant and privileged position as the guardian of this Christian nation. It was only in the late 1820s, less than 20 years before Victoria came to the throne, that Roman Catholics and Nonconformists had been allowed to hold public office. Other aspects of Anglican privilege, such as University Test Acts and compulsory church rates, were not abolished until well on in her reign. The Anglican Church remained established in Wales, despite its Nonconformist majority, and it was only in 1868, in the teeth of fierce opposition, that it was disestablished in Ireland.

The whole panoply of Church and State with its associated ceremonial was greatly developed in Victoria's reign, not least through the celebration of the monarch's jubilees and significant events in the lives of members of her family, for several of which Sullivan composed specific liturgical music or hymns. The increasingly grand state occasions and royal services, which usually took place in either Westminster Abbey or St Paul's Cathedral, enhanced the prestige and standing of the Church of England as well as linking it ever more closely to the monarchy and further reinforcing the religious and spiritual dimension of the nation. As a chorister in the Chapel Royal, Sullivan himself grew up at the very heart of this Anglican royal establishment, and he remained very much an establishment figure, although as we shall see his sacred music was taken up at least as enthusiastically by Nonconformists as by Anglicans.

The Victorian Church of England was far from being a monochrome institution. Within it, there were four very different theological groupings. The most important liturgically, driving up standards of church music and also bringing hymns into a somewhat reluctant Established Church, was the Tractarian or Oxford Movement, motivated by a desire to return to medieval principles of worship and connect with Anglicanism's pre-Reformation heritage. This relatively new movement, at its height in the 1840s and 1850s, to some extent eclipsed the older High Church tradition, characterized by a high and dry Toryism and much less enamoured of Catholic worship and innovation, which still nonetheless remained a significant force. At the other end of the theological spectrum were the Evangelicals, heirs to the eighteenth-century religious revival, which had spawned Methodism and deeply affected older Nonconformist denominations like the Baptists, Presbyterians and Congregationalists. More focused on sin, the atonement and personal salvation and favouring plainer styles of worship, they also played a significant part in bringing congregational hymns, which had initially been championed by Nonconformists, into Church of England services. The fourth significant movement was the so-called Broad Church, which was moderate, rational, urbane and less given to extremism and enthusiasm than either Tractarians or Evangelicals. To a large extent, the Queen herself favoured the Broad Church ethos, preferring her preachers to come from that tradition while also sharing the Evangelicals' preference for simple low-church worship. These divisions were mirrored in the Church of Scotland, where a smaller sacramentally and liturgically focused group of Scoto-Catholics coexisted with a large evangelical movement and a solid broad church group known as the moderates.

Alongside the national established churches stood the buoyant Nonconformist denominations who had a considerable following among the mercantile and industrial middle classes and a revived and newly tolerated Roman Catholic church, which under the leadership of John Henry Newman and Henry Manning was reaching many in the working classes. There was also a growing measure of agnosticism and doubt. The Victorian crisis of faith has been much written about in recent years, and there is perhaps a danger that its extent has been exaggerated.[4] It was first and foremost a movement among intellectuals, expressed in novels about agonized high-minded doubt like Mrs Humphrey Ward's *Robert Elsmere* (1888) and in the poems of Arthur Hugh Clough and Alfred Tennyson who famously observed in his *In Memoriam* (1849) 'there lives more faith in honest doubt, believe me than in half the creeds'. This intellectual doubt was fuelled by the effects of biblical criticism, which came into nineteenth-century Britain from Germany, dethroning the Bible from its revealed status and putting it on a par with other ancient texts of human composition. Sullivan's close friend George Grove was a keen devotee of this approach. The impact of Darwin's theory of evolution further eroded the literal authority of the Bible, challenging what is now called creationism and raising significant questions about humanity's place in the universe. A broader unease affected many sensitive Victorians about the prevalence of suffering in the world and how this could be reconciled with the idea of a beneficent loving God. There was also a growing moral revulsion over the doctrine of eternal punishment which figured so largely in many sermons and Christian tracts. The collapse of belief in hell is one of the most striking themes in the intellectual history of the nineteenth century.

If hell lost much of its force, the idea of heaven seemed to grow in importance in the popular as well as the cultured Victorian imagination, inspiring numerous paintings, poems, stories, songs and hymns. Sullivan wrote his first proper hymn tune to accompany the appearance of 'The Hymn of the Homeland', written by Hugh Haweis (1838–1901), vicar of St James's, Marylebone, in the popular magazine *Good Works* in 1867. In a way typical of many mid-Victorian poems, it painted a contrast between the trials and tribulations of this life and the idealized peace and rest of heaven, enhanced with the music of 'angels bright and fair':

> I'm sighing for that country, my heart is aching here;
> there is no pain in the homeland to which I'm drawing near.

This longing for heaven takes us to the heart of what is often seen as a key characteristic of Victorian religion and culture – and also in the eyes of many of his critics a dominant feature of Sullivan's sacred music – a rather maudlin sentimentality.

Sentimentalism was undoubtedly a marked feature of Victorian literature, art and music. It is usually defined in terms of indulgence in superficial emotion, over-reliance on feeling at the expense of reason and having a rather sickly sweet, saccharine quality often characterized as weak, effeminate and febrile. These are terms that their many detractors have applied to Victorian hymn tunes. They have also often been used about Victorian paintings, not least those of the Pre-Raphaelites, and about much Victorian literature, especially the novels of Charles Dickens, who stands accused of pushing his readers to emotional peaks through manipulation of scene and language. The most often cited example of this excessive sentimentality and ramped-up emotionalism is the harrowing child deathbed scene found in so many Victorian novels, the best known being those of Tiny Tim in *A Christmas Carol*, Paul in *Dombey and Son* and Little Nell in *The Old Curiosity Shop*.

Recent scholars have generally been much kinder and more nuanced about Victorian sentimentality than the many earlier critics who held it to be shallow, clichéd, mannered and manipulative. In his important study, *Sacred Tears: Sentimentality in Victorian Literature,* Fred Kaplan sees it as an attempt to express the basis of human nature in terms of feelings, not least moral feelings, and the ability to tell right from wrong. He regards Victorian sentimentality as a child of the philosophical idealism of the eighteenth century and a protest against realism, reductionism, cynicism and determinism. Novelists like Dickens and Thackeray were, in his view, motivated by a strong moral sense and a belief in the goodness of human nature and the ultimate triumph of good over evil: 'Victorian sentimentality defended the vision of the ideal against the claim that the universe and human history are governed by mechanical, or rational, or deterministic, or pragmatic forces.'[5]

It is important when reading today these harrowing infant deathbed scenes and the numerous poems and hymns longing for heaven to realize that they were a response to a grim reality from which we have now largely escaped in the developed world. One in five British children born alive in the 1830s and 1840s was dead by the age of five, and a third of burials in London in 1850 were of children under the age of nine. There were very few families who had not experienced the death of a loved one in infancy or childhood. This context helps to explain why childhood death, and an idolization of and yearning for heaven, are such prominent themes in Sullivan's sacred songs. As well as those who were carried away in childhood, there were also a good number who died in early adulthood. Average life expectancy in the year that Victoria came to the throne was just 39, the age at which Arthur Sullivan's beloved brother Fred succumbed to liver disease and pulmonary tuberculosis.

Bereavement and mourning were much more prominent, talked about and practised features of nineteenth-century life than they are today when we have done our best to sweep death under the carpet. Once again, the lead here came from the Queen herself, who withdrew from society after the death of Prince Albert and entered into a long period of mourning, which set something of a fashion among many of her subjects while at the same time exasperating several of her ministers. The prevalence of death, and the way in which it was dealt with both by copious quantities of grief and tears and also by extensive mourning rituals, undoubtedly enhanced the atmosphere of somewhat maudlin melancholy that hung over Victorian Britain and which critics have found in many of its characteristic cultural expressions. As Maurice Disher writes about Victorian song:

> 'With melancholy expression' had been insisted upon from the beginning of the century; looking backwards had always been the pet cause of it all, bereavement had constantly been harped upon, and more and more it had been felt that thoughts should be directed above, not overtly to religion when the words were for week-day use, but to heaven ... the cult of gravity was assisted by a luxurious pessimism, and in order to maintain this the entertainment of the drawing-room upheld the idea of the week of seven Sabbaths.[6]

The 'luxurious pessimism' that Disher rightly identifies as a major characteristic of Victorian parlour ballads was undoubtedly a marked feature of Victorian sentimentalism. The Victorian age is often seen as one of optimism and in many ways so it was. Yet it was also characterized by longing, nostalgia and a pervasive sense of loss, displayed most conspicuously in poems, songs and hymns. Was this simply an expression of the shallow, self-indulgent sentimentality of the comfortable bourgeoisie, as its critics have suggested, or was it rather an alternative and understandable response to economic progress and prosperity, a recognition of the loss of community, innocence and simple values in the face of rapid industrialization and the development of a complex modern capitalist society? If it was, indeed, the latter then that may also explain the religiosity that suffuses so much Victorian art, literature and music. Hoxie Fairchild has written that 'Victorian poetry of religious pertinence is torrentially abundant'.[7] The same could be said of mid nineteenth-century paintings and melodies. Was this religiosity another bourgeois affectation or was it born of a deeper longing for something lost?

There is, indeed, a strong case for seeing Victorian sentimentality, whether reflected in the idealization of childhood, the longing for heaven or the lingering deathbed scenes, as at root a reflection of and response to the increasing hold of religious doubts. This is broadly the thesis of Walter Houghton's classic study, *The Victorian Frame of Mind*, which rightly sees faith and doubt as two sides of the same phenomenon and points to the way that the critical movement gave birth to an anxious will to believe. Houghton quotes the positivist philosopher Frederic Harrison commenting in 1869 that there was 'abroad a strange consciousness of doubt, instability, and incoherence, and, withal, a secret yearning after certainty and reorganisation in thought and in life'.[8] For Harrison, the emotional attraction of belief counteracted the desire to question and examine. The essayist and historian Thomas Carlyle described the age in which he lived as 'at once destitute of faith and terrified of scepticism'.[9] Sentimentalism perhaps provided an escape from the terror of losing belief and from the social disintegration that many feared would result if religion were abandoned.

Houghton sees a clear religious purpose to the deathbed scenes which fill so many Victorian novels:

> They are intended to help the reader sustain his faith by dissolving religious doubt in a solution of warm sentiment. When the heart is so strongly moved, the sceptical intellect is silenced; and when feelings of profound love and pity are centred on a beautiful soul gone for ever, the least religious affirmation, the slightest reference to heaven or angels, or to reunion with those who have gone before was sufficient to invoke a powerful sense of reassurance.[10]

He also points to two other trends especially evident in the Victorian novel, the deterioration of benevolence into sentimentality and the enjoyment of tender emotions for their own sake:

The sentimental in art is betrayed by an emotional expression in excess of what the object of love or pity would normally arouse; or by the exaggeration of the benevolent character through bestowing upon it an incredibly warm heart that irradiates the soul with extraordinary kindness and pity. Both forms of sentimentality merge in the tears – tears of joy and tears of sweet sorrow – which flow through the Victorian novel whenever a loving heart catches a glimpse of either goodness or suffering.[11]

Tears played a hugely important part in the expression of Victorian sentimentality. Fred Kaplan, who takes the title of his study of the whole subject from Thackeray's evocation of 'sacred tears', suggests that their source was the moral spring of human nature. 'Tears, idle tears', written by Tennyson as a 'song' in his 1847 narrative epic *The Princess*, became one of the most popular poems of the age and was set by a number of prominent composers, including Sullivan in the last year of his life. Like so much of the Poet Laureate's work, it combines religious faith and doubt with an aching longing for a past that can never be brought back:

Tears, idle tears,
I know not what they mean,
Tears from the depth of some divine despair
Rise in the heart, and gather to the eyes,
In looking on the happy autumn fields,
And thinking, thinking of the days that are no more.

The effect of the Victorian crisis of faith can also be seen in the way that the home became an object of sentiment. As the influence of theological dogma and ecclesiastical authority declined, so the living Church became more and more the temple of the hearth. For agnostics as much as for religious believers, the home became a sacred place where people might learn the sentiments of attachment, friendship, reverence and love. With the cult of the home went a strong sense of family ties and affection. The 'strong family piety' that Arthur Jacobs identifies as the essence of Sullivan's religion and which was so movingly expressed in his relationship with his mother was by no means exceptional, even if he took it well above and beyond the call of duty in the extraordinary kindness that he showed to the family of his late brother.[12]

Sentimentalism clearly coloured Victorian Christianity. It is there in the emotionalism of Evangelical hymns, sermons and tracts with their dramatic heart-rending stories of sinners rescued from perdition and despair and in the emphasis which the Oxford Movement put on the sensory experience of worship through attention to its sound, colour and smell. Even the Broad Church and moderate movements had their own sentimental streak, expressed in a profound pastoral consciousness and a restrained expression of feeling which, while eschewing the emotional enthusiasm of the Evangelicals and Tractarians, was still capable of eliciting a tear.

Not least in its religious aspects, Victorian sentimentality was very much a child of the romantic movement, nurtured on the romantic poets, Walter Scott, the Arthurian legends, the revival of medievalism and the cult of the Gothic. In the words of Hoxie Fairchild, 'Christianity and romanticism wove themselves together in self-defence against their common enemies – utilitarianism, positivism and scientific materialism'.[13] Nineteenth-century British romanticism had deeply Germanic roots, drawing on the poetry of Schiller and Goethe and taking much from the land that provided the United Kingdom with its ruling house and the Queen with her beloved consort. It was wholly appropriate that the most potent symbols of the Victorian Christmas, itself surely the best-known and most enduring expression both of Victorian sentimentality and of the cult of the home, the Christmas tree in the hall and the Yule log in the hearth, should have come from Germany, perhaps, indeed, being brought over by Prince Albert himself.

It was also highly appropriate, and not at all coincidental, that in musical terms Victorian sentimentalism found expression in the huge popularity in Britain of the German composer Felix Mendelssohn, not least on the part of the Queen who regularly played his music on the piano and entertained him several times at Buckingham Palace. Mendelssohn, who made ten visits to England between 1829 and his death at the tragically early age of 38 in 1847, did more than anyone else both to popularize classical music among the British middle classes and to give it a distinctly sentimental hue. He himself was strongly influenced by the romantic movement while also remaining loyal to a more restrained classical tradition. His latest biographer, Larry Todd, describes him as reconciling the classical–romantic dichotomy by overlaying into his richly expressive music the classic attributes of poise, balance and clarity.[14] Born Jewish, he was baptized into the Christian faith at the age of seven and was a devout Lutheran for the rest of his life. His piety and irreproachable private life did much to boost his reputation among the British bourgeoisie. Much of his most sentimental work was done in England and aimed specifically at an English audience, including his anthem setting of Psalm 55, 'Hear my prayer', with its much-loved treble solo, 'O for the wings of a dove'.

Mendelssohn's influence on the musical life of Victorian Britain was immense and many-faceted. He was instrumental in stimulating the Bach revival, which found expression in the formation of the London Bach Society in 1849 and was carried forward by Sullivan in his performance of the B Minor Mass at the 1886 Leeds Festival. He wrote liturgical music for the Church of England, including a Magnificat, Nunc Dimittis, Te Deum and Jubilate, so encouraging its choral revival. His atmospheric orchestral music inspired by British subjects, notably the Hebridean overture and the incidental music for Shakespeare's *A Midsummer Night's Dream*, was hugely popular, as were his chamber pieces. In two areas, he was especially influential: his piano pieces, notably the eight volumes of his *Songs without Words* (1829–45), and his oratorios *St Paul*, which had its British premiere in Liverpool in 1836 and *Elijah*, written for the Birmingham Festival of 1846, made him the darling of both the drawing room and the provincial concert hall.

These were also his most obviously sentimental works. When the reaction against Victorian sentimentality kicked in at the end of the nineteenth century, they were singled out for particularly virulent criticism. George Bernard Shaw began the assault in 1888, denouncing 'his kid glove gentility, his conventional sentimentality and his despicable oratorio mongering'.[15] Indeed, Mendelssohn suffered very similar treatment to Sullivan at the hands of the musical establishment, being derided as a superficial, genteel lightweight. As the anti-Victorian reaction gathered pace in the twentieth century, he was dismissed as a composer of saccharin parlour room music of a sentimental, effeminate nature, rhythmically predictable and with few innovations in harmony and tonality. His pretty superficiality was contrasted to the weight and profundity of Beethoven and Wagner. In 1957, Wilfred Mellers attacked his anthems for 'spurious religiosity which reflected the element of unconscious humbug in our morality and beliefs', and in 1981, Stephen Banfield accused him of sterilizing British musical endeavour throughout the mid nineteenth century with the result that 'moments of sentimental religiosity became the norm'.[16]

In fact, the huge success of Mendelssohn's piano works and his oratorios owed almost as much to commercial, technological and sociological developments in the mid nineteenth century as to musical and moral tastes. The sale and manufacture of pianos soared through the 1850s and 1860s in one of the most spectacular manifestations of the Victorian consumer boom. By 1870, it was estimated that there were about 400,000 pianos in use across the British Isles, with 20,000 being manufactured every year in Britain and around 10,000 being imported annually from abroad. More than a million people were playing the instrument by this time, the great majority of them women who had taken it up as a suitable ladylike accomplishment. This army of female pianists provided the market for the publishing phenomenon of the drawing room ballad, itself a product of technological innovation in the field of printing, and its most successful and lucrative spin-off, the sacred song, both genres in which Sullivan was to excel. Similar technological developments and new techniques in organ building revolutionized church music and provided the perfect instrument to accompany anthems and oratorios.

On Saturday 9 July 1842, just eight weeks after Sullivan's birth, Felix Mendelssohn visited Buckingham Palace and played the chorus 'How Lovely are the Messengers' from his oratorio *St Paul* on the newly installed organ. Queen Victoria and Prince Albert sang along enthusiastically, and Albert pulled out the organ stops as the composer played. It was an iconic moment, setting the royal seal of approval on what was to become among the most popular musical genres of the Victorian age. Oratorio, strictly speaking a retelling of a Bible story based entirely on scriptural texts, appealed to the mid nineteenth-century British bourgeoisie not least because of its religious overtones and respectability. In the words of Colin Eatock, it was 'a vehicle for public, participatory music-making, and a pan-Protestant foil to Catholic musical genres such as the Mass. Furthermore, to those English people who viewed opera as a lurid and voluptuous art form, oratorio performances were, by contrast, morally respectable events.'[17] Mendelssohn personally did much to kindle the Victorians' love affair with the oratorio. His own *St Paul* and *Elijah* combined romanticism and Protestant evangelical Christian conviction in a way that perfectly caught, and indeed helped to shape, the tide of Victorian sentimentality. As Meirion Hughes says, these two works 'provided generations of amateurs on the choral festival circuit with an uncomplicated and sincerely felt Christianity expressed in a contemporary Romantic idiom'.[18]

The Victorians' enthusiasm for the oratorio took them back not just to Bach, the founder of the genre, but also to that other German composer who had done so much of his work in England, George Frederick Handel. Handel's oratorios were not as sentimental as those of Mendelssohn and his British imitators and successors like Sullivan, but that did not prevent them enjoying a huge revival in the later nineteenth century. The triennial Handel festivals at the Crystal Palace, which began in 1859 after trial runs in the two previous years with a choir of over 2,700, an orchestra of 450 and an audience of over 81,000, remained a highlight of the capital's musical life for the next 50 years, peaking in the 1880s with a chorus of 4,000, an orchestra of 500 and an audience of over 87,000. Handel was seen as a pre-eminently Christian and Protestant composer and, like Mendelssohn, he was lauded for his blameless character and charitable works. His string of Bible-based oratorios, with *Messiah*, the pearl at their centre, appealed to Victorian religiosity. They were especially popular with Nonconformists who, in the words of Donald Burrows 'formed the dedicated core of many choral societies, regarding the oratorio tradition as an acceptable artistic outlet for temperate society'.[19] After attending a performance of a Handel oratorio on a visit to England in 1855, Richard Wagner noted:

> It is closely entwined with the spirit of English Protestantism, and thus such an oratorio performance attracts the public far more than the opera; there is a further advantage in that attendance at such an oratorio is considered the equivalent of going to church. Everybody in the audience holds their Handel piano scores in the same way church-goers hold their prayer books.[20]

Oratorios provided the perfect fare for the newly formed choirs and choral societies, which were another Victorian invention. The first two decades of Victoria's reign saw a burst of musical education and an explosion of popular interest and involvement in choral singing unparalleled before or since. Much of this was driven by the thirst for self-improvement and adult education. On one evening in April 1837, a month before the Queen's accession, over 600 people assembled in the Mechanics Institute in Salisbury to hear a lecture on singing. It was also the result of a government initiative. As part of a wider drive for national education, Lord Melbourne's Whig administration sponsored mass weekly singing classes in London's Exeter Hall from 1839 to 1841. The moving spirit in this venture was Dr James Kay, first secretary of the Committee of the Privy Council for Education. He was convinced that singing had moral as well as educational benefits and offered 'an important means of forming an industrious, bright, loyal and religious nation'.[21] The classes which he organized were aimed particularly at schoolteachers. To teach them he hired John Hullah, the organist at Croydon Parish Church, who had made a special study of methods of vocal instruction in Paris and brought to the task of teaching singing a new and distinctive technique as well as dashing good looks, an almost permanently cheerful disposition and a fund of anecdotes with which he spiced his lessons. By the end of 1841 it was estimated that over 50,000 working-class children across London were learning singing from teachers taught by Hullah, who over the 20 years that he taught singing reckoned that more than 25,000 people, many of them teachers, had passed through his classes at Exeter Hall. Rival singing classes were run in the capital by Joseph Mainzer, a German priest who came to England in 1839 and produced a best-selling textbook, *Singing for the Millions*, in 1841.

Another key figure in getting the Victorians to sing was John Curwen, a Congregationalist pastor at Plaistow in Essex from 1844 to 1867, who developed and promoted the tonic sol-fa system, which had been invented by Sarah Ann Glover, a Norwich schoolmistress, in the early 1830s. He used the system to teach singing in his own chapel and in local schools and lectured on its benefits around the country. He founded the Tonic Sol-fa Association in 1853 and the Tonic Sol-fa College in 1862. In 1867, he resigned from his charge and established a printing and publishing business to make sol-fa material more widely and cheaply available. Although it is impossible to know for certain how many people learned to sing through this method, tonic sol-fa was taught systematically by thousands of teachers throughout Britain in the second half of the nineteenth century, and many choirs used it in preference to staff notation.[22]

Among the first-fruits of these efforts to promote singing were the numerous choral societies formed across the country in the early years of Victoria's reign. York and Bedford led the way in 1837, followed by Stockport in 1840, Glasgow in 1843, Wigan in 1847, Norwich in 1853 and Carlisle in 1854. Annual or biannual oratorio performances formed the staple of their repertoire. Bigger provincial cities established music festivals, lasting up to four days, which brought together local choirs to perform a mixture of sacred and secular works accompanied by the massive pipe organs installed in their great town halls which had been built to give architectural expression to Victorian provincial civic pride. Bradford began its festival in 1853 with Leeds following five years later. While initially relying largely on the existing repertoire of works by continental composers, the organizers of these festivals, which have been described in a recent study as 'the most significant cultural events to be held in provincial England during the nineteenth century', later took to commissioning works from contemporary British composers.[23] Sullivan's *The Light of the World* was premiered at the Birmingham Festival in 1873. *The Martyr of Antioch* made its debut seven years later at the Leeds Festival, of which he was conductor for 18 years.

The mid nineteenth-century crusade to encourage communal singing had its biggest and most lasting impact on the churches. Several of those most prominently involved in the choral revival movement were churchmen whose prime concern was to get worshippers to sing more and better. They had a big task on their hands. In most churches across the United Kingdom during the eighteenth and early nineteenth century, music was at a low ebb, being largely in the hands of ill-disciplined and anarchic west gallery instrumental bands and with congregational participation often limited to occasionally joining in slow and dirge-like metrical psalms. Echoing a commonly made complaint, John Hullah noted in 1843 that 'congregations generally do not sing at all ... it is not genteel to sing in church'.[24]

To remedy the sorry state of music in most churches, reformers like Hullah proposed the introduction of properly trained choirs, pipe organs and dignified and singable hymn tunes with strong melodies to replace the complex fuguing tunes favoured by the west gallery musicians. These innovations were also dear to the hearts of clergy influenced by the Oxford Movement, and in many places Tractarians and musical reformers worked hand in hand to eliminate metrical psalmody, instrumental bands and barrel organs and replace them with pipe organs and robed choirs singing services of a kind that had hitherto been heard only in cathedrals. Nonconformists were also keen on improving singing. As a minister, John Curwen's interest in promoting tonic sol-fa was first and foremost in order to teach people to sing in church and particularly to encourage the practice among Sunday school pupils. Another prominent campaigner for improved singing in church was Thomas Binney, the leading Congregational minister in London during the early decades of Victoria's reign. In 1848, he wrote an essay on 'The service of song in the House of the Lord', which argued for an end to the old practices of lining out hymns and psalms, using precentors and pitch pipes and accompanying the praise on stringed and wind instruments. Following his lead and under his influence, the ministers of many urban Nonconformist chapels introduced organs and robed choirs. The choir at Rusholme Road Congregational Church in Manchester was trained and conducted by Charles Dickens's sister, Fanny Burnett. More rural and remote congregations were not left untouched by the movement for better singing. John Waite, a blind Congregational minister, established himself as an itinerant singing master and visited Nonconformist chapels across the country promoting harmonized hymn singing. The Church of England also had similar travelling musical evangelists, the most notable being Frederick Helmore, who went round parish churches teaching congregations to sing in parts and setting up choirs.

The movement to improve singing in church even had its own pressure group, which used the tactics of lobbying and pamphleteering more usually associated with bodies like the Anti-Corn Law League. The Society for Promoting Church Music was the brainchild of Robert Druitt, a Mayfair medical practitioner who in 1845 wrote *A Popular Tract on Church Music, with Remarks on its Moral and Political Importance*. Like James

Kay, he was convinced of the moral benefits conferred by learning to sing and he sought to build on the work of Hullah at Exeter Hall. The society concentrated especially on promoting singing among children and amateur adult choirs and on improving music in worship. Druitt was passionately committed to the principle of congregational singing and had no truck with the idea of choirs as a separate entity from the rest of the worshipping community. Indeed, he advocated the distribution of choir members throughout the body of the congregation to encourage good singing and deplored their segregation in the chancel. Although he tirelessly lobbied clergy and choir leaders on the benefits of this practice, he persuaded few to implement it. In his wider aim of improving the standards of singing in church, however, Druitt's crusade was highly successful. He promoted it primarily through a journal, *The Parish Choir*, which appeared from 1846 to 1851 and had a wide circulation among the newly formed parish church and chapel choirs across the country thanks to the fact that each issue contained a generous amount of music, including hymn and psalm tunes, anthems, Gregorian tones, responses and canticles.

When in 1841 the Church of England set up its first national training establishment, St Mark's College, Chelsea, to train teachers for the National (i.e. Church of England) primary schools that were being set up throughout the land, choral singing was put at the heart of the curriculum. This was in large part due to the enthusiasm for church music of its first vice principal and precentor, Thomas Helmore, who was to play a major role in Sullivan's musical and religious education. Helmore engaged John Hullah to teach singing and the college's alumni went out across England, fired with enthusiasm to teach singing in schools and often also to set up choirs in their local parish churches.

As church choirs proliferated, diocesan choral festivals were founded on the model of the provincial music festivals. The first was held in 1856 in Lichfield Cathedral, where choirs sang chanted psalms and responses, hymns and anthems. In the same year, Frederick Ouseley, a moderate Tractarian clergyman who was professor of music at Oxford University, founded St Michael's College, Tenbury Wells, as a model choir school and training establishment with daily choral services. The trend towards cathedral-style choirs in parish churches singing full services, with canticles, psalms and anthems, received a further boost in 1864 with the founding of the College of Organists to promote the art of organ playing and choir training. Its system of examinations, introduced in 1866, did much to enhance the prestige of organists and improve standards of church music. Two more important organizations, the Church Choral Society and the College of Church Music, were established in 1872.

By the early 1870s, the great majority of Anglican parish churches had thrown out the 200-year-old macho tradition of the rough and ready, beer-swilling west gallery instrumental bands, so lovingly chronicled in the novels of Thomas Hardy, and replaced them with organs and harmoniums, more often than not played by demure young ladies. Nonconformist chapels had similarly abandoned pitch pipes and precentors, and even the initially reluctant Church of Scotland had begun to swallow its Presbyterian distaste for the 'kist o'whistles with a devil in every pipe' and embrace the pipe organ. In place of artisans blowing, scraping and bawling from the gallery, highly disciplined choirs robed either in surplices (in Anglican churches) or more sober academic-style gowns (in Nonconformist chapels) and positioned in the chancel sang four-part anthems, chanted prose psalms and canticles and led hymn singing accompanied by an organ.

Addressing a meeting of the Church Congress in Leeds in 1874, Frederick Ouseley pointed to the tremendous advances that had taken place in church music since the start of Victoria's reign. He singled out four factors as being largely responsible for the transformation: the sight-singing movement of John Hullah, the introduction of organs and harmoniums; the removal of the choir from the gallery to the chancel; and the impact of the railways in allowing choirs to come together in choral unions and for festivals. There were losses as well as gains in what had happened. Rough and untutored as they were, the west gallery bands stood in a genuinely populist folk tradition and displayed a contagious enthusiasm. The style of music that replaced them was much more controlled, more solemn, more reverential and more 'churchy'. It was also more bourgeois. The installation of massive pipe organs, their ornate cases embellished with angelic trumpeters and positioned, like the choir, in the heart of the sanctuary, perfectly expressed the respectable sentimentalism and religiosity of Victorian middle-class taste.[25]

These developments in church music presented professional musicians and composers with significant opportunities. For a start, they created numerous part-time and some full-time jobs as organists and choirmasters. Musicians employed by the major Tractarian churches in London could indulge themselves in performances of the great European choral classics. As organist of St Andrew's Church in Wells Street from 1863 to 1871, Sullivan's near contemporary and fellow finalist for the Mendelssohn Scholarship, Joseph Barnby, conducted entirely sung services with English adaptations of masses by Beethoven, Schubert, Haydn and Mozart. Later he moved to St Anne's Church in Soho, where in 1873 he inserted Bach's St John Passion into a communion service, deploying the full resources of his choir of 36 boys and 28 men. At the other end of the spectrum, organists at small Nonconformist chapels took their enthusiastic choirs every week through anthems and hymn tunes and lovingly prepared them for their annual oratorio performance.

The revival of both choir and congregational singing across all churches in Victorian Britain produced an insatiable demand for new hymns, anthems, service settings and larger-scale sacred works. Sullivan was one of many composers who responded to this demand, not just for economic reasons but also out of religious feelings and a sense that this was an exciting and creative area of endeavour. His first oratorio, *The Prodigal Son*, was commissioned by the Three Choirs Festival, which had begun early in the eighteenth century. Premiered at Worcester Cathedral in 1869, it was reprised at Hereford the following year. Victorian composers sought to make church music more artistic and more interesting. The developments of recent decades allowed them to do this. The introduction of pipe organs in nearly every church allowed much more colour and elaboration in the accompaniment of hymns and anthems – indeed the whole palate of the orchestra was available to those writing for the more elaborate organs found in an increasing number of churches. The existence of trained choirs allowed for part-song writing and more complex polyphony.

Alongside these hugely important developments in church music, government support for music teaching in schools and in adult education continued throughout the nineteenth century. The Education Act of 1870 made singing classes a central part of the elementary school curriculum, thanks in part to lobbying by John Hullah, who had acted as music tutor at the first teacher training college, set up in Battersea in 1839 as well as at the first church college at St Mark's. Hullah was appointed Inspector of Music in Training Schools for the United Kingdom in 1872. When he retired ten years later, the post was widened to cover all the elementary schools of England and given to John Stainer. This commitment to musical education in the maintained sector was matched in private schools where hearty congregational hymn singing was encouraged in chapel. Efforts were also made to improve the standards of musical education at a higher level. The National Training School for Music was opened in 1876 on land in South Kensington provided by the Commissioners of the Great Exhibition of 1851 with Sullivan as its first principal. The brainchild of Sir Henry Cole, Secretary of the Society of Arts, and backed both by the Duke of Edinburgh and the Prince of Wales, it was modelled on the state-supported Continental conservatoires and intended to pioneer free music education in Britain and to be the official training school for prospective music teachers as well as composers and performers. Sadly, the expected level of government funding was not forthcoming and the founders were unable to realize their original goal of establishing 300 free scholarships. However, in 1883 the Training School was reborn with state support as the Royal College of Music.

Behind all these developments, both sacred and secular, lay a strong conviction that music-making was not just to be encouraged for its own sake but had moral as well as artistic benefits. This idea was forcefully expressed in an influential book entitled *Music and Morals* by Hugh Haweis, the author of the 'Hymn to the Homeland' for which Sullivan had written his first proper hymn tune. First published in 1871, it went through 20 editions and was still in print in 1906. Haweis's book was instrumental in dispelling middle-class suspicion about music. In Meirion Hughes's words, 'it was a turning point in the cultural climate of Victorian Britain, providing that powerful moral defence of music that had so long been absent'.[26]

In many ways, *Music and Morals* can be read as a checklist of the most significant developments in British musical life in the first three decades of Queen Victoria's reign and their beneficent moral effects. The growth of school singing classes was commended for its effect on young hearts and minds:

> Since young people will have amusement, what more delightful pursuit could be found for them than music? And since they persist in taking a peculiar delight in each other's society, where could they better meet than at the music class in the schoolroom, or town hall, when their minds are to some extent occupied, discipline maintained, and a healthy and exhilarating recreation provided for them?[27]

Haweis particularly singled out what might be called the representative role of singing and the way it allowed emotions to be expressed and distress to be dispelled: 'That girl who sings to herself her favourite songs of Schubert, Mendelssohn, or Schumann, sings more than a song: it is her own plaint of suffering floating away on the wings of melody.'[28]

There was much in the book about the effect of the choral revival in churches. The Tractarians were singled out for special praise for pulling the 'wheezy organs out of their dingy nooks' and sweeping away the gallery bands:

> Then arose the age of white surplices, and new hymn tunes and decent versicles and anthems ...Whatever we may think of their doctrines, the High Church party have stood up for the aesthetic element in devotion, and by introducing a respectable amount of ritual, with good music,

they have shown us how it was possible to be emotional without being vulgar.[29]

While rejoicing in the spread of hearty hymn singing, Haweis was also keen to defend the anthem against those who saw it as an 'unwarrantable interloper' or a 'show off for the choir': 'Rightly understood, it may be quite as blessed a thing to allow music to flow into the soul as to pour forth actively songs of praise.'[30]

Oratorio came in for particular praise as 'a form of art capable of expressing the noblest progressions of the religious sentiment in the highest plains of emotion' and for displaying

> the effect which is produced by arranging the magnificent episodes of scripture in a dramatic – not operatic – form, and translating their emotional significance into the universal language of music. In the oratorio, unlike the opera there is nothing absurd or outré. The fact of Elijah standing before us in a well-trimmed moustache and clean kid gloves does not in the least shock our sense of propriety, because no impersonation is attempted. The singers are there, not to personate character, but to help us to realise the force and procession of certain emotions through which the characters in the sacred drama are supposed to pass ...
>
> I have known the oratorio of the *Messiah* draw the lowest dregs of Whitechapel into a church to hear it, and during the performance sobs have broken forth from the silent and attentive throng ... If such performances of both sacred and secular music were more frequent, we should have less drunkenness, less wife-beating, less spending of summer gains, less pauperism in winter.[31]

Haweis reserved his most purple prose for discussion of the impact of the huge rise in piano playing, especially among the female sex:

> Let no one say that the moral effects of music are small or insignificant. That domestic and long-suffering instrument, the cottage piano, has probably done more to sweeten existence and bring peace and happiness to families in general, and to young women in particular, than all the homilies on the domestic virtues ever yet penned.[32]

Piano playing had all sorts of moral benefits. Just as 'Latin grammar strengthens a boy's memory, and teaches him to study the meaning of words', so 'the piano makes a girl sit upright and pay attention to details'.[33] The 'poor lonely little sorrower, hardly more than a child, who sits dreaming at her piano, whilst her fingers, caressing the deliciously cool ivory keys, glide through a weird nocturne of Chopin' finds that 'the angel of music has come down' and her 'restless, unsatisfied longing has passed ... She has been taken away from the commonplace and dullness of life.' Music has brought back 'freshness to the tired life and buoyancy to the heavy heart'.[34] Once again, the emphasis is on the way music supplied a healthy outlet for emotion, especially for women, so often called by society to repress their feelings:

> Joy flows naturally into ringing harmonies, while music has the subtle power to soften melancholy by presenting it with its fine emotional counterpart. A good play on the piano has not infrequently taken the place of a good cry upstairs, and a cloud of ill-temper has often been disbursed by a timely practice.[35]

Haweis's *Music and Morals* perfectly expressed the central role that music played in the sentimentality, restrained emotionalism and religiosity of Victorian culture. It is essentially an optimistic book, chronicling the huge strides made and pointing to a bright future in which 'music promises to become in England what it has long been in Germany, a running commentary upon all life, the solace of a nation's cares, the companion of its revelry, the Minister of its pleasure, and the inspired aid to its devotion'.[36]

In fact, Britain was well ahead of Germany in the strength of its choral movement, its church music and in terms of the proportion of the population who played the piano. Yet it still felt a great sense of inferiority and was dismissed by the Germans and the Austrians as the land without music. This was because it had not produced a great composer. There was no British Brahms or Beethoven, not even an English Mendelssohn. Into this void stepped the young Arthur Sullivan, the *wunderkind* of British music, the first recipient of the prestigious Mendelssohn Prize, which took him to Leipzig as a 16-year-old in 1858 to immerse himself in the German tradition. Many believed and hoped that he would come back to be the great serious composer, who would finally allow the English to hold their heads high among their cultural despisers. Yet strongly influenced by German music as he was, Sullivan was also, despite his mixed Italian and Irish blood, essentially English in his cultural sympathies and character. More formative than his years in Leipzig was his prior schooling in the Anglican choral tradition. This was the source of the flowing fount of sentiment that poured forth from his pen in the hymns, sacred songs, anthems and oratorios which proved so popular with his countrymen and his Queen.

3

When I First Put this Uniform On: Sullivan's Upbringing and Formative Years

Uniforms were an important feature of Arthur Sullivan's childhood. Among his earliest memories must surely have been of his beloved father dressed as sergeant bandmaster of the Royal Military College at Sandhurst, a post which he held from 1845 until 1856. At the age of 12, it was his own turn to put on a uniform. His excitement at donning the scarlet coat edged with gold worn by the children of the Chapel Royal is evident in a letter to his father: 'We have got the gold clothes to-day ... Will you come to Chapel? If you do, you will have the double pleasure of seeing me togged out and hearing me sing a solo.'[1]

These two uniforms – his father's and his own – and what they represented were hugely influential on Sullivan's development as a musician and as a person. Military music was in his blood, as it was in that of the great Continental operetta composer Franz Lehár, who similarly grew up as the son of an army bandmaster. It allowed him as a boy to learn to play pretty well every brass and woodwind instrument and to discover the particular limitations and potential of each, providing the basis for his great facility for orchestration. It also gave him a penchant for martial airs and marching rhythms, demonstrated especially effectively in hymn tunes like ST GERTRUDE and BISHOPGARTH and more daringly in the way that he set his two Te Deums. The striking uniform worn by the boy choristers of the Chapel Royal was even more significant in his development. It seems to have been what principally attracted him to join this elite choir, which transported him in his early teens to the heart of the Anglican establishment and immersed him in its rich choral tradition. It was his experience and enjoyment of church music while singing in the Chapel Royal that led him into this area of composition and profoundly influenced his style and subject matter. More widely, performing for royalty and at great state occasions undoubtedly fostered in him the unmistakable sense of patriotic Protestantism that characterizes so much of his sacred and secular music.

Patriotic Protestantism is not, in fact, what one would expect to distinguish Sullivan's work or outlook. His genes from both sides of the family were non-English and Roman Catholic. His paternal grandfather, Thomas, hailed from County Cork. Like many poor Irishmen of the time, he enlisted in the British Army, serving in the Peninsular Wars and, according to one possibly fanciful story, guarding the exiled Napoleon Bonaparte on St Helena before ending his days as a Chelsea Pensioner. Although we know nothing of his religious background or convictions, it seems highly likely that he would have been brought up as a Catholic, although his career in the British Army would inevitably have involved a degree of Anglicization. His wife, Mary, however, may have been a Protestant. She hailed from Bandon, famous for being the most staunchly Protestant town in Ireland, 'the inhabitants not permitting papists to reside there as they had been so cruelly treated by men of that persuasion'.[2] According to Herbert Sullivan and Newman Flower, Thomas and Mary's daughter, Elizabeth, Arthur Sullivan's aunt, became a nun and ended her life as mother superior of a convent near Bruges in Belgium. Their younger son, John, was certainly a Catholic, but their older son, Thomas, Arthur's father, seems to have attended the Anglican parish church at Sandhurst during the 12 years that he spent as bandmaster at the Royal Military College there, before becoming professor of clarinet at the new military school of music at Kneller Hall.

Catholicism was a much more definite and distinct influence on Sullivan's mother, Mary Clementina Coghlan, who had an Irish father and an Italian grandfather on her mother's side and was herself educated at a convent school in Hampstead. Sullivan described her as descending from 'an old Italian family'. This was often given as the explanation for his own dark features and olive skin, although there were also suggestions that he had Jewish or even negro blood in his veins – the Victorian novelist Samuel Butler described him as 'the Irish Jew' and one contemporary, Robert Francillon, went so far as to suggest that there was 'a strong strain of African blood that became increasingly perceptible with increasing age. He was, in fact, an Octoroon [a person of one eighth black ancestry].'[3] Detailed research by his most recent English biographer, Arthur Jacobs, turned up no evidence of Jewish ancestry.[4] The Roman Catholic influence, however, is uncontestable. Mary Sullivan seems to have remained a practising Catholic throughout her life. According to Francis Burnand, the librettist of Cox and Box and himself a Catholic, Sullivan occasionally accompanied his mother to the Catholic Church of St Peter and St Edward in Palace Street, Westminster. This was probably largely out of filial devotion on his part, although it may also have had something to do with the music there. Seeking to rebut an erroneous story that he and Sullivan had cooked up the idea of *Cox and Box* while walking back together from church one Sunday, Burnard observed: 'my early hours for going to Mass would never have suited Arthur S. who if he ever visited a Catholic Church would have visited it on account of the music, that is at High Mass at 11am'.[5]

Did Sullivan take any of his mother's Catholicism into his own religious formation or his sacred music? The only evidence of possible pro-Catholic sympathies that I can find is a letter written at the age of 14 to his parents in which he reports learning about the Crimean War and also notes that there is talk of abandoning the virulently anti-Catholic commemoration of Guy Fawkes Day, celebrating the foiling of a plot in 1605 to assassinate James I while opening Parliament and restore a Catholic monarch to the throne: 'They talk of doing away with the services for that day altogether, and let the poor fellow sleep in his grave in peace, and only remember that it was the day the battle of Inkerman was fought, since the Roman Catholics helped us to win the day, and we speak so badly of them in the service.'[6] His Irish ancestry was clearly important to him, as demonstrated in the name he chose for his one and only symphony ('the Irish') and the haunting quality of the music that he wrote for his last stage work, *The Emerald Isle*. His Italian ancestry perhaps at least partly explains his sunny disposition as well as his looks. It is, however, difficult to see any Catholic influences at work in either his own faith or his music. The sacred music that he most admired and which was most clearly influential on his own work – the oratorios of Bach, Handel and Mendelssohn – was Protestant and in the Lutheran tradition. These distinctly Protestant musical influences can only have been reinforced during his time studying composition at Leipzig, among the most Protestant of all German cities with its particular associations with Bach and Mendelssohn. There is no sense in any of Sullivan's sacred works of any Catholic influences, although perhaps we can find lingering echoes of his mother's faith in his particularly sensitive setting of prayers to the Virgin Mary in *The Golden Legend* and in his 1898 opera *The Beauty Stone*.

Much more important and formative was his upbringing in the Church of England. Despite his mother's Catholicism, he was baptized at the age of two months on 31 July 1842 at St Mary's Parish Church in Lambeth, close to the family home. When the Sullivans moved to Sandhurst three years later, Thomas at least seems to have attended the parish church there, and there is evidence that he had some involvement in the music at the services. Arthur recalled to his first biographer, Arthur Lawrence:

> Sometimes I used to go to Sunday afternoon service at the old church at Sandhurst. The church was old in every respect: old-fashioned, high-backed, whitewashed pews, with a gallery at one end for the musicians. What used to interest me most was the little ceremony that the clerk performed so solemnly in regard to the hymns. After he had, from his desk, given out the hymn, always from Tate and Brady's Psalter, he would walk solemnly to the other end of the church, mount to the large empty gallery by means of a ladder, and picking up his clarionet, would lead the musical accompaniment, which consisted only of his own instrument, the clarionet, a bassoon and a violoncello.[7]

This early reminiscence provides a vivid description of the old ways of singing in the Church of England with the Tate and Brady Psalms and west gallery band so beloved of Thomas Hardy that were about to be swept away by the arrival of organs and hymns. According to Henry Saxe Wyndham, Sullivan himself led the gallery band at Sandhurst church, playing either bassoon or cello. His youthful fascination with church music is confirmed by the nature of his first known composition, an anthem setting words from Psalm 137 'By the waters of Babylon', written at the age of eight in 1850.

A further sign of young Arthur's interest in church music was his determination to sing in one of London's great church choirs. Arthur Lawrence records that as a boy 'his great ambition was to become a member of the choir of either the Chapel Royal or Westminster Abbey'.[8] Significantly, it was the uniforms worn by the boys of the Chapel Royal – scarlet and gold coats for special occasions and navy blue jackets and trousers with red cord stripes and crown buttons at other times – which determined his choice. Having been told about them by William Plees, headmaster of the small prep school in Bayswater, where he boarded from the age of nine, he set his heart on going there.[9] His parents were uneasy about the quality of education that would be offered, but he persisted, and in 1854 prevailed on Plees to take him to see Sir George Smart, organist and composer to the Chapels Royal. Sullivan sang the aria 'With verdure clad' from Haydn's *Creation*, accompanying himself on the piano. Smart was impressed by the quality of his voice and told him to report immediately to Thomas Helmore, the master of the children in the Chapel Royal. He sang the same song to Helmore, who quizzed him about the basics of the Christian faith, it being a rule that no boy was to be admitted as a chorister who 'cannot answer the questions in the Church Catechism'. The fact that he was able to impress Helmore with his religious knowledge as well as his musical ability confirms that he must have had more than just a peremptory upbringing in the Church of England. Although he was just short of 12, and choristers were not usually admitted beyond the age of nine, he was enrolled as a boy treble on 12 April 1854.

Arthur Sullivan's time in the Chapel Royal was without doubt the single most decisive influence both in shaping his future career as a church musician and in determining the style of his sacred compositions. Its importance is acknowledged equally by those who regarded it as a benign influence and by those for whom it was a wholly malign one. Thomas Helmore's brother Frederick believed that 'being established in his new abode, the future Sir Arthur found himself in an atmosphere of music in accordance with his own spiritual longings'.[10] For David Eden, by contrast, 'his entry into the Chapel Royal may be regarded as the most grievous blow ever suffered by English music, for it tainted him with the spiritual bankruptcy of Victorian Anglicanism'.[11]

Before assessing what Sullivan did learn as a chorister between 1854 and 1857, it is worth pausing to examine the role and nature of this unique institution. Tracing its origins back to Anglo-Saxon times and still in existence today, the Chapel Royal essentially makes up the monarch's ecclesiastical household and is one of the key links between royalty and the Established Church. The main function of its choir, which in Sullivan's time was made up of ten boys and sixteen gentlemen, split into two eight-man divisions who sang during alternate months, is to sing services in the private royal chapels and perform at important royal occasions, such as christenings, weddings and funerals. As one of the children of the Chapel Royal, Sullivan not only gained a superb grounding in English church music, comparable if not superior to what he would have received as a cathedral chorister, but found himself at the heart of the Establishment with easy access to leading musicians and churchmen as well as to others in high society and Court circles. He also joined a long line of distinguished musicians who had sung in the Chapel Royal, either as children or gentlemen, among them Thomas Tallis, Thomas Morley, Thomas Attwood, John Blow and William Croft as well as contemporary composers such as George Smart, John Goss and Edward John Hopkins.[12]

The choristers' weekly regime centred around singing at morning and evening services in the chapel at St James's Palace every Sunday. They frequently joined the choir for weekday morning services at St Mark's Training College for Schoolmasters, where Thomas Helmore was precentor, and were also expected to attend and perform in the Motet and Madrigal societies, both, in the words of Bernarr Rainbow, 'being conservative institutions where boy trebles and male altos had not yet given place to female singers'.[13] There were further opportunities to perform with the Sacred Harmonic Society and at the regular musical matinees held at Thomas Helmore's house in 6 Cheyne Walk, Chelsea, where the choristers boarded.

From the first, it was clear that Sullivan had an exceptional voice. Within two days of joining the Chapel Royal choir, he was singing the duet in Nares's anthem, 'Blessed is he that considereth the poor and the needy' at the Maundy Thursday service at the Royal Chapel in Whitehall at which Maundy money and shoes and stockings were distributed to 35 aged men and 35 aged women. Christopher Bridgman, a fellow treble, recalled many years later: 'His voice was a very pure high soprano. His top A or B flat used to ring out with brilliant effect, and apparently without effort. The enunciation of his words was very distinct and, moreover, he sang from his heart.'[14] Thomas Helmore noted that 'his voice was very sweet and his style of singing far more sympathetic than that of most boys'.[15] Perhaps the most remarkable testament to the quality of his voice, and also to his wider musical abilities, comes from the reminiscences of Charles John Corfe, who became the first Anglican bishop of Korea in 1889. As a boy, he was one of the first batch of choristers at St Michael's College, Tenbury Wells, the training school set up by Frederick Ouseley to promote choral music throughout the Church of England. He recalled the service of consecration on 29 September 1856, the Feast of St Michael and All Angels:

> The morning anthem was 'Praise the Lord' (Goss) and never have I forgotten the voice of the boy who sang the treble part in the verse, 'O pray for the peace of Jerusalem'. That boy was from the Chapel Royal Choir, and his name was Arthur Sullivan. He was then sixteen [a mistake – he was actually 14], and the voice, wonderfully preserved and developed, was then at its best.[16]

Corfe went on to recall that following the consecration service, Ouseley gave a musical party and challenged Sullivan to play an extempore duet with him. The teenager immediately accepted the challenge and took the treble part to Ouseley's bass: 'how long they played I do not remember, nor, of course, do I remember any of the tunes. They played for some time, however, and even my untutored ear could tell that it was all right – without any breakdown or hesitation.' The following month Sullivan became the first (i.e. senior) boy in the Chapel Royal choir.

It is difficult to judge what effect membership of the Chapel Royal had on Sullivan's own religious beliefs. Choirboys are not generally renowned for their sanctity or theological grasp, although a fair few have found their way in later life into ordained ministry. Twice every year all the boy choristers were examined by the sub-dean as to their scriptural knowledge. It is clear that this side of their education was taken seriously by their teachers, if not necessarily by the boys themselves. A letter home records 'We have had the Gospel to write out ten times for not knowing it.'[17] Probably what was more important and exciting to Sullivan was the opportunity to be involved in grand occasions and to mix with high society, both activities which he developed a taste for and continued to relish in adult life. A certain amount of myth making surrounds some of the royal events in which he supposedly took part. Bridgman claimed that he sang the solo in an anthem specially written by Michael Costa for the service of christening for Queen Victoria's son, Leopold, Duke of Albany. However, this service took place in the private chapel of Buckingham Palace on 28 June 1853, nearly a year before Sullivan joined the Chapel Royal and it is clear that this story, repeated by both Newman Flower and Percy Young in their biographies, is apocryphal. He was certainly present for another royal baptism, that of Princess Beatrice in Buckingham Palace in July 1857, and was impressed by the ceremonial and pageantry of this and other similar occasions, with the Yeomen of the Guard on parade and the presence of crowned heads of state from abroad in their full regalia. He regularly performed before members of the royal family and other celebrities and was rewarded for his singing with half a sovereign by both Prince Albert and the Duke of Wellington.

Sullivan's years in the Chapel Royal contributed hugely to his musical education and exposed him to a very wide range of sacred music. Helmore himself was an enthusiastic devotee of plainsong and Anglican chant, which consequently featured prominently in the services sung by the choristers at St James's Chapel and St Mark's College. Much use was also made of the anthems written by Tudor composers. A month after joining the Chapel Royal, Sullivan sang an Orlando Gibbons anthem in the Festival for the Sons of Clergy service at St Paul's Cathedral. Tallis and Byrd also featured prominently in the choir's repertoire, as did anthems and chants by their lesser-known early sixteenth-century predecessors and their eighteenth-century successors, Boyce and Handel. Arias and choruses from *Messiah* were a staple of the public concerts given by the Chapel Royal choir. Shortly after his admission, Sullivan sang the soprano aria 'Rejoice greatly' in a concert at St Mark's College, and he was in the 1,500-strong chorus that performed the 'Hallelujah' chorus, when Queen Victoria reopened the Crystal Palace at its new Sydenham site in June 1855. He also sang the soprano solos in Handel's *Judas Maccabeus* in a concert in Battersea.

He was also introduced to more recent works. Extracts from Mendelssohn's *Elijah* were a staple of the musical matinees held at 6 Cheyne Walk, which the composer himself had attended before his early death in 1847 and where Jenny Lind often sang the soprano arias, entrancing Sullivan by her vocal quality and sensitive interpretation. He was also much taken by the anthems written by John Goss, who took over as composer to the Chapel Royal in 1856, and enthused to his father about 'Praise the Lord, O my soul', the same anthem that he was to sing at St Michael's College, Tenbury Wells, 'I like Mr Goss' anthem very much; it is very fine.'[18] He sang the solo soprano part in the first performance of Frederick Gore Ouseley's oratorio *The Martyrdom of St Polycarp* in the Sheldonian Theatre, Oxford, on 9 December 1854. This work, which had been written as an exercise for the composer's doctoral thesis, appealed to Sullivan so much that he copied the trio from it into his music book. Returning home some time later for the Christmas holidays, he recommended the march to his father, who was by now at the Military School of Music in Kneller Hall, and copied it out from memory with full band parts. The march, which denoted the advance of the heathens, was described by one reviewer as 'a most spirited and heart-stirring piece of composition, reminding one forcibly of Mendelssohn's Wedding March'.[19] It was received so warmly by the audience that it was given an immediate encore but even allowing for the fact that he had heard it twice, Sullivan's ability to recall it *in toto* and complete with parts a week later is impressive and suggestive of an exceptional musical ear.

Sullivan developed a particular love of oratorios in his teens, amassing a collection of scores using the money that he received for singing. A letter to his father, probably written in 1857, notes that he put half a crown given to him by the Bishop of London for singing 'With verdure clad' towards buying a copy of Handel's *Samson* at Novello's. On the same expedition he also bought a score of *Judas Maccabeus*. Noting that the cover of the Novello editions 'is scarlet cloth and gold' (shades of his love of uniforms), he gleefully pointed out 'Shan't we be well stocked with oratorios?' before signing off with his customary 'God bless you'.[20] In rather more serious vein, at the age of 17, he reprimanded his brother Frederick for his frivolous remarks about the most famous of all sacred oratorios: 'The slighting manner in which you speak of Handel's *Messiah* is an insult to sacred music and – besides it is no fault [of his] if it is not exactly lively. Perhaps you would have liked him to have interpolated a few comic songs in each act.'[21] Ironically, in later years, Sullivan would be accused by his sterner critics of doing exactly that in his own sacred works.

If the scolding of his brother shows how seriously Sullivan took sacred music, he was not above having a little fun with it as well. On a wet half holiday, Bridgman recalled, he would compose impromptu pieces and conduct his fellow choristers, each with a comb covered with paper:

> It was a great delight to him to take some popular comic song or common tune of the day and turn it into a psalm or hymn tune. Some of his best hymn tunes, if played in appropriate time and method, will be found to have originated in this way. He was very clever at fugue. He would frequently say to one of us, 'Now, like a good chap, hum or whistle me something', and his request being complied with, he would rush off to the pianoforte and make a good fugue from the subject given him.[22]

Sullivan's efforts at composing during his three years in the Chapel Royal were not confined to these parodies and light-hearted fugues. They included at least three significant pieces which really set him off on his career as a composer of church music. The first, an anthem, 'Sing unto the Lord and bless his name', was written when he was just 12. He showed it to George Smart, who was sufficiently impressed to tell him to copy out the parts. In May 1855, Smart conducted a performance of it in the Chapel Royal. Afterwards C. J. Blomfield, the dean of the Chapel Royal, then as now an office undertaken by the Bishop of London, called the young composer into the vestry, shook his hand, told him that perhaps he would be writing an oratorio some day and rewarded him with a half sovereign. Bridgman, who claimed that the original manuscript came into his possession, recalled taking it many years later to the Savoy Theatre, when Sullivan was rehearsing *The Gondoliers*. Francois Cellier, the resident conductor for the D'Oyly Carte Opera Company, who had himself been a chorister at the Chapel Royal, 'took the manuscript to the pianoforte, and, running over the first few bars, he turned to Sullivan and said: "Why, Sir Arthur, here is the refrain of H. M. S. Pinafore!"'.[23] It is not clear which song from *Pinafore* Cellier recognized in this youthful anthem, and there must be some doubt as to whether Bridgman's story is again apocryphal, since other sources suggest that the anthem was given by Sullivan not to him but to the singer and conductor W. H. Cummings, after whose death in 1915 it was sold at Sotheby's, but it is too good a tale not to tell!

The second major sacred work that Sullivan composed during his time at the Chapel Royal, which was to be his first published work, was written, when he was just 13. It was a sacred song based on the two opening verses of Hosea 14, as they appear in the Authorized Version of the Bible:

    O Israel return, return,
Return unto the Lord thy God:
O Israel return,
Return unto the Lord thy God:
For thou hast fall'n by thine iniquity,
Hast fall'n by thine iniquity.

Take with you words, and turn to the Lord.
Say unto him,
Take away all iniquity,
Take away all iniquity and receive us graciously.

    Return to the Lord,
Return to the Lord thy God;
Return O Israel, unto the Lord thy God.

This is a fascinating work in a number of respects. It is an unusual text for a song setting; I am not aware of these verses being used as the basis for any other song or anthem. Sullivan may well have been influenced by the great soprano aria that begins Part Two of Mendelssohn's *Elijah*, 'Hear ye, Israel', which he had heard Jenny Lind singing. Based on verses from Isaiah, it has a somewhat similar message both about Israel not heeding God's commandments and also of God being 'He that comforteth'. There are undoubtedly echoes of Mendelssohn in Sullivan's song, although it is altogether simpler, gentler, more wistful and much less bright and bombastic than 'Hear ye, Israel'. Set for boy soprano voices, it begins on a high F sharp and goes up to a high A, giving it a floating, ethereal quality. It also has an underlying sense of reassurance. It is interesting that Sullivan chose a text that is about rebelliousness, backsliding and falling through iniquity but which also asks the Lord to 'receive us graciously' and which, in his setting, emphasizes particularly the theme of returning to God. This is very much the theme of the story of the Prodigal Son, especially as it was understood by Sullivan and interpreted in his own first oratorio. The fact that he fixed on verses about being wayward and returning to a gracious God perhaps provides an early hint of a theological motif; the forgiving, gracious nature of God and his embrace of the returning sinner, which returns several times in his sacred works. Does it also give a pointer to his own emerging religious beliefs? He wrote it in Tavistock, while staying with his fellow chorister, Christopher Bridgman, to whose mother he dedicated it. Thomas Helmore arranged for a small quantity of copies to be printed and published by Novello in November 1855.

His third sacred composition during this period was a setting of Psalm 103, 'Bless the Lord, O my soul, and all that is within me bless his holy name'. Composed in 1856, it was unpublished, but is contained in an autograph manuscript book sold at Sotheby's on 13 June 1966. A letter to his father, asking 'When are you going to sing my Psalm?', suggests that Thomas Sullivan had some involvement in the music at Sandhurst Parish Church. Aside from these sacred compositions, Sullivan also tried his hand at secular songs, including a madrigal, 'O lady dear', which carries the annotation, 'Written while lying outside the bed one night, un-dressed, and in deadly fear lest Mr. Helmore should come in'.[24]

The most abiding influence during Sullivan's time at the Chapel Royal – he left when his voice broke in 1857 – was that of his teachers. Of these the most important by far was Thomas Helmore (1811–90). The son of a Congregational minister, he was attracted to Anglicanism through the Tractarian Movement's emphasis on liturgy and recovering ancient church music and was ordained into the Church of England. He served as vice-principal and precentor of St Mark's College, Chelsea, the first Church of England teacher training college, where, under his direction, prayers and responses were intoned and psalms sung unaccompanied either to Gregorian or Anglican chant by the entire student body gathered every morning in the Chapel. He retained the precentorship, when in 1846 he became master of the children of the Chapel Royal, with responsibility for the choristers' education and pastoral care. He was the first clergyman to hold this office since the Reformation and did much to improve the boys' moral and physical welfare following a lax and cruel regime under his predecessor.

A distinguished musician in his own right, Helmore played a decisive role in raising the standards and changing the face of Victorian church music. Together with his younger brother Frederick, he was largely instrumental in establishing choral services, with sung anthems and chanted psalms and responses, in parish churches throughout the Church of England. His own particular passion was for plainsong, which he believed to be the perfect form of congregational singing. As Sullivan himself noted, Helmore 'was enthusiastic for the revival of old Church music, and was at the head of the movement for the use of Gregorian music in the Church'.[25] Central to his efforts to restore its use were his publications *The Psalter Noted* (1849), *A Manual of Plainsong* (1850) and the *Hymnal Noted*, which appeared in two parts in 1851 and 1856, a collection of plainsong melodies attached to translations of early Latin hymn texts by J. M. Neale, which included 'Of the Father's love begotten' and 'O come, O come, Emmanuel'. Helmore and Neale also collaborated on a volume of *Carols for Christmastide* which appeared in 1853 and launched 'Good King Wenceslas' on the world.

Helmore recognized Sullivan's huge potential both as a performer and a composer and did much to establish the foundations of his career. He was particularly taken with the sensitivity of his interpretation of sacred music. A moving letter sent to Sullivan's mother following a service at St Neots Church in Cambridgeshire records: 'Arthur sang a very elaborate solo in church today ... his expression was beautiful. It brought tears very near my eyes (although the music itself was rubbish), but as I was immediately to enter the pulpit, I was obliged to restrain myself.'[26] He gave Sullivan a good deal of solo work and encouraged him greatly, not just with singing but with composing, telling his mother that, as well as getting on with his Latin and not neglecting his general education, every week 'he should compose a little something, a song or a sanctus, or an anthem of his own. This is the practical way of testing his industry.'[27]

It was Helmore more than anyone else who kindled and nurtured Sullivan's love of church music. He had three specific influences on both the nature and style of his pupil's future work in this particular area of composition. The first came through Sullivan's immersion in plainsong and Anglican chant. This may, I suspect, lie at the root of his frequent use of repeated notes, particularly although not exclusively at the beginning of pieces, a practice, especially noticeable in his hymn tunes, which his detractors have singled out for criticism. Sullivan used plainchant in several of his anthems and liturgical settings, most strikingly, perhaps, in the middle section of 'The Strain Upraise'. More generally, I wonder if the grounding in plainsong and its virtues which he received from Helmore was a factor in making him such a master of word setting. Plainchant follows the natural rhythms and cadences of speech. It is, indeed, in some senses an enhanced form of speaking. It is surely not being too fanciful to suggest that Sullivan's schooling in this particular technique gave him a particular concern with setting words clearly and economically, generally eschewing melisma and lengthy trills and cadenzas, as well as making him the master of the patter song.

The second area where Helmore made a distinctive and lasting contribution to Sullivan's musical style was through introducing him to the work of the early sixteenth-century English composers, who were so prominently featured in the Chapel Royal repertoire. Their influence surely in part lies behind the clean, bright, straightforwardness of so much of Sullivan's music, both in the secular and the sacred spheres, the quality which makes it so English. It is significant that in the lecture which he delivered on music in Birmingham in 1888, where he is perhaps at his most profound and also his most self-revealing, he enthused about the superiority of the English predecessors of Tallis and Byrd – he cited specifically Edwards, Redford, Shepperd, Tye, White, Johnson and Merbecke – over the Continental predecessors of Palestrina:

> They were their equals in science, and they far surpassed them in the tunefulness and what I may call the common sense of their music. Their compositions display a 'sweet reasonableness', a human feeling, a suitability to the words, and a determination to be something more than a mere scientific and mechanical puzzle, which few, if any, of the Continental composers before 1550 can be said to exhibit.[28]

The attributes that Sullivan singled out as distinguishing the work of these early Tudor composers – sweet reasonableness, human feeling, and suitability of setting to the words – were precisely those that characterized so much of his own music.

The third major way in which Helmore influenced Sullivan musically was more direct and immediate. He got him started on the business of writing and arranging hymn tunes. For an edition of harmonies to accompany the plainsong melodies in the second part of the *Hymnal Noted*, published in 1858, Sullivan supplied harmonized accompaniments to four plainsong melodies, three of which came from the Salisbury Hymnary and one from the Spanish Graduals. It was his first commission and his first experience of working on hymn tunes. He later wrote: 'The knowledge and experience I gained in this way in regard to hymn tunes assisted me materially in making my big collection of hymn tunes for the Society for the Promotion of Christian Knowledge, entitled "Church Hymns".'[29] Without Helmore, there might have been no ST GERTRUDE or GOLDEN SHEAVES.

Helmore shaped Sullivan's character as well as his musical tastes and direction. It could hardly be otherwise, when he was for three years effectively a second father, as he was for the other choristers living in Cheyne Walk, who saw considerably more of him than of their own parents. Although High Church in his attitude to worship and music, in other respects, Helmore held to the liberal creed of his Congregationalist father. He had a broad outlook and a generous spirit, and he almost certainly recognized and nurtured these same qualities in the young chorister under his care. A deep and genuine bond of mutual affection and admiration developed between them. In a moving and heartfelt letter sent to his old master in 1862, when he was back from studies at Leipzig and setting out on his professional career as composer and conductor, Sullivan wrote:

To you I owe more than to anyone else perhaps. The high principles and elevated tone applying equally to Art as to morals with which you strove more by example than by precept to imbue me (God grant that it may have been with some success!), the care and attention bestowed upon every branch of my education, and the constant and kindly interest taken in my progress, have been in no small manner influential in making me what I am – viz: an earnest labourer in the cause of true Art.[30]

Sullivan continued to revere Helmore, after he had become a highly successful composer and achieved fame and fortune through the Savoy operas. He wrote to his mother in 1875, 'he is good in every sense – a thoroughly good and religious man, and a kindly man of the world as well' and asked him to take the funeral services for both his parents. For his part, Helmore sought to keep his former pupil in the Christian faith, which he had played an important role in instilling into him. The year before he died, he sent Sullivan as a Christmas present a copy of a new translation of Thomas à Kempis's classic of spiritual devotion, *The Imitation of Christ*. In his letter of thanks, written in the midst of rehearsals for the American premiere of *The Gondoliers*, Sullivan wrote: 'It seems to me, from the hasty glance that I have been able to throw at the book, that the lines require no music – the rhythm itself is music, and of a most beautiful character'.[31] It was not perhaps quite the lesson that the aged cleric, who noted on the envelope, 'Interesting letter from Sir Arthur Sullivan on the reception of a new translation of Thomas à Kempis', had hoped that his former pupil would draw from the medieval manual of spiritual instruction. However, Sullivan's response demonstrated the almost mystical quality of his spirituality, something which Helmore had recognized early on and helped to nurture.

Two other older musicians also had an important formative influence on Sullivan in his Chapel Royal days. George Smart (1776–1867), who first heard Sullivan sing and recommended him to Helmore, had himself been a chorister in the Chapel Royal in the 1780s. He had sung in the first great Handel commemoration in 1784, played the drums for Josef Haydn and known Beethoven, Weber and Mendelssohn. He was organist to the Chapel Royal from 1822 to 1856 and composer there from 1838 to 1856. Smart greatly encouraged Sullivan, conducting his first anthem and showing a keen interest in his work. He was chairman of the committee which awarded him the first Mendelssohn Scholarship, which sent him initially to the Royal Academy of Music and then to Leipzig. He wrote a glowing testimonial to his professors there and did all he could to further the young composer's career. Sullivan characteristically reciprocated this kindness, continuing to see his old benefactor, when he was well in his eighties and writing a moving letter to his widow after his death (page 12). Smart did not have as much direct influence as Helmore on Sullivan's musical development but it is worth pointing out that his own most lasting legacy, the psalm and hymn tune WILTSHIRE, was written when he was just 19 and organist at St James's Chapel, London. Still regularly used for the metrical version of Psalm 23 and for the hymn 'Through all the changing scenes of life', its gentle melodic sweep, lyricism and sense of assurance anticipate features in several of Sullivan's hymn tunes, written at a similar stage of his own life.

John Goss (1800–80), another former Chapel Royal chorister, went on to become professor of harmony at the Royal Academy of Music and organist of St Paul's Cathedral from 1838 to 1872. In 1856, he succeeded Smart as composer to the Chapel Royal, and it was in this capacity that he got to know and admire Sullivan, although he probably also met him socially, as he was a near neighbour of Helmore, living two doors away in Cheyne Walk. Goss was among the leading church composers in mid Victorian Britain, turning out a stream of anthems and hymn tunes, his best-known and most enduring being PRAISE MY SOUL written for Henry Lyte's 'Praise my soul, the King of heaven' in 1869 and HUMILITY for 'See amid the winter's snow' in 1871. Goss taught Sullivan harmony and counterpoint at the Royal Academy of Music. The two men were great admirers of each other's work – Goss was particularly enthusiastic about Sullivan's symphony – and it was fitting that despite the 40-year age gap between them they received their Cambridge doctorates of music together in 1876. If Goss had a particular influence on Sullivan, it was perhaps in reinforcing the importance of taking great care over setting the words of hymns and anthems. This was a characteristic that both teacher and pupil shared. The judgement that W. A. Barrett made about Goss in 1882 could equally have applied to his pupil: 'his music is always melodious and beautifully written for the voice, and is remarkable for a union of solidity and grace, with a certain unaffected native charm'.[32]

Alongside these contacts with leading church musicians of the day, Sullivan also forged close relationships with young musicians of his own generation. Joseph Barnby (1838–96) was a boy chorister at York Minster and came to London in 1854 to study at the Royal Academy of Music. It is not entirely clear when he first met Sullivan: his brother sang in the choir of Westminster Abbey, and there is a Barnby mentioned as singing with the gentlemen of the Chapel Royal at the Maundy Thursday service in 1854, where Sullivan made his debut as a soloist, although I have not been able to discover his Christian name. Despite being pipped at the post for the Mendelssohn Scholarship by his younger competitor,

Joseph Barnby remained good friends with Sullivan throughout his life. Barnby went on to have a distinguished musical career as precentor (head of music) at Eton and principal of the Guildhall School of Music.

Another contemporary with whom Sullivan became friendly was John Stainer (1840–1901), a chorister at St Paul's Cathedral. They almost certainly met through singing together at the grand occasions, which brought together the choirs of the Chapel Royal, Westminster Abbey, St Paul's Cathedral, St Michael's College, Tenbury, and Oxford and Cambridge college chapels. Sullivan's obituary in the *Musical Times* noted that 'the two lads, when off duty, were wont to delight in penny trips together on Thames steamboats, their enjoyment of those water excursions being considerably enhanced by a copious consumption of nuts and oranges'.[33] Stainer later recalled a hilarious incident around 1856, when he would have been 16 and Sullivan 14, and they were both up in the organ loft at St Paul's. John Goss inadvertently walked across the pedals in the middle of a service, sending a sustained roar of 'alarming thunderings', which frightened the congregation and put a temporary stop to the sermon. Around the same time, the two teenagers sought to assist Frederick Ouseley's efforts to build a new organ in the chapel of St Michael's College, Tenbury Wells, by trying out gutta-percha, a natural form of rubber obtained from trees in South East Asia, for the pipes. The experiment was abandoned, when Ouseley complained about the strong smell. Stainer, who succeeded Goss as organist at St Paul's Cathedral in 1872, remained a close friend and supporter of Sullivan throughout his life and was one of the pall-bearers at his funeral.[34]

These mentors and friends whom Sullivan acquired during his formative years in the Chapel Royal were all first and foremost church musicians. Helmore, Smart, Goss and Stainer hardly wrote a note of secular music between them. Barnby did turn his hand to part-songs and parlour ballads but devoted most of his efforts to sacred works. Sullivan retained very close friendships with these and other church musicians in later life, and they were often his strongest champions and defenders when he was assailed by the musical establishment. William Parry observes:

It was strange that it was the musicians of the church – John Stainer, George Martin and Frederick Bridge [organist of Westminster Abbey] – who seemed to understand Sullivan best: where Stanford and Parry worried that Sullivan had let the sacred calling of music down by writing comic opera, Sullivan's ecclesiastical contemporaries appreciated the composer whose love of life and its pleasures was the *sine qua non* of his music.[35]

Perhaps it is not so strange that it was those who grew up, like Sullivan, steeped in church music and who shared his early fascination and love for it who became his natural soul mates.

Sullivan's three years as a chorister in the Chapel Royal greatly influenced his style and direction as a composer as well as initiating several of his deepest and most enduring friendships. They immersed him in the world of church music, which he relished as a singer, a listener and, increasingly, a composer. Did they also 'taint him with the spiritual bankruptcy of Victorian Anglicanism', as David Eden has suggested? Were they the source of that artificially sanctimonious style and the dull religiosity, which critics like Erik Routley have identified as his besetting sin? A relatively early biographer, Henry Saxe Wyndham, suggested that 'Sullivan's early musical education ... had been much too exclusively ecclesiastical'.[36] It is true that he was exposed to little other than liturgical and sacred music in these formative teenage years. As we have seen, however, it was music of a broad and varied scope, encompassing plainsong, chant, the work of the English composers of the sixteenth century and the oratorios of Handel and Mendelssohn as well as contemporary compositions.

A specific legacy of his Chapel Royal days was perhaps Sullivan's tendency to write the soprano parts in his oratorios as though for boy trebles with a high tessitura and a pure ethereal floating quality. It is also true that they have a distinctly 'churchy' feel redolent of Anglican cathedral music. More broadly, his nephew Herbert was surely right to say that the Chapel Royal gave him 'the note of religious melody which coloured his own composing in later years and often stole, as if unaware, into his operas'.[37] There was undoubtedly a religious note in much of Sullivan's subsequent work, but it was hardly spiritually bankrupt or dull. Rather it was characterized by the melodic as much as by the religious element – and that too was perhaps a direct legacy of his time as a chorister and also of his early years listening to and learning to play the instruments in his father's military band, a combination which, as Percy Young has observed, meant that his introduction to music 'was by way of melody', a quality which continued to infuse his own work, both sacred and secular.[38]

Sullivan himself looked back to his days in the scarlet and gold uniform as the happiest of his life. I have dwelt at length on them in this chapter, because I believe they were formative in determining his direction and style as a composer of sacred and church music. The succeeding years of study, at the Royal Academy of Music from 1856 to 1858 (during the first of which Sullivan was still singing in the Chapel Royal) and at Leipzig from 1858 to 1861, can be dealt with much more briefly as they were much less important in this respect. As the author of an article on his church music published shortly after his death commented somewhat clumsily, 'During his Royal Academy of Music and Leipzig pupilage there are no evidences that Sullivan cultivated his church music muse in the matter of production.'[39] He did, in fact, compose one anthem while at Leipzig, 'We have heard with our ears' which was dedicated to Sir George Smart and performed at the Chapel Royal in January 1860. His time in Germany does offer one interesting insight into his religious attitudes. In his first month in Leipzig, he wrote to his mother saying that he would not be attending the first two Gewandhaus concerts 'as they are on a Sunday'.[40] He clearly stuck to these strict Sabbatarian principles throughout his time there, giving a negative answer to the first question that Smart put to him on his return home, 'Did you go to any concerts on a Sunday?', thereby delighting his pious patron.[41] Later in life, Sullivan dropped these youthful puritan scruples and became a strong advocate of Sunday afternoon concerts in London.

On returning from Leipzig in May 1861, Sullivan threw himself back into the world of church music. This was in truth probably as much in order to earn some money as to pursue what he saw as his particular vocation. One of the main opportunities for an aspiring professional musician to make money was through becoming a church organist. As soon as he returned to London, Sullivan took up organ lessons for five months with George Cooper, who had succeeded Smart as organist at the Chapel Royal in 1856. He turned down the first job opportunity that was suggested to him, by Jenny Lind's husband Otto Goldschmidt, at the Lutheran Church in London, declining it 'on religious grounds', which presumably meant his Anglican affiliations. Shortly afterwards, he secured the organist's post at St Michael's Church, Chester Square, less than two miles from the house in Pimlico where he was now living with his parents. He had been recommended strongly to the vicar, Joseph Hamilton, by Captain C. J. Ottley, a friend of Thomas Helmore. At his audition, Sullivan also scored a hit with the vicar's daughter, Mary, who later confessed that she 'was quite enthralled by the performance of the E minor fugue of Bach, one of the pieces played by the slim, curly-headed, black-eyed youth'.[42] She went on to become Sullivan's organ pupil, to deputize for him at Wednesday morning and Sunday afternoon services at St Michael's and to 'save his life' by copying out the violin parts of his first comic opera, *Cox and Box*, on the morning of its first band rehearsal. A strong bond clearly developed between the new organist and the vicar's daughter; in a moving reminiscence shortly after his death she wrote that 'for many years our friendship was very close' and that 'when we were all young it was a joke among us that I was to write Sir Arthur's life'. It is interesting to speculate what would have happened had Sullivan married this early admirer. In the event, Mary married a clergyman, Walter Carr, who became vicar of St John's Church in Worcester.

St Michael's had a mixed congregation, which included MPs, barristers, surgeons and army officers as well as bricklayers, butlers, engine-drivers and grooms. According to Percy Young, Sullivan received an annual stipend of £80. If this figure is correct, he was getting considerably more than other, better qualified London organists – Joseph Barnby received just £30 at St Andrew's Wells Street, which was in the van of the choral revival in the Church of England and prided itself on having entirely sung services. St Michael's had a three-manual organ built by Flight and Robson, which occupied three-quarters of the west gallery. Edward Mills, who acted as Sullivan's deputy from 1867, has left this description of his talents as an organist:

> His style of playing was eminently legato and quiet, and scrupulously in keeping with the general feeling of the words; but when occasion required, the louder portions of the instrument would gradually be drawn upon for a well-conceived climax, such as is found in Haydn's tune 'Austria'. He rightly considered his thoughtful accompaniment of the service to be his strongest point as an organist.[43]

Mary Carr, the vicar's daughter and Sullivan's erstwhile admirer, reminisced after his death about another of his talents:

> Arthur Sullivan's conducting power was shown still more in what he could make the congregation do. As a rule, the hymns were sung very heartily by everybody in the congregation, but he could subdue the whole body of voices to a whisper when he chose; as, for instance, in such passages as the last verse of 'Rock of Ages' sung to a German tune named 'Cassell'.[44]

The choir at St Michael's gave Sullivan his first experience of choral conducting and a good deal of pleasure and amusement:

> We were well off for soprani and contralti but at first I was at my wit's end for tenors and basses. However, close by St Michael's Church was Cottage Row police station, and here I completed my choir. The Chief Superintendent threw himself heartily into my scheme, and from the police I gathered six tenors, and six basses, with a small reserve. And capital fellows they were. However tired they might be when they came

off duty, they never missed a practice. I used to think of them sometimes when I was composing the music for the *Pirates of Penzance*.[45]

Mary Carr had a slightly different recollection of how the choir of singing
policemen came about which gave the initiative to her father:

> The origin of the policeman choir was this: cordial relations had always
> existed between the police station, situated close to St Michael's, and
> the Church – indeed a special service was held for the constables every
> Wednesday morning. So when there was a difficulty about procuring
> tenors and basses, it occurred to my father that there was this raw
> material ready to hand. Raw material indeed it was at first, but with
> patience and perseverance it proved capable of results surprising to
> those who knew the beginning. Many, doubtless, have heard Sir Arthur
> tell in later days the story of that Easter evening when the Psalms were
> chanted for the first time. How, after weeks of patient teaching them
> their parts, his tenors and basses having got through a couple of verses,
> feebly and tentatively in harmony, burst into a joyful unison, the mel-
> ody of Mornington in E flat. The 'harmonious Bluebottles', however,
> completely wiped out this disgrace afterwards, and made an efficient
> and steady choir, if not one distinguished for beauty of tone.[46]

The recruitment of the singing policemen was assisted by the fact that the
Chief Commissioner of the Metropolitan Police, Sir Richard Mayne, was
a member of the congregation. The police station had opened in what was
then called Cottage Row in 1846. The street changed its name to Gerald
Road in 1885, and the police station remained there, until it was closed in
1993. A letter written in 1863 shows Sullivan's amusement and frustra-
tion with his constabulary choir:

> I returned home tired to death with teaching my gallant constables a
> tune in G minor. No easy task, I can assure you.
> 'Now my men what key is this in?'
> Dead silence.
> Organist – 'Don't all speak at once. One at a time if you please.'
> Shy Tenor (B47) – 'B, sir.'
> 'Major or minor?'
> 'Minor, sir.'
> The force looks approvingly at B47 for having thus defended its hon-
> our.
> Organist – 'No that won't do.'

The force now looks suspiciously at Mr Sullivan and B47 alternately.
Mr S. – 'It's G minor.'
Deep sigh from the force and sympathising looks at each other. This is
the way things go on.[47]

Let the last words on this subject come from Sullivan's close friend, Joseph
Bennett, music critic of the *Daily Telegraph* and organist at the Westminster Chapel who sometimes attended rehearsals at St Michael's:

> I never ceased to admire the way in which he kept the constables at
> the boiling point of enthusiasm, as well as on brink of laughter. The
> organist's good spirits were infectious, and though, as he himself sang
> in after years,
>> Taking one consideration with another,
>> A policeman's life [*sic*] is not a happy one,
> I would be bound that the 'able-bodied' of St Michael's were, during
> rehearsal, as cheerful as all the birds in the air. They could not help it,
> neither could their musical chief help it either, so ebullient was his good
> nature, and so captivating his charm.[48]

On a more sober note, it was while he was at St Michael's that Sullivan's
beloved father died. Mary Carr provides a poignant memory of this time:

> My most vivid recollection of Arthur Sullivan in the old organ loft is on
> the day he came for sympathy after his father's death. He was dressed
> entirely in black, his usually brilliant eyes were dull and lifeless and his
> face deadly pale, so that he looked the embodiment of grief. As was his
> custom when writing anything new, he played me portions of the *In
> Memoriam* overture which I heard subsequently at the Crystal Palace. I
> shall never forget seeing the occupants of the side gallery start to their
> feet by an uncontrollable impulse at the first crash of those triumphant
> chords in C major, just before the close.[49]

In June 1867, Sullivan became organist at the newly built church of St
Peter's in Cranley Gardens in South Kensington. According to what he
told his first biographer, Arthur Lawrence, his appointment there came
about by accident because of his friendship with the first vicar, Francis
Byng:

> I designed the new organ for him and undertook to find an organist.
> When the day arrived for the consecration I hadn't obtained the organ-
> ist for him, so I volunteered to play for two or three Sundays until I

could find some one else, with the result, however, that I played there for two or three years.[50]

In fact, Sullivan remained as organist of St Peter's for five years until 1872. He retained his post at St Michael's until 1869, regularly using Edward Mills as his deputy there. In contrast to St Michael's, where, in Mills's words 'the services were of a very plain type', the fashionable St Peter's had a surpliced choir in the chancel, where the organ was also sited, and put on full cathedral-style choral services of the kind that Sullivan had experienced under Helmore's direction at St Mark's Training College.[51] Not that the services were without their more humorous moments:

> I remember that at the consecration of the church by the then Bishop of London, the hour fixed was twelve o'clock, and by some misunderstanding the Bishop didn't arrive until one. Consequently I had to play the organ the whole time in order to occupy the attention of the congregation. As the minutes went by and the Bishop didn't arrive I began to play appropriate music. First I played 'I waited for the Lord', and then went on with a song of mine which is entitled 'Will he come?' The appropriateness of the pieces was perfectly apprehended by the congregation.[52]

During his time at St Peter's, Sullivan made full use of his contacts in the church music world. For the consecration service in June 1867, he chose Goss's anthem 'Praise the Lord', the same one that he had praised to his father and sung as a 14-year-old soloist at St Michael's Tenbury, and augmented the church choir with boys from the Chapel Royal. Goss was present for the consecration and quite often attended the evening service at St Peter's. On one occasion, when he came up to the organ at the end, Sullivan got the choir to sing 'Praise my soul, the King of Heaven', for which Goss had written the well-known tune PRAISE MY SOUL in 1869 and which Sullivan praised as the 'finest hymn tune in existence'.[53] The choir then sang Sullivan's 'The strain upraise', which Goss praised in similarly effusive terms, or as Mills put it, 'Goss kindly retaliated on his pupil'. Percy Young asserts that thereafter, whenever Goss attended St Peter's, Sullivan always made sure that 'Praise my soul' was sung at evensong.[54] Whether he was tipped off in advance or simply looked down the nave at the start of the service to check if he was there, is not recorded.

Frederick Ouseley was another occasional attender at St Peter's, on one occasion extemporizing a fugue on the opening phrase of the hymn tune 'Hanover'. Sullivan recognized that his own strong point as an organist lay in accompanying the choir, and he eschewed complex virtuoso performances on the instrument. Edward Mills recalled that his voluntaries 'which were mostly drawn from vocal or instrumental works – Mendelssohn perhaps being the favourite – were as orchestral in colour as the small organ would admit, a soft 16 feet reed on the swell being the chief solo stop'.[55]

His work as an organist brought him into contact with clergy as well as with fellow church musicians, and he struck up a particularly close friendship with three clergymen. The most colourful was the aristocratic Revd the Hon. Francis Byng (1835–1919), vicar of St Peter's, Cranley Gardens from 1867 to 1889. A chaplain both to the Queen and to the Speaker of the House of Commons, his imposing presence, beautiful voice and high birth made him a favourite with couples seeking to be married in his fashionable church. He was an active Freemason and was elected in 1889 as the Grand Chaplain of the United Kingdom Lodge. Later the same year, however, he suddenly resigned all his benefices and left London, supposedly owing to a gambling debt. He was said to be 'addicted to cards', an affliction that he perhaps passed on to his organist, who was a chronic gambler throughout his adult life. In 1899, Byng became the fifth Earl of Strafford, when his brother, the fourth Earl, was decapitated in a railway accident. He remained a close friend of Sullivan, who jokingly pointed out his musical limitations in a letter written just a year before his own death:

> In endeavouring to intone, you led choir, congregation, and organist an exciting chase over a gamut of about two octaves, we vainly doing our utmost to follow you. You were heroic – we never could run you to earth; that is, pin you to the same note for two consecutive prayers or collects.[56]

Another more musically accomplished clergyman with whom Sullivan struck up a close friendship at this time was Robert Brown, known as Brown-Borthwick after his marriage at Westminster Abbey in 1868 at which Sullivan was a groomsman and for which he wrote a four-part unaccompanied anthem, 'Rejoice in the Lord' based on Psalm 33. Curate at the Quebec Chapel, Marble Arch, he was a leading hymnologist and gave Sullivan his first substantial commission for hymn tunes in 1869. Clement Cotterill Scholefield (1839–1904), curate at St Peter's, Cranley Gardens from 1871 to 1879, also became a close friend. Although lacking any formal musical education, he was commissioned by Sullivan to write several tunes for the hymn book that he edited in 1874, among them the immortal ST CLEMENT (see Appendix 3).

Of all the friends that Sullivan made following his return from Leipzig the most significant was almost certainly George Grove (1820–1900). Best remembered as organizer of concerts in the Crystal Palace, first director of the Royal College of Music and founding editor of the Dictionary of Music that still bears his name, Grove was a polymath, whose interests encompassed engineering and biblical scholarship. He became particularly close to Sullivan, when they journeyed together to Vienna in 1867 in search of long-lost musical manuscripts by Schubert. Their letters to each other, which are preserved in the Pierpont Morgan Library, reveal a level of affection and intimacy unmatched anywhere else in Sullivan's correspondence. Grove produced his own biblical concordance in 1854 and contributed more than 1,000 pages to a Bible Dictionary edited in the early 1860s by the lexicographer, Sir William Smith. Of advanced liberal theological views, he was an early British enthusiast for the movement which originated in Germany to treat the Bible like other ancient texts and subject it to scientific study and historical criticism. He deplored literal readings of the Bible, which he felt was 'set up as an idol' and was 'full of crude, horrid ideas about God ... formed in a dark ignorant age'.[57] I suspect that Grove's liberal theology may have influenced the religious views of Sullivan, who called him in to advise on the selection of scriptural texts for *The Light of the World* and on the libretto of *The Martyr of Antioch*. Although there is no direct evidence of this, I also wonder if Grove had a hand in constructing the libretto of Sullivan's other major sacred choral work, *The Prodigal Son* (see pages 113–21).

Church music was not the centre of Sullivan's world in the 1860s, as it had been in the Chapel Royal days. In terms of composing, which was his driving purpose in the ten years after he returned from Leipzig, sacred pieces took their place alongside many others. He himself said of this period:

I was ready to undertake anything that came my way, symphonies, overtures, ballets, anthems, hymn tunes, songs, part songs, a concerto for the cello, and eventually comic and light operas – nothing came amiss to me, and I gladly accepted what the publishers offered me, so long as I could get the things published.[58]

Most of the music that he composed between 1861 and 1871 was secular. It included the incidental music to *The Tempest* (1862), which established his reputation as the leading up-and-coming British composer, the ballet *L'Ile Enchantée* and the cantata *Kenilworth* in 1864, the Cello Concerto, Irish Symphony and *In Memoriam* overture in 1866, the *Marmion* overture in 1867 and the overture *Di Ballo* in 1870. There were also chamber music pieces, numerous song settings and the initial ventures into the genre which would bring him lasting fame and fortune with *Cox and Box* in 1866, the *Contrabandista* in 1867 and *Thespis*, his first collaboration with W. S. Gilbert, in 1871. Set alongside this substantial corpus, Sullivan's sacred output in the ten years following his return from Leipzig seems relatively modest. It encompassed seven hymn tunes, seven anthems, a Te Deum, Jubilate and Kyrie published by Novello in 1866 and more substantially, his own first oratorio, *The Prodigal Son* (1869).

Sullivan's resignation from his post as organist of St Peter's in February 1872 marked the end of his time as a musician working in a church context. Coming less than two months after the opening of *Thespis* at the Gaiety Theatre, it is tempting to see it, as several biographers have, as signalling a decisive turning away from the world of sacred music which had so gripped and enthralled him as a boy and throughout his teenage years. On the eve of his thirtieth birthday, he was firmly established as the great hope of British music in all its aspects, not just the narrowly ecclesiastical, with a reputation rivalling that of Mendelssohn as the man who might at last end the old canard that England was the land without music.

Did his departure from the organ loft signal a more fundamental move at the end of his twenties away from the faith of his childhood and teenage years towards a more secular, agnostic outlook? It is difficult to say. As has already been pointed out, the letters written in the first three decades of his life display a greater sense of the presence of God, or at least more often invoke God's name, than do those that he wrote in later years. That may simply be because so many of them were written to his parents and express tender filial affection. He clearly enjoyed his ten years as a church organist – he was probably earning enough from his songs by the mid 1860s to have quitted earlier if his motives for doing the job were purely financial – but he was becoming increasingly busy on the conducting circuit and immersed in social and other distractions. Perhaps the decision to stop being a church organist and choirmaster, with the regular weekend commitments that the job entailed, was more what would now be called a lifestyle choice than an indication of waning religious commitment.

Although he certainly stopped being in church every Sunday, Sullivan did not give up the practice of churchgoing after leaving his post at St Peter's. His diary records that while he seldom seems to have attended a Sunday service while on his own in London or in one of the country retreats where he escaped to work, he almost always worshipped at the local parish church or private chapel when staying as a weekend guest with his aristocratic friends and patrons. He was often prevailed on to play the organ or harmonium at such services, something which he was always happy to do. He particularly commented on and enjoyed hearty hymn singing. An entry in his diary for 9 September 1874, while staying at Balcarres, the Scottish home of Sir Coutts and Lady Lindsay, is typical: 'We had a heavenly day yesterday and drove in the morning to the English Church, six miles distant. There was a very nice service, and we all sang the hymn lustily, to the accompaniment of a small organ, played by one young lady and blown by another.'[59] The journey to the 'English' (i.e. Episcopal) church, rather than the nearer Presbyterian parish church, where the musical diet was still probably restricted to unaccompanied metrical psalms, would certainly have met with his approval. In a letter to his mother from Glasgow the following year, he complained 'I tried to find a good Anglican church, but they are all dull or else Kirks.'[60] Much more to his taste was the style of worship that he experienced on board HMS *Hercules*, the flagship of his good friend the Duke of Edinburgh, who had invited him as guest on a cruise round the Baltic in June 1881: 'Yesterday being Sunday there was a church service and I played the harmonium. I was greatly delighted with the singing of the crew. They roared out the chants and the hymn tunes lustily and loved to dwell on the high notes.'[61]

He also often attended and participated in church services on his many visits abroad. In a letter to his mother on Christmas Day 1877 he reported that 'by the help of a stalwart gendarme' he had managed to gain access to the crowded Midnight Mass at St Sulpice in Paris 'where my friend Widor is organist' and noted that 'when the mass was over – that is the communion – judge my surprise and pleasure when they struck up the Adeste Fideles!'.[62] Five years later he wrote to her from Cairo to say that he had played the organ at the English church service where 'our gallant band sang very well, especially "Onward, Christian Soldiers" (my tune).'[63] A visit to Monaco in 1878 'to have a look at the gaming tables' prompted the resolution 'Tomorrow I shall make a colossal effort and go to Church – to counterbalance the wickedness of gambling'.[64] It is a rare but perhaps telling acknowledgement of his weakness for gambling and resolve to atone for it in some measure through religious observance.

Whatever led Sullivan to end his weekly active involvement in making church music, he did not stop composing in this area. On the contrary, in the two years following his resignation from St Peter's, he wrote relatively few secular works and devoted himself very largely to sacred compositions. They include the *Festival Te Deum* of 1872, the oratorio *The Light of the World* (1873) and the great majority of his hymn tunes – 25 original tunes and 69 arrangements for the major hymn book which he edited in 1874. It is to his hymn tunes that I now turn as I begin a systematic exploration of his output in the field of church and sacred music.

4

They Only Suffer Dr Watts' Hymns: Hymn Tunes and Arrangements

Of all Sullivan's sacred music, indeed of all his work aside from the Savoy operas, it is his congregational hymn and carol tunes and arrangements that are the best known and most frequently performed today. Despite the best efforts of politically correct and pacifist-inclined clergy and hymn book editors to stop us singing 'Onward, Christian soldiers', ST GERTRUDE remains among the most popular and instantly recognizable of all British hymn tunes. Indeed, it is a tribute to its potency and popularity that there have been so many attempts to fit it with less militaristic words and also to parody it, as the examples in Appendix 2 testify (pages 199–200). NOEL, Sullivan's arrangement and extension of a traditional folk melody, is sung every Christmas to Edmund Sears's carol 'It came upon the midnight clear'. LUX EOI, GOLDEN SHEAVES and BISHOPGARTH are regularly used for a variety of hymns in most of the major British churches. In the Episcopal Church of the United States of America ST KEVIN is the preferred tune for the Easter hymn 'Come, ye faithful, raise the strain'. Less often heard today, but still to be found in several hymn books, are SAMUEL (for 'Hushed was the evening hymn'), COURAGE BROTHER (for 'Courage, brother, do not stumble') and PROPIOR DEO (for 'Nearer, my God, to Thee').

The writing and arranging of hymn tunes were among Sullivan's earliest activities as a composer and the first to earn him money. The harmonized accompaniments, which he made at the age of 15 for four plainsong melodies attached to ancient Latin hymns and which appeared in the 1858 edition of Thomas Helmore's *Hymnal Noted*, constituted his first commission. The great majority of his hymn tunes were composed early on in his career, although he went on writing them throughout his life, one of his most enduring and characteristic, BISHOPGARTH, being composed three years before his death for the diamond jubilee of Queen Victoria. Overall, I calculate that Sullivan wrote 61 original hymn tunes and 75 harmonizations and arrangements of existing melodies. The full list, with the first line of the text to which each was first set and the date and place of first publication, appears in Appendix 1 (pages 188–198). Most of the tunes can be found in the excellent booklet published by Richard Cockaday.[1] The great majority were written specifically for two hymn books, *The Hymnary* (1872), to which Sullivan contributed 12 original tunes, and *Church Hymns with Tunes* (1874), for which he himself was musical editor and supplied 25 new tunes and 69 arrangements.

In writing hymn tunes, Sullivan was contributing along with other leading English composers of the period to one of the most significant musical and cultural movements of the Victorian age. It was only in the 1840s and 1850s that the Church of England fully embraced hymn singing, allowing congregations to extend their repertoire beyond the narrow confines of metrical psalmody and following the example of Nonconformist churches, led by the Baptists and Independents, who had been lustily singing hymns of human composure for a century or more, and poaching worshippers from Anglican churches as a result. The most important and influential hymn book of the Victorian age, and arguably of all time, *Hymns Ancient and Modern*, published in 1861, firmly established hymn singing at the heart of Church of England worship. In its wake came a shoal of Anglican hymn books, including the two to which Sullivan contributed so extensively, *The Hymnary* and *Church Hymns with Tunes*. His tunes were widely taken up by Nonconformists, notably Baptists, Methodists, Congregationalists and Presbyterians; indeed it was an English Presbyterian hymnal, *Psalms and Hymns for Divine Worship* (1867) which provided his first commissions. They were also very popular with the Presbyterian churches of Scotland, who finally weaned themselves away from an exclusive diet of metrical psalms in the 1870s and 1880s.

Hymn tunes were far from being a musical backwater in the latter half of the nineteenth century and were rather at the cutting edge of contemporary composition. Nicholas Temperley has rightly described the Victorian hymn tune as 'the greatest musical achievement of the period ... which brought together all parties in the Church and gave congregations a genuine and appropriate part to play in a joint performance with choir and organ'.[2] The choral movement and the introduction of organs into most churches encouraged the writing of hymn tunes in four part harmony with a range of tone colours to enhance their mood, the melody sometimes being tossed around between parts and the old four-square psalm tune giving way to continuous musical compositions more akin to part-songs or oratorio choruses with more daring harmonies and progressions. It was natural that as a young up-and-coming composer schooled in church music, Sullivan should turn his hand to writing hymn tunes which provided such creative possibilities and for which there was a huge demand, especially in the 1860s and 1870s, when new texts and hymn books came thick and fast at the height of the Victorian hymn explosion. It is significant that the overwhelming majority of his original tunes (55 out of 61) were written for new texts and translations written by his contemporaries. He set the words of many of the great Victorian hymn writers, including John Ellerton, John Henry Newman, John Mason Neale, Horatius Bonar and William Walsham How. He also supplied new tunes for a classic seventeenth-century text, John Milton's 'Let us with a gladsome mind' (his EVER FAITHFUL EVER SURE arguably provides a more varied and less banal accompaniment than the generally used MONKLAND), and for three outstandingly popular eighteenth-century hymns, William Cowper's 'God moves in a mysterious way' (ST LUKE), Augustus Toplady's 'Rock of Ages' (MOUNT ZION) and Charles Wesley's 'Love Divine all Loves Excelling' (FORMOSA).

Rivalry between publishers in their determination to cash in on the new and growing market for hymns helped hymn writers by providing an insatiable demand for new tunes. Sullivan himself alluded to this rivalry when he wrote that 'one of my best known hymn tunes was the result of a quarrel'.[3] The proprietors of *Hymns Ancient and Modern* fell out with their original publishers, Novello, who proceeded to commission a rival book, *The Hymnary*, for the same predominantly High Church market. The musical editor of *The Hymnary*, Joseph Barnby, commissioned Sullivan to write a new tune for Sabine Baring Gould's 'Onward, Christian soldiers', which had been set when it first appeared in the 1868 appendix to the first edition of *Hymns Ancient and Modern* to ST ALBAN, an uninspiring arrangement of a tune from the slow movement of Haydn's Symphony No. 53 in D. Sullivan's stirring ST GERTRUDE, which first appeared in print in advance of the publication of *The Hymnary* in the December 1871 issue of the *Musical Times*, soon supplanted it and gave the hymn a new popularity and long life.

In terms of his representation in the hymn books of the period, Sullivan stands firmly within the top ten Victorian hymn tune composers. In an analysis which I made for my book *Abide With Me: The World of Victorian Hymns*, based on the tunes used in four of the most popular hymn books of the last three decades of the nineteenth century, he ranks sixth, coming below John Bacchus Dykes, Joseph Barnby, Henry Gauntlett, Henry Smart and Edward John Hopkins, and above John Stainer, Samuel Sebastian Wesley, William Henry Monk and Richard Redhead. Subsequent research across a wider range of hymnals has confirmed that he consistently maintained his position roughly halfway up the top ten, with a tally of between 25 and 30 original tunes in virtually every hymnal published in the late nineteenth and early twentieth centuries. This was quite an achievement considering that in terms of overall output, he came considerably lower down the pecking order. Stainer, for example, wrote 157 original tunes, Dykes 276 and the exceptionally prolific Henry Gauntlett churned out around 10,000.

Sullivan was unusual among the leading Victorian composers of hymn tunes in that much of his career was devoted to writing secular music. The only other one who conceivably falls into this category was Joseph Barnby, whose compositions included the Eton school song, 'Carmen Etonse', and the best-selling ballad 'Sweet and Low'. The rest were church musicians whose output was almost entirely confined to sacred music. It is tempting to see Sullivan as an essentially secular musician who dabbled in writing hymn tunes without any great conviction and simply as a way of making money when he was struggling as a young composer. This is the verdict of David Eden: 'I think it is safe to conclude that Sullivan's considerable output in this area came into existence simply because he needed the money … His reason for writing had nothing to do with religious conviction as such.'[4] It is certainly true that writing hymn tunes was a lucrative occupation for those making their way in the musical profession. The booming market in hymn books provided commissions and substantial sales and frequent reprints brought in regular royalty payments.

It is also true that more than three-quarters of Sullivan's hymn tunes and all his harmonizations and arrangements were written before the start of his successful collaboration with Gilbert and D'Oyly Carte in 1875. There were, however, good reasons, other than a mere desire to make money, why most of his work in this area was done in the years between 1867 and 1874. This was the height of the Victorian hymn boom, when, in Temperley's words, 'the torrent of hymns and hymn tunes unequalled before or since … appears to have reached its height'.[5] It was also the period when Sullivan was himself a church organist and was much involved in the world of church music. As we have already observed, many of his closest friends during this period of his life were church musicians, and it was partly at their prompting that he wrote hymn tunes and arrangements. It was, for example, at the behest of Robert Brown-Borthwick, editor of the *Supplemental Hymn and Tune Book*, published in 1869, that he wrote his arrangement of the tune ST ANN, attributed to William Croft, to accompany Reginald Heber's hymn 'The Son of God goes forth to war'.

The other image that tends to prevail is of Sullivan not putting much care into his hymn tunes and dashing them off quickly and casually, often while staying with his aristocratic friends. This is hardly surprising, given that his best-known tune, ST GERTRUDE, seems to have been composed in a matter of a few minutes in the drawing room at Hanford, a large house near Blanford in Dorset, where he was staying as the guest of Ernest and Gertrude Clay Ker Seymer (Ernest, the elder brother of the composer Frederic Clay, had added his wife's surname to his own on his marriage). Sullivan named the tune after his hostess who ended her account of the tune's hasty composition: 'We sang it in the private chapel attached to the house, Sir Arthur playing the harmonium.'[6] The fact is that it was not just hymn tunes that Sullivan wrote at some speed while staying in country houses. He seems to have composed several songs for *The Sorcerer* during a brief visit to Balcarres House in Fife as guest of Sir Coutts and Lady Lindsay. Much of his composing was done at breakneck speed, and there is no evidence to suggest that his hymn tunes received more perfunctory or casual treatment than any other class of work. On the contrary, his boyhood experience of singing hymns in the Chapel Royal made him conscious of the importance of this aspect of church music, and when he came to compiling and arranging the tunes for the hymn book, which he himself edited in 1874, he seems to have taken the whole business very seriously and devoted a considerable amount of time and effort to it.

Sullivan is usually ranked alongside Barnby and Stainer as a leading exponent of the high Victorian hymn tune, distinguished by an emotional and sentimental style achieved through intricate part writing, chromatic progressions and other devices designed to enhance the impact of the text. The three composers were good friends and much of an age: Barnby was four years older and Stainer two years older than Sullivan. They are often seen as following the lead of their seniors Dykes and Monk, both of whom were born in 1823, in eschewing the restraint, austerity and classical harmony of an earlier generation of nineteenth-century composers, led by John Goss (born in 1810) and Henry Smart (born in 1813). In terms of his style, Sullivan is perhaps best placed alongside Dykes as well as Stainer and Barnby. All four wrote in a characteristically sentimental Victorian idiom, and it is notable that each had a collection of his hymn tunes published by Novello shortly after his death, an accolade accorded to few other composers.

Sullivan had considerable respect for the work of older composers like Goss and retained a fondness for the plainchant in which he had been schooled by Thomas Helmore. Several of his own hymn tunes use Anglican chant – notably VENI CREATOR, about which he wrote to William Walsham How, 'it is a favourite of mine and has a most peculiar effect on me', LITANY NO. 2 and HOLY CITY – and he wrote a chant for Psalm 150 (see page 151). The great majority of his tunes, however, are distinctively high Victorian in being lyrical and flowing, written and harmonized like part-songs and carefully crafted to heighten the emotional impact of the text. They are more sentimental and less austere and restrained than what had gone before and what would come after in the tunes of Vaughan Williams, Stanford and Parry. For most of Sullivan's contemporaries, the motivation for this style of writing came principally from the Tractarian or Oxford Movement within the Church of England, of which Dykes was a leading exponent and Barnby and Stainer keen disciples. Although a cardinal principle of Tractarianism was the doctrine of reserve, it also sought to bring more colour and drama into worship and was often characterized by an intense emotionalism, which its critics felt displayed a rather maudlin effeminacy summed up by the lace cottas worn by Anglo-Catholic priests. Sullivan himself did not inhabit this world. There is no evidence that he had Tractarian leanings, although the churchmanship at St Peter's, Cranley Gardens, where he was organist from 1867 to 1872, tended in that direction. For him, perhaps more than for most of the other leading Victorian hymn tune composers, musical influences were more important than theological or ecclesiological principles. The influence of Schubert and Mendelssohn was particularly strong in terms of an emphasis on a firm lyrical melodic line and lush harmonies.

Where Sullivan stands very clearly alongside Dykes, Stainer and other leading exponents of the high Victorian hymn tune is in his almost evangelistic determination to enhance the meaning of the texts he set, pointing up their poignancy and drama and eliciting the maximum response from those singing them. Most of the hymn tunes written by these composers were carefully tailored to a particular set of words. They were not stock tunes written for general use with any text of the right metre. To this extent, they were written with an evangelistic and spiritual intent and not as exercises in perfect harmony and counterpart according to the principles of J. S. Bach. Stainer pointed to this spiritual purpose when he defended the hymns of his contemporaries against their academic critics who saw them as vulgar and lacking in high artistic standards:

> Many of our most valuable words and hymns ... would fail to satisfy the artificial requirements of the learned poet, but they uplift the heart and emotions as if by some hidden magic. Alas for the day if such a path for spiritual influence should ever be lightly set aside in order to make room for words and music intended to teach the higher rules of poetry and a cold respectability in music.[7]

Although certainly not an Evangelical in the partisan sense of the word, Sullivan would have shared Stainer's view that the 'true estimate of a hymn tune cannot be found by principles of abstract criticism' but rather in 'something indefinable and intangible which can render it, not only a winning musical melody, but also a most powerful evangeliser'.[8] He would also have agreed with Dykes that 'music should be beautiful, that it may be a more fitting offering for Him, and better calculated to impress, soften, humanise and win' and that his one desire was that 'each hymn should be so set to music (by whomsoever God wills to select for that purpose) that its power for influencing and teaching may be best brought out'.[9] This twin emphasis on creating beautiful music and enhancing the meaning and message of the text is evident in Sullivan's hymn tunes just as much as it is in his settings of Gilbert's lyrics in the Savoy operas.

The extent to which Sullivan was a disciple of Dykes is very clear from his setting of Horatius Bonar's very popular and avowedly sentimental 'I heard the voice of Jesus say':

> I heard the voice of Jesus say,
> 'Come unto me and rest;
> Lay down, thou weary one, lay down
> Thy head upon my breast':
> I came to Jesus as I was,
> So weary, worn and sad;
> I found in him a resting-place,
> And he has made me glad.

Sullivan's AUDITE AUDIENTES ME, which first appeared in the *New Church Tune Book* of 1874, follows the precedent set by Dykes in his VOX DILECTI, written for the 1868 appendix to *Hymns Ancient and Modern*, in modulating from the minor to the major halfway through the verse to fit the change in tone of Bonar's text. While Sullivan was almost certainly following Dykes's lead in using this device, he went even further in emphasizing the message of the hymn by setting the first half of each verse, which is essentially made up of Jesus' words of invitation, in unison over sustained organ chords and the second half, which describes the believer's response, in harmony. Although AUDITE AUDIENTES ME is weaker and less memorable than VOX DILECTI, it strives even harder to reflect and enhance the change of mood in the text. There are other Sullivan tunes which are clearly derivative – it is hard to hear his 1874 tune CORONAE for 'Crown him with many crowns', for example, without feeling that it is closely modelled on George Elvey's DIADEMATA, set to the same hymn in the 1868 appendix to *Hymns Ancient and Modern*.

Sullivan's hymn tunes encompass a huge range of styles and moods, reflecting the very different themes of the texts to which they were set. Some, like ST GERTRUDE, BISHOPGARTH and LUX EOI, come straight off the parade ground and could have been written for the chorus of heavy dragoons in *Patience*. In this, they are entirely in keeping with the triumphant words to which they are set. ST GERTRUDE fits the mood of Sabine Baring Gould's 'Onward, Christian Soldiers', which was originally written as a 'Hymn for Procession with Cross and Banners' to be sung outdoors by children processing on Whit Monday from one Yorkshire village to another, much better than the sluggish ST ALBAN to which it was initially set. BISHOPGARTH was written for a patriotic hymn celebrating Queen Victoria's Diamond Jubilee. Sullivan excelled in producing stirring patriotic tunes and he was called on to provide a suitable melody for a Canadian national hymn, 'God bless our wide Dominion, our fathers' chosen land' written by the Marquess of Lorne while Governor General in 1880. He obliged with DOMINION HYMN. LUX EOI was written for a triumphalist hymn about the second coming of Christ, 'Hark a thrilling voice is sounding: "Christ is nigh!" it seems to say'. It also fits supremely well the great resurrection hymn of praise 'Alleluia! Alleluia! Hearts to heaven and voices raise' to which it is now almost universally sung.

Other similarly bouncy affirmative tunes express Sullivan's own simple, trusting faith, which was, like his approach to life more generally, uncomplicated, generous, open and hopeful. As I have already suggested, I think his faith is clearly represented in his setting of Norman MacLeod's hymn 'Courage, brother, do not stumble', itself a great statement of straightforward manly muscular faith, which has much the same message as Harry Lauder's popular music hall song 'Keep right on to the end of the road' and could happily be sung by Muslims and Jews as well as by Christians. Sullivan's tune COURAGE BROTHER reinforces the hymn's central message 'Trust in God' by repeating it not just once but twice so that it rings out three times as a stirring clarion call above the bouncy march-like setting of the verses. A similar affinity with the text informs CONSTANCE, written for the hymn 'Who trusts in God a strong abode in heaven and earth possesses'. It is a tune that could have come straight out of *The Sorcerer* – and it would be tempting to suggest that the composer named it after the delightfully trusting and innocent character of Constance in that piece were it not for the fact that it pre-dates the opera by three years.

Sullivan's intrinsic optimism and love of life come across in other tunes which are not so obviously bouncy and 'rumpty tumpty'. The lyrical but gentle GOLDEN SHEAVES perfectly fits William Chatterton Dix's harvest hymn 'To Thee, O Lord, our hearts we raise in hymns of adoration' with its wonderful rich imagery of bright robes of gold adorning the fields and the valleys standing so rich with corn that they are singing. Sullivan provides this pastoral hymn of thanksgiving with a melody so appropriate and vivid that you can almost smell the newly mown hay and hear the threshing machines as you sing it. In its way, it is as evocative of the English landscape as the music of Delius or Vaughan Williams but in a lusher, more comfortable and more Victorian way. There is a similarly gentle but affirmative quality in Sullivan's setting of Sarah Flowers Adams's 'Nearer my God to thee', another sentimental hymn of personal faith that was immensely popular with the Victorians. It is significant that in this case he adopts a very different approach to Dykes whose tune HORBURY, written for the same hymn, could be taken almost as a textbook example of the high Victorian hymn tune at its most dreary – achingly slow, full of chromatic slides and infused with a soporific, maudlin quality. In contrast, Sullivan's PROPIOR DEO manages to be much more affirmative and filled with hope without losing a sense of the poignancy and yearning conveyed in the words. It is not as full of suspensions as Dykes's tune, the melodic flow is better and the harmonies are not so cloying. Once again, it seems to me to express the composer's simple, trusting faith.

There are strong grounds for believing that PROPIOR DEO was the tune used by the musicians on the *Titanic* when they played 'Nearer my God to Thee' shortly before the liner went down on the night of 15 April 1912. Sarah Adams's hymn seems to have been sung to Sullivan's tune in the Bethel Independent Methodist Chapel in Colne, Lancashire, where the *Titanic*'s bandmaster, Wallace Hartley, had been a chorister and played the violin and where his father was choirmaster. Edward Moody, a close friend of Hartley's, told the *London Daily News* in an interview shortly after the tragedy: 'When I speak of "Nearer my God to Thee", I mean Sullivan's setting. That would be what the orchestra played on the sinking Titanic.' Hartley's body was recovered from the sea, according to one account with his violin strapped to his chest, and brought back by liner across the Atlantic. PROPIOR DEO was played at his funeral in the Bethel Chapel and as his coffin was lowered into the ground at Colne Cemetery. It was also sung at a concert to raise money for a memorial to him. His memorial, which stands in Colne churchyard, has carved into its base a violin and the opening bars of PROPIOR DEO accompanying the first two lines of the hymn.[10]

Other Sullivan tunes are equally if not more touched with pathos and poignancy. They include the restrained COENA DOMINI which provides a rather understated accompaniment to the communion hymn 'Draw nigh and take the body of the Lord', a translation by J. M. Neale from a Latin original found in a seventh-century Irish Antiphoner. Perhaps the most nuanced and sensitive is LUX IN TENEBRIS, written for John Henry Newman's 'Lead, kindly light', another favourite, which was regularly at the top of the Victorian hymnological hit parade. It is essentially an expression of doubt-filled faith, penned by Newman, when he was at the height of the spiritual crisis, which was to find its resolution in his reception into the Roman Catholic Church, and its wide popularity surely had much to do with the Victorian crisis of faith. Many composers tried their hand at setting it. Probably its best known accompaniment is Dykes's LUX BENIGNA, which although commended by Newman himself, hardly reflects the hesitant, tentative nature of his text, being altogether too positive, with a strong forward movement in its steady, reassuring repeated minims. Sullivan's LUX IN TENEBRIS, which is perhaps better suited to choirs than congregations and has appeared as a choir anthem in several hymnals, provides a much more sensitive and honest reflection of Newman's ambiguity and expressions of doubt. The supposedly worldly Sullivan understood and captured the mood of this classic spiritual text better than the pious Dykes.

It is significant that LUX IN TENEBRIS first appeared in a selection of sacred part-songs. The dividing line between the Victorian hymn and the sacred parlour ballad was distinctly blurred and authors like Adelaide Ann Procter as well as composers like Sullivan and Barnby regularly crossed over between the two genres. Like other composers of high Victorian hymn tunes, Sullivan was often accused by critics of writing in the style of part-songs with the implication that this brought a secular sentimentalism into the worship of God. It was probably not an accusation that greatly bothered him. He would almost certainly have agreed with Dykes, who was not averse to the term 'part-song' being applied to his hymn tunes and maintained 'that every age should contribute to the store of the church's music according to the spirit of its own time and that the Victorian age should contribute in that of the part-song, so essentially associated with that time'.[11]

Sullivan was perhaps at his best when setting hymns that were themselves written in the style of sacred songs and parlour ballads in telling a strong human story and eliciting a moral and emotional response. A good example is James Drummond Burns's dramatic retelling of the story of the Lord's appearance to Samuel, 'Hushed was the evening hymn'. The opening verse sets the tone of colourful descriptive writing and dramatic narrative:

Hushed was the evening hymn,
The temple courts were dark,

The light was burning dim
Before the sacred ark;
When suddenly a voice divine
Rang through the silence of the shrine.

Subsequent verses vividly retell the story of Eli and Samuel, and the last
stanza calls for a clear and direct response with a typical Victorian commendation of the values of resignation and obedience and an idealization
of simple childlike faith:

Oh! give me Samuel's mind,
A sweet unmurmuring faith,
Obedient and resigned
To Thee in life and death,
That I may read with childlike eyes
Truths that are hidden from the wise.

Sullivan related strongly both to Burns's dramatic narrative and to his
evocation of simple, innocent faith. His setting of this text, SAMUEL, is
adjudged his best hymn tune by several musicologists, among them the
distinguished twentieth-century hymnologist, John Wilson, who wrote
that 'the text caught him more than half way to his "G & S" mood'.[12]

Sullivan was undoubtedly more at home with hymn texts which told a
story and expressed a simple, hope-filled faith than with those expressing
deep and mystical theology. Among his worst tunes is CHAPEL ROYAL
written for George Matheson's 'O Love that wilt let not let me go', a text
that is full of powerful but complex theological imagery centred on the
theme of sacrifice. He lacked the theological grasp displayed by Stainer
in his tunes CROSS OF JESUS and ALL FOR JESUS, which handle the
doctrine of the atonement and the power of the cross with a subtlety
and understanding that Sullivan never really demonstrated. He was not
interested in exploring and interpreting theological themes and the finer
points of Christian doctrine. The hymns that brought out the best in him
were those with relatively simple expressions of faith, although they did
not need to be triumphalistic and devoid of ambiguity and doubt. One of
his earliest hymn tunes, initially called ST LUKE and later ST NATHANIEL,
was written for William Cowper's 'God moves in a mysterious way'. A
chromatic progression at the end of the second line leading into an octave
leap on the first two words of the third line, particularly appropriate for
the phrases 'he plants' in the first verse and 'are big' in the third, gives the
tune an angular, mysterious feel wholly appropriate to the words.

Sullivan's contribution to Victorian hymnody did not just consist in supplying tunes. He also acted as musical editor for a major mid-Victorian hymn book, *Church Hymns with Tunes*, published by the Society for Promoting Christian Knowledge in 1874 and intended to provide a middle-of-the-road alternative to High Church hymnals like Helmore's *The Hymnal Noted* and Barnby's *The Hymnary*. Less sacramental and more low church in ethos than *Hymns Ancient and Modern*, it was at the same time less markedly Evangelical than the other widely used Victorian Anglican hymn book, *The Hymnal Companion to the Book of Common Prayer*. In editing a major hymnal Sullivan was following the example of two of his close musical friends: Robert Brown-Borthwick had edited the *Supplemental Hymn and Tune Book* in 1869 and Barnby *The Hymnary* in 1874. Stainer would later perform the same task for the main Presbyterian hymnal, *The Church Hymnary*. Musical editorship of these large and complex volumes brought some financial rewards but also a great deal of hard work in commissioning, selecting and arranging tunes and it was generally undertaken as a form of ministry and service to the church. In the midst of his labours over *Church Hymns With Tunes*, Sullivan wrote to Brown-Borthwick, 'Had I known the wearisome labours of it, I would not have undertaken it for a <u>thousand pounds</u>' and to his mother, 'I hope that the hymn-book will be a blessing to the Church. It's a curse to me.'[13] Most of his biographers have tended to emphasize the negative aspect of these remarks and suggest that they showed that the project was a tiresome chore, which he only undertook for the money. However, we should perhaps take the remark to his mother expressing his hope that the book would be a blessing for the Church at face value. The same sentiment is expressed at the end of his preface to the hymnal, 'the Editor trusts that this book may prove one more step towards the advancement of good and worthy music in the service of God'.[14]

In preparing his hymnal, Sullivan enlisted the help of and commissioned tunes from his friends Clement Scholefield, Robert Brown-Borthwick and James Elliott. He also worked very closely with William Walsham How, rector of Whittington in Shropshire and a leading hymn writer in the Victorian Church of England, best known today for his authorship of 'For all the Saints who from their labours rest'. In the preface, he thanked How, who was one of the editors of *Church Hymns*, 'for his kindness in undertaking the work of inserting Expression Marks, a work which the Editor cannot but think he has carried out with great discretion and taste'. The two men became friends and mutual admirers and were later to collaborate, at Sullivan's instigation, on the Diamond Jubilee hymn for Queen Victoria.

We can learn something of Sullivan's own taste in hymn tunes from the collection that he edited. *Church Hymns With Tunes* contains 38 different German chorale melodies, predominantly from the seventeenth century, many of which are used several times. There are also tunes by Gibbons, Tallis, Bach and Handel and plainsong melodies. The great majority of the tunes, however, were written by living Victorian composers. Sullivan himself contributed 36 original tunes. Elliott, who was organist at three fashionable London churches between 1864 and 1909, had 14 tunes in the book, Dykes 13, Gauntlett 10, Barnby 8, Henry Smart (nephew of Sullivan's mentor at the Chapel Royal) 7 and Brown-Borthwick and Scholefield each had 6. The tunes attributed to Scholefield, all specially commissioned for *Church Hymns With Tunes*, include ST CLEMENT, set to John Ellerton's 'The day Thou gavest' and destined to be one of the most enduring and popular of all Victorian hymn tunes. The possibility that Sullivan may have had a rather greater hand in it than the attribution suggests is discussed in Appendix 3.

Other contemporaries were not so favoured. W. H. Monk, the musical editor of *Hymns Ancient and Modern*, had only two tunes in *Church Hymns with Tunes*, the same number as Prince Albert, while S. S. Wesley fared little better with three and Stainer had only one. These poor showings are almost certainly a result of copyright restrictions imposed by the editors of *Hymns Ancient and Modern* rather than any prejudice against them on the part of Sullivan.

In compiling *Church Hymns with Tunes*, Sullivan went above all for good, singable tunes. The melody was clearly uppermost in his mind, as it surely should be in a good hymn tune, but harmony was also important to him. In most of the 69 arrangements that he made for this book, he rendered the harmonies stronger and more interesting. His overriding concern was to find a good match for the words, as an interesting remark in the preface confirms:

> Adaptations from popular works are, as a rule, much to be deprecated, as presenting original compositions in a garbled form only. But exceptions may occasionally be made with advantage, and the Editor accepts without any very grave apprehension, the responsibility of such an arrangement, for instance as 'Come unto me', the original melody, which it closely follows, being so linked with the feeling of the words, that separation would seem unwarrantable.[15]

The particular tune to which Sullivan was referring here is an adaptation of Handel's melody from *Messiah* for the aria 'He shall feed his flock'. He used an arrangement of the part of the aria set to the familiar words from Matthew 11.28 'Come unto me, all ye that labour and are heavy laden, and I will give you rest' as the tune for a hymn based on the same biblical text, William Chatterton Dix's 'Come unto me, ye weary'. This rather daring interpolation of the Handel melody to replace a slightly dreary and pedestrian tune by Dykes, COME UNTO ME, to which this hymn was usually sung, could be seen as slightly corny and gimmicky but it brings us back to the central importance for Sullivan of using music to reinforce and enhance the meaning of words – in this case because a particular tune was so indissolubly linked to a scriptural text. The musical editor of the next edition of *Church Hymns with Tunes*, Basil Harwood, reverted to the Dykes tune.

Church Hymns with Tunes had substantial sales and influence within the Church of England. By 1890, it had sold over 85,000 copies and established itself as the second most used hymn book in Anglican churches after *Hymns Ancient and Modern*, with *The Hymnal Companion to the Book of Common Prayer* running a poor third. Its two most enduring contributions to hymnody were to launch ST CLEMENT on its way and to provide in NOEL the perfect accompaniment for Edmund Sears's wistful Christmas hymn, 'It came upon the midnight clear'. Sears's hymn, written in 1849, when he was pastor of a Unitarian church in Massachusetts, had first appeared in Britain in 1870 in *The Hymnal Companion to the Book of Common Prayer* set to FLENSBURG, a melody derived from a tune by Ludwig Spohr. For its appearance in *Church Hymns*, Sullivan reworked a traditional carol tune which had been sent to him by a friend. It has been identified as a Herefordshire tune called EARDISLEY and apparently used for the carol 'Dives and Lazarus', and it also bears a strong resemblance to the melody of the Sussex Mummers Carol. The eight opening bars which constitute the first half of NOEL are made up of Sullivan's arrangement of the traditional tune and the last nine bars, which make up the second half are his own original composition. Although more than half of the tune is an original Sullivan composition, with characteristic modesty he published it with the attribution 'Traditional Air arranged'.

Sullivan's love of hymn tunes is further demonstrated in the way that he brought them into some of his grand liturgical pieces. He based his *Festival Te Deum* around ST ANN, a tune probably written by William Croft, who had been a chorister in the Chapel Royal in the late seventeenth century, and firmly wedded by *Hymns Ancient and Modern* to Isaac Watts's 'O God, our help in ages past'. In somewhat similar fashion, he introduced his own tune ST GERTRUDE prominently into his *Boer War Te Deum*. Other composers used hymns in a more straightforward way in their oratorios, as Stainer did in *The Crucifixion* and Elgar in *The Dream of Gerontius*. Sullivan's employment of hymn tunes in his two Te Deums was more idiosyncratic but it demonstrates his clear fondness for this particular form of church music.

How were Sullivan's hymn tunes regarded by his contemporaries? Among his fellow musicians, Stainer was one of the most enthusiastic. He tried to persuade Sullivan to contribute some original tunes for his collection of *Carols for Christmastide* in 1867. Sullivan declined on the grounds that he had so many uncompleted commissions and all his time was taken up, although he did manage to contribute an exquisite arrangement of an old tune for 'All this night bright angels sing' for the second series of *Carols for Christmastide* in 1871. Stainer's high regard is evident from the fact that he used 28 Sullivan tunes in the first edition of the 1898 Presbyterian *Church Hymnary*, of which he was musical editor. John Curwen, the Congregationalist minister, who founded the tonic sol-fa system of music education, was another enthusiast for Sullivan's hymn tunes and arrangements. He recommended an arrangement of ST ANN in *Church Hymns with Tunes*, which uses simple unaccompanied harmony for the quieter verses as interludes between unison verses dominated by the organ, as a model of free accompaniment. From other quarters, however, Sullivan suffered in the general assault that was launched on the high Victorian hymn tunes by many in the church musical establishment. In a typical attack, John Heywood, organist of St Paul, Balsall Heath, near Coventry, published a book in 1881 criticizing contemporary hymn tunes as 'outrageously boisterous and vulgar'. Too many were 'pretty tunes', where the emphasis was on popularity rather than musical quality, and falling into what he called the 'tum tum' class with repeated notes and chords.[16] He did not mention names but Sullivan was undoubtedly in his mind, as well as Dykes and Stainer. In similar vein, Thomas Helmore wrote that 'most modern hymn tunes are nauseous' although he loyally forbore from singling out his old Chapel Royal pupil for disparaging comment.[17]

The views of hymn writers on Sullivan's tunes were equally varied. The ultra-Tractarian Francis Pott was not a fan of the tune written to accompany his 'Angel voices, ever singing':

I am afraid some of its popularity arose from Sullivan having, contrary to my desire, set it in 'The Hymnary' to a trivial, pretty but altogether unfit tune of his own – which caught the ear of people who did not trouble themselves to see that the hymn was of quite another character. In giving permission since for the printing of the hymn I have always made it a condition that Sullivan's tune shall not be in any way referred to.[18]

Doubtless it was the waltz-like lilt and chromatic swoops of ANGEL VOICES which made Pott feel that Sullivan's tune was trivial and inappropriate for his angelic meditations. Other leading hymn writers, however, did not share such misgivings about their hymns being made more popular by a rousing if slightly vulgar tune. John Ellerton thanked the editors of *Hymns Ancient and Modern* for Joseph Barnby's HEBRON, which they had commissioned for his 'Now the labourer's task is o'er': 'It seems to me nearly as perfect in its way as Sullivan's tune for 'Let no tears today be shed' [ST MILLICENT] – I mean as an interpretation of the words.'[19] It is significant that Ellerton, Broad Church in sympathy, a friend of working men and perhaps of all clerical Victorian hymn writers the one most attuned to popular taste, should have singled out for special praise the two least 'churchy' of the major hymn tune composers. The quality for which he praised them was, of course, exactly what made Barnby such a master of the parlour ballad and Sullivan the king of the patter song, their skill in setting words to give them prominence and bring out their meaning.

In 1898, Sullivan was asked by Rudyard Kipling to set his hymn text 'Recessional' which begins with the verse:

God of our fathers, known of old
Lord of the far-flung battle-line,
Beneath whose awful hand we hold
Dominion over palm and pine –
Lord God of Hosts, be with us yet,
Lest we forget – lest we forget!

In a letter to Kipling, Sullivan wrote that the task of setting 'Recessional' presented unusual difficulties, but did not elaborate on what they were. Was it that he found it difficult to capture the ambiguity at the heart of a text filled as much with doubts about Britain's imperial mission as pride in it and which warned of the danger of being 'drunk with sight of power'? Kipling replied to the composer asking him to accept what he called his 'hymn in spirit' as 'yours if you care to use it, and when you care to use it' and assuring him that 'there will be no other setting authorised by me'. He pressed Sullivan again on the subject of 'Recessional' two years later after the two men had collaborated on the song 'The Absent-Minded Beggar' to raise funds for the families of soldiers fighting in the Boer War, expressing the hope that 'the spirit will move you to set it'.[20] It is a moving testimony by one of the greatest poets of the late Victorian age to his faith in Sullivan's ability to capture the meaning of a hymn text which was not shallowly triumphalistic but deeply penitential and shot through with ambiguity.

Sullivan's hymn tunes were at their most popular in the years following his death. Writing in 1905, James Lightwood, the Methodist
hymnologist, commented enthusiastically: 'The distinguishing features of
Sullivan's tunes are their solid diatonic harmonies, and the easy flowing
melodiousness of the different parts. Thus they are eminently fitted for
congregational use, and a considerable number of them find a place in
most modern hymnals.'[21] Nonconformist hymnals from the early years of
the twentieth century especially favoured his tunes. The 1904 *Methodist
Hymn Book* contains 25 and the 1916 *Congregational Hymnary* 31. The
highest score of Sullivan tunes that I have been able to find in any hymn
book apart from the one that he himself edited is in a somewhat eccentric
Anglican volume, *The Church Hymnal for the Christian Year*, edited by
Victoria, Lady Carbery and published in 1917, where there are 34.

In his generally complimentary remarks, Lightwood pointed with less
enthusiasm to the use as hymn tunes of several of Sullivan's melodies
written for other purposes. He noted that 'Sullivan's celebrated song,
"The Lost Chord", has been set to "Jerusalem the golden"; but this exists
only in MS., and it is sincerely to be hoped it will never get beyond this
stage.' Although a footnote in his 1905 book records somewhat puzzling-
ly (given that Sullivan died in 1900) that 'it is now printed as a hymn-tune
with the composer's permission', I have failed to find it anywhere in print.
At least one other well-known Sullivan melody directly inspired a hymn
during the composer's lifetime. Finding that Phoebe's song 'Were I thy
bride' from *The Yeomen of the Guard* kept floating into his mind, the poet
and journalist, William Canton, best known for his children's poems and
hymns, wrote a hymn, 'Hold thou my hands' to fit it in 1893. He commented later 'these words seemed to grow into it and out of it'.

Hold thou my hands!
In grief and joy, in hope and fear,
Lord, let me feel that thou art near:
hold thou my hands![22]

It is not clear whether Sullivan was ever told about this hymn or whether
it ever appeared in print set to the tune which had inspired it. In both
the 1906 *English Hymnal* and *Songs of Praise* it was accompanied by a
sixteenth-century tune, MISERERE MEI.

The adoption of Sullivan melodies as hymn tunes continued in a more
marked fashion after his death. The 1900 *Baptist Church Hymnal* set
J. S. B. Monsell's 'When I had wandered from His fold' to the tune Sullivan
had written to accompany Adeline Procter's sacred song, 'Through sorrow's path'. The 1904 *Methodist Hymn Book* used the solemn opening

refrain of his overture 'In Memoriam' for Isaac Watts's hymn 'Not all the blood of beasts/On Jewish altars slain'. As far as I can see, this was the first appearance as a hymn tune of a melody that was subsequently taken up to accompany a number of hymns, including Edwin Hatch's 'Breathe on me, breath of God', Henry Lyte's 'My spirit on Thy care', John Ellerton's 'Our day of praise is done' and the vesper hymn 'Lord, keep us safe this night', which appeared in two settings in Novello's *Parish Choir Book*. In jollier vein, King Henry's song 'Youth will needs have dalliance' from the *Incidental Music to Henry VIII* was adopted for Ernest Smith's carol, 'We sing a song of Christmas time' in an American collection, *Carols Old and New*, edited by L. L. Hutchings and published in Boston in 1916. A later American hymn book, *The Army and Navy Hymnal* (1942), set William Walsham How's hymn 'The joyous life that year by year/Within these walls is stored' to Sullivan's carol tune 'Upon the snow clad earth'.

While Nonconformist hymnals were enthusiastically embracing Sullivan, a contrary campaign was in progress to keep his tunes out of early twentieth-century Anglican hymnals on the grounds of their Victorian sentimentality and vulgarity. Vaughan Williams made HAYDN, as he re-named ST ALBAN, the preferred tune for 'Onward, Christians Soldiers' in the 1906 *English Hymnal*, grudgingly allowing ST GERTRUDE in as an alternative. There were no other Sullivan tunes in the main body of the hymnal. GOLDEN SHEAVES was consigned, alongside Scholefield's ST CLEMENT, three tunes by Monk, two by Barnby and one by Dykes, to the appendix, which he famously described as 'The Chamber of Horrors', where one might 'dwell in the miasma of the languishing and sentimental hymn tunes which so often disfigure our services'.[23] Percy Dearmer did not include a single Sullivan tune in his 1926 *Songs of Praise,* a self-consciously modern collection, which eschewed Victorian sentimentality.

The musical establishment in the early twentieth century tore into Victorian hymn tunes for their sickly sweet, cloying, effeminate, sanctimonious quality, achieved through too much chromaticism, close harmony and over use of diminished and dominant sevenths. The tone was set by Henry Hadow, a leading academic musicologist, who wrote in 1900: 'They seek the honeyed cadence and the perfumed phrase ... they can touch the surface of emotion, but can never sound its depths.'[24] Vaughan Williams, writing in the preface to the *English Hymnal*, went so far as to say that the majority of Victorian hymn tunes, which he characterized as 'enervating, languishing and sentimental', were 'positively harmful to those who sing and hear them'.[25] Ernest Walker, writing in 1907, criticized their 'cheaply sugary harmony and palsied part-writing'.[26] For Charles Villiers Stanford, writing in 1914, Victorian hymn tunes were 'sentimentalized rubbish, decked out in gegaws, and as ill-suited to their surroundings as a music hall song in the Bayreuth Theatre ... they degrade religion and its services with slimy and sticky appeals to the senses, instead of ennobling and strengthening the higher instincts'.[27]

Dykes, Barnby, Stainer and Sullivan were the main victims of this ferocious assault. In the mid twentieth century, the attack became more narrowly focused on the hymn tunes of Sullivan. This is particularly evident in the writings of the distinguished hymnologist, Erik Routley, whose more general attacks on Sullivan's sacred music have already been quoted (pages 6–7). Routley directed his fiercest criticism on Sullivan's hymn tunes, launching his attack in an article in the Hymn Society Bulletin in 1942.

> Could 'Nearer, my God, to Thee' conceivably be given a setting more completely impercipient of its spirit than the almost outrageously unsuitable PROPIOR DEO, which has not a single throb of spiritual feeling in it? ... and is it possible to imagine any composer more utterly failing to feel, much less express, the deep and moving spiritual passion of 'Rock of Ages', perhaps the very greatest of all English hymns, than Sullivan does in MOUNT ZION?[28]

He went on to congratulate the editors of *Songs of Praise* for consigning all of Sullivan's tunes to the scrapheap and to assert 'the truth is that Sullivan was out of his element altogether in this field'.

Routley returned to the fray with even more vigour seven years later. As has already been pointed out, he shifted the grounds of his attack somewhat, suggesting that while writing sacred music was what Sullivan believed to be his true vocation, he felt that he had to subjugate his natural melodic gifts when composing for the Church and cultivate dullness. His criticisms of the hymn tunes remained withering: 'We look in vain for a really good tune by Sullivan ... the predominant characteristic is dreariness ... there is a shameless secularism and bad technique.' Routley castigated Sullivan's hymn tunes for their 'weak craftsmanship' and identified two specific faults in them: the persistent use of repeated notes in the melody, a sign of vulgarity especially evident in ST GERTRUDE, LUX EOI and RESURREXIT; and the unskilful and uncomfortable placing of high notes 'which gives to several of this composer's tunes a rather hectic tone and an unusually insistent and irritating stridency', especially noticeable in the Easter hymn tunes LUX EOI, FORTUNATUS and RESURREXIT. He also reiterated his earlier argument that Sullivan was out of his depth and comfort zone in writing church music. Too often, his hymn tunes are banal, secular and vulgar: 'And if you want music which is far beyond the border of secularism, being eminently suitable for the stage of the Savoy Theatre and not at all to public worship, you can find examples in ST THERESA and ANGEL VOICES.'[29]

Routley returned to batter Sullivan again in the 1950s, describing his hymn tunes as 'vacillating between appalling vulgarity and glum monotony' and representing 'the disastrous rubbish which a musician of outstanding gifts thought appropriate for church use ... Sullivan wrote hardly a tune that is not virtually intolerable for modern singing.'[30] A slightly more emollient tone entered Routley's writing in the late 1960s. He acknowledged Sullivan as the one English Victorian church composer 'in whom we can see the influence of an eminent European musician' and pointed to the significance of his visit to Vienna in 1866 when he discovered some of Schubert's music. However, his fundamental emphasis was still negative: 'If his church music had not been corrupted by sentimental notions of the church's dignity, he would have mediated Schubert to the singing congregation. As it is, only faint and usually incongruous traces of the Viennese style appear in his church music – for example, in his tune ANGEL VOICES.'[31]

Routley's repeated attacks on Sullivan's hymn tunes are particularly vicious but not unrepresentative of what was being said and written by many in the musical establishment in the mid twentieth century. They need to be addressed in any serious analysis of this part of the composer's output. Let us take first his two specific technical criticisms about the excessive use of repeated notes and high registers. It is certainly true that the use of repeated notes particularly at or towards the beginning of phrases is a favourite Sullivan device, used to enhance the didactic quality and marching rhythm of a melody and perhaps displayed most conspicuously in BISHOPGARTH which strangely is not cited by Routley. I have already suggested that it may at least partly reflect the influence of the plainsong and chant in which he was schooled by Helmore (page 49). However, Sullivan was by no means alone among Victorian hymn tune composers in having a penchant for repeated notes. Barnby was equally fond of them. Stainer used them in DOMINUS MISERICORDIAE and Ouseley in GETHSEMANE. Dykes's ST ANDREW OF CRETE, for J. M. Neale's 'Christian, dost thou see them', begins with 12 repeated Gs with the result that the first and second lines of the hymn are sung entirely on the same note. S. S. Wesley, who was a fierce critic of Dykes and other practitioners of the high Victorian hymn tune, was himself not immune from the temptation to use repeated notes, as witnessed by the beginning of his AURELIA. Nor were those leading exemplars of an earlier and more restrained generation of hymn tune composers, George Smart and John Goss, as shown in REGENT SQUARE and PRAISE MY SOUL. In this particular failing, if such it be, Sullivan was no worse than most of his contemporaries.

Routley's second technical criticism, about the excessive number of high notes, has been echoed by others. Kenneth Trickett, a leading Methodist hymnologist of the later twentieth century, once complained to me that 'the trouble with LUX EOI is the tendency to turn that top F sharp into a horrible shriek, yet if the tune is transposed down, it loses its characteristic brightness'.[32] Sullivan did certainly use a lot of high notes. As originally set, ANGEL VOICES, CONSTANCE, BISHOPGARTH, CHAPEL ROYAL, VALETE, LUX IN TENEBRIS, WELCOME, HAPPY MORNING and FATHERLAND all contain a high F and ST GERTRUDE has five. High F sharps occur in SAFE HOME, COURAGE, BROTHER and LUX EOI. In its original part-song incarnation, the soprano line in LUX IN TENEBRIS went up to a high G, although when used as a hymn tune in *Church Hymns with Tunes*, it was taken down to F. The purpose of these high notes was undoubtedly to emphasize certain words in the texts to which the tunes were originally set, which they do very dramatically. I wonder if their prevalence is another legacy of Sullivan's Chapel Royal days, in this case reflecting his own exceptionally high reach as a boy soprano.

The frequent use of both repeated and high notes could be interpreted as showing Sullivan in his Savoy mode, striving for effect and seeking to make his hymn tunes as dramatic as possible. They also reveal a characteristic which he shared with many of his contemporaries, identified by Routley as 'the assiduous, and sometimes anxious, and even frantic, desire of the Victorian hymn-tune writer to be sure that at every beat there will be something to catch the listener's attention ... Just as in architecture, empty space is intolerable without some kind of decoration, so in music, silence and repose are emotionally taboo. All must be picturesque.'[33]

This criticism conflicts with Routley's other great complaint about Sullivan's hymn tunes, which is that they are fundamentally dreary and represent a sacrifice of the composer's natural melodic gifts in favour of a dull religiosity. In fact, I wonder if the perceived dreariness of several of Sullivan's hymn tunes derives from the very same impulse that makes others so up-beat and bouncy, namely his striving to be faithful to the spirit of the words which he is setting and to enhance their meaning and atmosphere. The fact is that many of the texts that Sullivan was called upon to set are profoundly maudlin and depressing. A high proportion of Victorian hymns focused on the topics of distress, weariness, suffering, dying and grieving. This was an aspect of Victorian sentimentalism for which there were good reasons as we have already observed (page 22). How could Sullivan, for all his own great love of life and optimistic, genial personality, escape a note of dreariness when setting texts such as 'Art thou weary, art thou languid, art thou sore distressed?', 'In the hour of my distress, when temptations me oppress' or 'I'm but a stranger here, heaven is my home' with its life-denying message and sense that heaven rather than earth is where we are meant and want to be. The first hymn for which Sullivan supplied an original tune, The Hymn of the Homeland, describes a dying man contemplating the heavenly homeland to which he is drawing near and singing 'when I think of the homeland my eyes are filled with tears'. It was hardly a congenial subject for a lively 25-year-old. If some of Sullivan's tunes do have a rather maudlin, gloomy quality, that is surely because they seek faithfully to reflect and bring out the message of the texts for which they were written rather than out of any studied religiosity and cultivation of dullness.

Several musicologists writing in the 1960s and early 1970s echoed Routley's criticisms of Victorian hymn tunes in general and those of Arthur Sullivan in particular. In his important and scholarly study, *Church Music in the Nineteenth Century* (1967), Arthur Hutchings, professor of music at Durham University, criticized 'the Victorian fault of sentimentality' from which, rather surprisingly but perhaps because of the Durham connection, he absolved Dykes but singled out for blame Sullivan and Barnby.[34] In his equally scholarly 1971 study *The Music of the English Church*, Kenneth Long took a further sideswipe at Victorian hymnody, bracketing Sullivan, Stainer, Dykes, Gauntlett and Barnby together as displaying 'the comforting warm glow of spurious religiosity induced by trivial and sentimental ear-ticklers'. Long was, in fact, slightly less damning about Sullivan than he was about some of his contemporaries. While Dykes is castigated for 'weaknesses that make musicians blush' and Barnby for tunes that are 'simply mawkish', Sullivan receives a rather milder ticking off, being guilty only 'of the far more healthy fault of sheer vulgarity'.[35]

An interesting if seriously flawed analysis of Sullivan's motivation for writing hymn tunes was made in a paper delivered to a conference on Gilbert and Sullivan at the University of Kansas in 1970 by Samuel Rogal, an academic at State University College, Oswego, New York. Ignoring or unaware of the clear evidence to the contrary, Rogal suggested that his hymn tunes post-dated Sullivan's collaboration with Gilbert and were written during the period when he was spending more and more time in the orchestra pit of the comic opera house, a place which was far from congenial for someone desperately wanting recognition as a serious composer. Rogal argued that the hymn tunes were a way out of the pit both literally and metaphorically for Sullivan, providing spiritual release from the comic opera stage and also from his own pain and loneliness: 'Arthur Sullivan found religion not within the walls of a church or the tenets of a denomination, but from the balm provided by his own genius for composing music for hymns and sacred song.'[36] While there may be some truth in this statement, it is based on a false premise. As has already been pointed out, the great majority of Sullivan's hymn tunes were written before he was immersed in the world of comic opera. They may conceivably have provided a balm in terms of relief and distraction from the pain of his kidney stones, which, as Rogal notes, began to cause serious trouble in 1872, but it is difficult to agree with him that they offered an escape from the world of the theatre.

The later twentieth century saw a more positive attitude emerging towards Sullivan's hymn tunes on the part of academic musicologists. Perhaps the turning point came with the publication of Nicholas Temperley's superb study of *The Music of the English Parish Church* in 1979. It is much more sympathetic to what Victorian hymn tune composers were trying to do and much more complimentary of what they achieved than any previous study. Temperley describes the Victorian hymn tune as 'a lasting success' while acknowledging that 'it has been almost universally condemned by music critics from its own time to the present'.[37] Sullivan has two entries in Temperley's list of the greatest Victorian hymn tunes, of which there are 16 in total, with LUX EOI and ST GERTRUDE, and is the only composer apart from Dykes to make more than one appearance in the list. His editorship of *Church Hymns with Tunes* is praised for introducing ST CLEMENT, which also features in the list of great Victorian hymn tunes, and Temperley notes that '[t]wo distinguished tunes by Sullivan himself appeared in this book: LUX EOI and NOEL, the latter associated with the Christmas carol "It came upon the midnight clear" and skilfully based on a traditional carol melody.'[38] The companion volume, which includes musical examples, contains two Sullivan hymn tunes, ST FRANCIS and his setting of Heber's 'The Son of God goes forth to war' to Croft's psalm tune ST ANN.

Prejudice against Sullivan's hymn tunes still lingers among academic musicologists and practising church musicians. Arthur Jacobs does not disguise his contempt for some of them in his broadly sympathetic biography published in 1984 and revised in 1992. Organists of my own acquaintance have delighted in unpicking the harmonies in ST GERTRUDE and LUX EOI and showing me how they break all the rules of harmony laid down by Bach. Not long ago, I carefully selected 'Hushed was the evening hymn' for an evening service confident in the assumption that we would sing it to the glorious SAMUEL, only to find that the organist struck up John Ireland's LOVE UNKNOWN, which, however fine a melody it is, does not do the same justice to this particular text. Such informed musical analysis as has been made in recent years of this aspect of Sullivan's work tends to reinforce the view that it inclines towards the vulgar and populist. In a chapter on 'The Music of Dissent' in a book published in 2011 about Nonconformist hymnody in Britain, for example, Nicholas Temperley singles out ST THERESA, which he prints in full set to 'Brightly gleams our banner' from the 1900 *Baptist Church Hymnal*, as exhibiting 'the more exuberant rhythms of revival hymnody' and having a distinctly non-Anglican flavour.[39]

I have myself conducted a one-man crusade over the last 25 years to rehabilitate Sullivan's hymn tunes and encourage their wider appreciation and use. This began with a lecture to the Sir Arthur Sullivan Society and an article on 'Sullivan's Hymn Tunes Re-Considered' for the Bulletin of the Hymn Society of Great Britain and Ireland in 1992. A live broadcast Sunday morning service for BBC Radio 4, which I led from a Traction Engine Rally at Astle Park in Cheshire in August 1992, had an all Sullivan praise list. It elicited many letters from listeners enthusing about the hymns and asking more about them, especially LUX EOI and BISHOP-GARTH. A memorable open-air *Songs of Praise* televised from the Gilbert and Sullivan Festival in Buxton in 1997 included 'Lead, kindly light' sung to LUX IN TENEBRIS, which I also included in a live Radio 4 *Sunday Worship*, which I led from Buxton in 2000. I am delighted to say that as a result of these broadcasts, and of other occasions when I have used this tune, I have had a steady stream of requests for copies of it for use by church choirs around the country. In 2000, I persuaded Kingsway Music to record and release a CD of 14 Sullivan hymn tunes as part of their popular Hymn Makers series. It remains the only disc in the collection devoted to a composer rather than a hymn writer. Sullivan hymn tunes featured prominently in the Sullivan matins which I conducted in Keble College Chapel, Oxford, as part of the English Music Festival in May 2008 and in the choral evensong from the Savoy Chapel broadcast live on BBC Radio 3 as part of the Light Fantastic festival of light music in June 2011, although sadly 'Onward, Christian soldiers' had to be cut at the last minute, as the programme was over-running.

The hugely popular service of worship held in the middle Sunday of the annual International Gilbert and Sullivan Festival in Buxton and the Sunday services, which are an important and valued part of the regular weekend conferences and festivals organized by the Sullivan Society, have done much to promote Sullivan's hymn tunes and expand the repertoire of those still sung today. The reaction that I have had to these and other occasions, where I have introduced Sullivan hymn tunes into public worship, confirms that the British public still loves singing them, whatever the critics may say.

Sullivan's representation in currently used hymn books is considerably poorer than in those published in the early part of the twentieth century but is no worse than that of most of his contemporaries. Rather surprisingly, he fares better in the hymnals of the established churches of England and Scotland than in those of the Nonconformist denominations where once he was so popular. *Common Praise*, the successor to *Hymns Ancient and Modern*, which came out in 2000 and can perhaps be taken as a barometer of mainstream Church of England taste in hymnody, contains three original Sullivan tunes: LUX EOI, which is used twice, GOLDEN SHEAVES and ST GERTRUDE, together with the harmonization of NOEL and the almost certainly erroneously attributed harmonization of ELLERS (see Observations to Appendix 1 on page 197). This is a considerably poorer showing than that of John Stainer, who has 7 tunes and John Bacchus Dykes, who has 17. However, Sullivan fares better than the contemporary with whom he is often compared, Joseph Barnby, who has only two tunes in *Common Praise*. Among other leading Victorian composers, S. S. Wesley and W. H. Monk fare better, but E. J. Hopkins and John Goss only have two tunes apiece, and Richard Redhead is on an equal footing with Sullivan with three tunes, one of which is used twice. Another popular current Church of England hymnal, the Anglican edition of *Hymns Old and New* (Kevin Mayhew, 2000), has the same three Sullivan tunes, with LUX EOI being used for three different hymns. The widely used interdenominational hymnal, *The Complete Mission Praise* (Marshall Pickering, 1999) also includes three Sullivan tunes, in this case SAMUEL, LUX EOI and ST GERTRUDE together with the arrangement of NOEL and the misattributed ELLERS. *Sing Praise*, the supplement to *Common Praise* published in 2011, has just one Sullivan tune, LUX EOI, used for both Timothy Dudley Smith's 'We believe in God the Father' and James Seddon's 'Church of God, elect and glorious'. The new edition of *Ancient & Modern* published in 2013, includes NOEL, ST GERTRUDE, GOLDEN SHEAVES and LUX EOI which is used four times.

It is worth noting that Sullivan's representation is rather better in the hymn book currently used in the Episcopal Church of the United States of America. The Episcopal Hymnal, which dates from 1982, includes four original Sullivan tunes, LUX EOI, ST GERTRUDE, ST KEVIN for 'Come ye faithful raise the strain' and FORTUNATUS for 'Welcome, happy morn', together with NOEL, which is used twice. Only Dykes, with six tunes, has a better showing among Victorian composers. Stainer and Barnby lag behind with just two tunes each.

Sullivan also fares reasonably well in the Church of Scotland's *Church Hymnary*. The current (fourth) edition, which came out in 2005, includes LUX EOI (which I can claim the credit for getting back into the hymnal after a long absence and which appears twice), BISHOPGARTH, COURAGE BROTHER and ST GERTRUDE and two arrangements: NOEL and LEOMINSTER. Sadly, SAMUEL and PROPIOR DEO, which were both in the third edition published in 1973, have been dropped, not because of any antipathy to the tunes, but because the texts which they accompanied, 'Hushed was the evening hymn' and 'Nearer my God to Thee', were deemed to be rather dated. Sullivan trails behind Dykes, who has nine tunes and one harmonization in the *Church Hymnary*, but comes out ahead of Stainer, who has only three tunes. A comparison of the number of original Sullivan tunes in successive editions of the *Church Hymnary* shows the extent to which his stock fell through the twentieth century. The first edition, published in 1898, contained 23, the second revised edition (1927) 12, the third (1973) 5 and the fourth (2005) 4. However, this is a less steep decline in popularity than that experienced by many of his contemporaries. In the 1927 *Revised Church Hymnary*, Stainer had 12 original tunes, Monk 14, and Gauntlett and Barnby 11 each. In the current edition, Stainer and Gauntlett are down to three each, Monk has two and Barnby has none.

The Nonconformist hymnals, which were once so fond of Sullivan, now largely shun him. The United Reformed Church's *Rejoice and Sing* (1991) has just one original tune, SAMUEL, plus the arrangement of NOEL. *Baptist Praise and Worship* (1991) similarly has just one tune, LUX EOI, used twice. The new Methodist hymnal, *Singing the Faith* (2011) has two Sullivan tunes: BISHOPGARTH, set to 'To thee, O Lord our hearts we raise' and LUX EOI used for Timothy Dudley Smith's 'We believe in God the Father' and Michael Saward's 'Wind of God, dynamic spirit'. This is one down on his representation in the 1983 Methodist book *Hymns & Psalms* and ten down on his representation in the 1933 *Methodist Hymn Book*.

Despite their disappearance from the hymn books, Sullivan tunes continue to inspire and appeal to modern hymn writers. Timothy Dudley Smith suggests SAMUEL as the best tune for his morning hymn 'Lord, as the day begins', and it has appeared in four hymnals set to that text. In 1983, John Dalles, an American Presbyterian hymn writer, responded to a request for a new hymn on Pentecost with 'Come, O Spirit, with your sound'. He noted that 'I wrote the text with Sir Arthur Sullivan's hymn tune ST KEVIN in my head, because I am a long-time admirer of his musical genius.'[40] This tune also appealed to the great twentieth-century English Methodist hymn writer, Fred Pratt Green, who died in 2000 at the age of 97. When he wrote a hymn for the dedication of an organ in a Bristol Methodist Church in 1981, 'What a joy it is to sing/When the Spirit moves us', he wrote it with ST KEVIN in mind. He had discovered it in *The Hymn Book of the Church of England in Canada*, published in 1938, and in the words of his biographer, Bernard Braley, 'it charmed him – and the organist concerned'.[41] More recently, Christopher Idle, the prominent Anglican hymn writer, chose LUX EOI as the tune for his hymn written for the 2012 Olympic Games, 'Let us run with perseverance', on the grounds of its liveliness and sense of movement.

The tradition of setting hymns to tunes from the Savoy operas continues. In 1991, while rector of Islip in Oxfordshire, Richard Sturch wrote a hymn 'A man set out to build himself a tower' to be sung to the tune of the company promoter's song, 'Some seven men form an association', from *Utopia Limited*. Gatherings of the Sullivan Society are regularly enlivened by the singing of 'The king of love my shepherd is' to 'In enterprise of martial kind' from *The Gondoliers,* 'Abide with me' to 'When I was a lad' from *H.M.S. Pinafore,* 'Now thank we all our God' to 'The Soldiers of Our Queen' from *Patience,* 'Christ, whose glory fills the skies' to 'Take a pair of sparkling eyes' from *The Gondoliers* and 'While shepherds watched their flocks by night' to 'The sun whose rays' from *The Mikado*.

Critics and scoffers will doubtless continue to maintain that Sullivan dashed off his hymn tunes without much thought or commitment in order to make money. The more I have studied this part of his output, however, the more I have become convinced that while financial considerations undoubtedly played a part, his motivation in writing hymns and editing a major hymn book was also spiritual and sprang from his own simple and trusting faith, his love of church music and his desire to help the Church and his many friends among the clergy. This last motive was clearly to the fore in the case of what was almost certainly the last hymn tune that he ever wrote, BISHOPGARTH, which he composed to accompany 'O King of Kings Whose reign of old', written by his old friend, William Walsham How, who was by now Bishop of Wakefield, to celebrate Queen Victoria's Diamond Jubilee in 1897.

How's hymn takes us to the heart of High Victorian hymnody. Intensely patriotic and unashamedly sentimental, it also had a broad inclusiveness and sought to articulate the shared values of the community and a sense of the common good. It was, in fact, written at the suggestion of Sullivan and as a result of his direct lobbying of the Royal Household. Keen to contribute to the Queen's Diamond Jubilee celebrations, he wrote from France to the Prince of Wales on 1 April 1897 expressing his desire 'to receive the Queen's command to compose something special for this wondrous occasion'. Significantly, he specifically suggested a hymn tune, 'to be sung at the service at St Paul's with military band accompaniment ... I think I should reach *the hearts of the people* best in a hymn tune, such a one as "Onward, Christian Soldiers".'[42] He had in mind here the brief open-air service that the Queen herself would be attending outside St Paul's Cathedral on 22 June in the course of processing through the streets of London.

As a result of this overture, Sir Arthur Bigge, the Queen's private secretary, met Sullivan in Cimiez, where Victoria was staying, on 6 April and told him that the Queen wanted any hymn used at the St Paul's service to be sung to a popular and well-known tune. Sullivan reported that he had heard 'that this was a German chorale which he deplored' and suggested that the Queen might ask How, with whom he had collaborated so happily on *Church Hymns with Tunes*, to write a new hymn for the occasion which he himself would set to music. This was communicated in a letter to the Queen from Bigge who added: 'Sir Arthur Sullivan knows no one to whose writing he would have greater pleasure in composing than the Bishop of Wakefield. This hymn might be sung in the churches on 20 June [the day which marked the sixtieth anniversary of Victoria's accession and had been designated as a 'Day of General Thanksgiving'].'[43]

How was duly approached by the Prince of Wales to write a suitable text. He felt daunted by the task, telling Sullivan that although he felt 'awfully dry and dusty', he found consolation in the fact that 'you have promised to write a tune for it. That may possibly redeem it'. Before embarking on the hymn, he consulted the composer as to whether he had any preference as to metre and refrain 'as I would try to adapt myself to you if such is the case'. How expressed his own preference for 8.7 metre, as in 'The King of Love My Shepherd is', or its Trochaic form, as in 'Glorious Things of Thee are Spoken', and also for including 'an "Alleluia", or some such refrain, after each verse on so jubilant an occasion.'[44] In the event, he settled on a double 8.7 metre and produced four verses without refrain which brimmed over with heartfelt patriotism and portrayed the Queen as the much-loved mother of the nation:

Oh Royal heart, with wide embrace
For all her children yearning!
Oh happy realm, such mother-grace
With loyal love returning!
Where England's flag flies wide unfurl'd,
All tyrant wrongs repelling;

God make the world a better world
For man's brief earthly dwelling!

How's hymn 'O King of Kings, Whose reign of old/Hath been from ever-lasting' was shown to the Queen who gave it her approval. Bigge sent it to Sullivan, passing on Bishop How's comment that 'Sir Arthur Sullivan's genius will light it up a little'.[45] When he received the verses, Sullivan told How: 'I have rarely come across so beautiful a combination of poetry and deep religious feeling.'[46] Both staunch monarchists and populists (How was known as the omnibus bishop because he scorned an episcopal car-riage and preferred to travel round his urban diocese on public transport), they were the perfect pair to catch the celebratory mood of the nation, and Sullivan came up with a strong march tune, BISHOPGARTH, which reinforced How's triumphalist and exhortatory message. 'When you sing it properly in church,' How told a young boy who had written to say how much he liked the hymn, 'you must try to think you are singing it to God, and thanking him for giving us so good a Queen.'[47]

On 27 May Sullivan wrote to How to report that he had secured royal endorsement for the hymn:

> The first batch of copies will go out to all the beneficed clergy from the Queen's printers on Saturday and copies will be on sale everywhere after that at a price which no one can complain at! We shall also dis-patch to the nearest colonies at once so that they can have it in good time.
>
> My only regret is that I don't think the music is quite up to the level of the words, but I did my best, and it is not easy to be devotional, effective, original and simple at the same time.[48]

'O King of Kings' was first sung on the morning of Sunday 20 June 1897 at the thanksgiving service in St George's Chapel, Windsor, attended by the Queen herself, as the processional hymn beginning the national thanks-giving service at St Paul's Cathedral, and by congregations in churches across the land. It was not used, as Sullivan had originally hoped and suggested, at the brief thanksgiving service held two days later outside the cathedral's west door, while the Queen, who felt too frail to climb up the steps, remained in her carriage. At least Sullivan, who according to the historian Jeffrey Richards was among a group of distinguished musicians, including Hubert Parry, Walter Parratt and Frederick Bridge, who sang in the choir at the top of the cathedral steps for this service, was spared the German chorale, which he had deplored – the only hymn sung outside St

Paul's was 'All people that on earth do dwell' to the Old Hundredth.[49] The German chorale tune, NUN DANKET, was, however, used in the service at St George's Windsor, accompanying 'Now thank we all our God'.

The jubilee hymn on which How and Sullivan had collaborated was instantly popular with the public. At the composer's suggestion, all royalties from the sale of copies went to the Prince of Wales Hospital Fund. Within three months of its publication, the fund had benefited to the tune of over £200 through this arrangement. Another Victorian bishop, Edward Bickersteth of Exeter, was so taken with the vigorous, muscular, uplifting quality of BISHOPGARTH that he wrote a stirring gospel hymn 'For my sake and the Gospel's, go and tell redemption's story' especially for it, so ensuring that the tune would not be lost once the jubilee celebrations were over but would continue to do its evangelistic work for many years to come, as, indeed, it has for more than a century. His hymn first appeared in the *Church Missionary Hymnbook* of 1899 set to BISHOPGARTH and is still a favourite in the Church of Scotland. In 1902, Mary Bradford Whiting wrote a hymn 'O God, the Ruler of our race' to BISHOPGARTH for use in celebrations of Edward VII's coronation in churches across the land. In the 1903 edition of *Church Hymns with Tunes*, it was paired with 'Great God, to Thee our hearts we raise', a hymn written by the eminent hymnologist, John Julian, vicar of Wincobank, Sheffield, in 1898. I cannot establish whether Julian had Sullivan's tune in mind when he wrote this hymn, which has appeared in several editions of the Church of Ireland's *Church Hymnal*, although not always set to BISHOPGARTH.

BISHOPGARTH displays the classic faults and strengths of Sullivan's hymn tunes. It has been castigated by academic musicologists, including those usually friendly to Sullivan like Arthur Jacobs, who called it 'a weak tune, weakly harmonized: the repeated notes of "Onward, Christian Soldiers" were heard again, feebly'.[50] It is vulgar in the best sense of the word, catchy, popular and calculated to leave those singing it full of patriotic or evangelistic fervour. Loved by congregations and by many clergy, it is, like so many of Sullivan's hymn tunes, memorable, simple and stirring. It may not conform to the principles of harmony laid down by Bach and it may have a superfluity of repeated notes, but it is eminently singable. It shows the varied influences of the parade ground, the Chapel Royal and the simple trusting faith of its composer who himself wrote: 'It is not a part song, nor an exercise in harmony. It is a tune which everyone will, I hope, be able to pick up quickly and sing heartily.'[51] There is Sullivan's credo as a hymn tune writer.

5

Ballads, Songs and Snatches:
Sacred Ballads and Part-Songs

Solo and part-songs designed for singing in parlours and drawing rooms as well as on the concert platform were among the most popular features of Victorian middle-class culture. As Nicholas Temperley notes, 'the Victorian ballad was one of the most characteristic musical expressions of its age'.[1]

Several factors contributed to the popularity of parlour ballads, which reached its height in the last three decades of the nineteenth century. Among the most important were the effects of the rise in singing classes and musical literacy noted in Chapter 2, the boom in piano sales and the technological innovation of chromolithographic printing, which enabled the mass production of cheap and legible sheet music and of the attractive coloured song sheet covers, which remain among the most collected items of Victoriana. More broadly, the prevailing sentimentalism of the age favoured an art form which was both safely domestic and centred on the home and yet at the same time emotionally charged and tugging at the heart strings.

Within the overall genre of Victorian ballads, sacred solo and part-songs were recognized as a discrete and important category. They had a specific function in providing suitable musical fare for Sunday afternoons and evenings, when only sacred texts might with propriety be sung, but they also had a wider appeal in an age where religious sentiment was so prevalent. Music publishers were not slow to see their commercial potential. Vincent Novello, son of an Italian immigrant, had launched his music publishing business in 1811 with *A Collection of Sacred Music*. His firm, along with those started shortly afterwards by Samuel Chappell in partnership with John Cramer and by Thomas Boosey, came to dominate the mass production of Victorian sheet music. Collections of sacred songs were produced to supplement the hymns increasingly being sung by families around the piano on Sunday evenings. Among the first was Caroline

Norton's *Sabbath Lays*, published in 1853. In 1875, Boosey began *The Sacred Music Cabinet*, a series which ran to 28 parts over the next ten years. Numerous other volumes of sacred songs appeared in the 1870s with titles like *Sabbath Strains* and *Sunday at Home*.

Arthur Sullivan was one of the leading composers of Victorian ballads and arguably the supreme exponent of the sacred song. In his standard work on the subject, *The Singing Bourgeois*, Derek Scott describes him as 'one of the four enduringly popular ballad composers of the latter half of the nineteenth century' (the others being Frederic Cowen, James Molloy and Stephen Adams) and singles him out as 'the most melodically imaginative and rhythmically varied'.[2] In 'The Lost Chord', Sullivan produced the single most successful and iconic Victorian sacred ballad, which outsold its chief rivals, Adams's 'The Holy City' and Henry Lamb's 'The Volunteer Organist'. His 'The Long Day Closes' has proved perhaps the most enduring of all the Victorian sacred part-songs. Sullivan's recognized pre-eminence in this field in his own day is indicated by his showing in John Hiles's *Sacred Songs, Ancient and Modern: A Complete Collection of Sacred Vocal Music, by Celebrated Composers, suitable for Home Use*, published by Boosey in 1874. Only Beethoven and Handel have more songs in this collection. Sullivan, with eight entries, is well ahead of his nearest British rival, the Irish composer, Sir John Stevenson, who has five.

It is difficult to provide a definitive total of Sullivan's sacred solo and part-songs. This is because there is no hard and fast definition of what constitutes a sacred rather than a secular song. As Maurice Disher points out, Victorian poets generally felt a compulsion to preach with the result that when set as songs their texts often sound like hymns and display a combination of 'melancholy music and moralizing verse'.[3] Few 'secular' Victorian ballads are devoid of expressions of religious or sanctimonious sentiment. Lionel Lewin's hugely popular 'Birds in the Night', set by Sullivan, for example, contains the (somewhat opaque) line: 'Soon is the sleep but God can break when angels whisper Lullaby'. Yet this kind of interpolation does not of itself make it a sacred song. The list which appears in Appendix 4 (pp. 205–6), containing 18 solo ballads and 8 part-songs, constitutes what I take to be the corpus of Sullivan's settings of sacred texts, by which I mean those where the main thrust is religious or spiritual rather than where there are incidental moral or spiritual allusions. There is inevitably an element of subjectivity about this selection, but I have consulted with several Sullivan experts in drawing it up, and I hope that it provides a reasonably comprehensive list of his sacred work in this area.

As with his hymn tunes, most of Sullivan's sacred songs were written in his early years as a composer – the great majority in the late 1860s and early 1870s. He did occasionally return to the genre later in life, but for the most part his output in this area was the product of his youthful and more obviously faith-filled decades.

Sacred Part-Songs

There is a clear cross-over between Sullivan's hymn tunes and his sacred part-songs. Two carol melodies which were published as part-songs, 'All this night' and 'Upon the snow-clad earth', are included with his hymn tunes in Appendix, 1 because they are set in four-square hymnodic form and clearly designed for congregational singing. There are three other Christmas song settings, which can more appropriately be described as part-songs, 'I sing the birth was born tonight', written by the Tudor poet and dramatist Ben Jonson, John Cawood's 'Hark! What mean those holy voices sweetly sounding through the skies', and 'It came upon the midnight clear', where, in contrast to his congregational setting NOEL, Sullivan set Edmund Sears's ever popular Christmas hymn for soprano solo and choir.

These songs could as appropriately be sung in the chancel as in the parlour. Others of Sullivan's sacred part-songs have a similarly dual identity, later being taken up as hymn tunes. LUX IN TENEBRIS, his setting of John Henry Newman's 'Lead, kindly light' (page 73), first appeared in a selection of five sacred part-songs published in 1871. Another tune published in this selection, set to Henry Kirke White's 'Through sorrow's path', was later taken up as a hymn tune, being set in the 1900 *Baptist Church Hymnal* to J. S. B. Monsell's hymn 'When I had wandered from His fold'.

The 1871 collection of *Five Sacred Part Songs* contains some of Sullivan's most characteristic work in this genre. In addition to his settings of 'Lead, kindly light', 'It came upon the midnight clear' and 'Through sorrow's path', it includes a song for soprano, alto and tenor soloists and choir taking as its starting point the question posed in Isaiah 21.11: 'Say watchman, what of the night?' and continuing with characteristically Victorian reflections on death, resurrection and eternal life:

That night is near, and the cheerless tomb
Shall keep thy body in store
Till the morn of eternity rise on the gloom,
And night shall be no more.

The fifth item in this collection is a setting of one of Adelaide Anne Procter's poems, 'The way is long and dreary', which again is characteristically Victorian in its emphasis on the dreariness and bleakness of life, in this case compared to the even greater sufferings endured by Christ and punctuated by frequent invocations of the prayer 'O Lamb of God who takest away the sins of the world, have mercy upon us' in a way that makes it almost a liturgical piece:

> The way is long and dreary,
> The path is bleak and bare;
> Our feet are worn and weary,
> But we will not despair;
> More heavy was Thy burden,
> More desolate Thy way.

Both 'Say watchmen' and 'The way is long and dreary' found their way into the 1900 *Baptist Church Hymnal*, further underlining the cross-over between the hymn and the sacred part-song. All five items in Sullivan's 1871 collection of sacred part-songs were included in Hiles's 1874 volume of sacred vocal music along with 'I sing the birth' and two numbers from *The Prodigal Son*.

Along with the two Christmas songs and the items in the 1871 collection, I have included one other Sullivan part-song in Appendix 4. 'The Long Day Closes' is perhaps the most enduring of all his part-songs, although it is debatable as to whether it should be counted as a sacred work. There is no mention of God or Christ in it. The emphasis in the text, written by Henry Chorley, a prolific author and journalist of Lancashire Quaker stock, is rather on fate – 'Heed not how hope believes and fate disposes'. It does, however, have an undeniably spiritual feel, especially in its closing lines: 'Thy book of toil is read, go to the dreamless bed, the long day closes.' What makes it sacred is not so much the text but the way Sullivan set it, with hushed tones and churchy harmonies. It is a good example of what he did so often with Gilbert (who also seems to have been a believer in fate more than anything else), taking not very sacred or elevated words and investing them with a spiritual quality (see pages 175–7). Unashamedly sentimental, it still tugs at the heart strings – I have seen grown men reduced to tears by it – and is, in the words of John Caldwell, 'a perfectly tuned miniature of its kind', which epitomizes the best of Victorian sentimentality.[4] It is significant, and highly appropriate, that shortly after Sullivan's death, the tune of 'The Long Day Closes' was used for a church anthem, 'Saviour, Thy children keep'.

Sacred Solo Ballads

Sullivan's first published composition was a sacred song. 'O Israel', written when he was 13 and based on verses from Hosea, has already been discussed at some length (pages 46–7). His next venture into this field came when he was 22 and set a poem entitled 'Virtue' by the seventeenth-century Anglican divine, George Herbert, which begins 'Sweet day, so cool, so calm, so bright' and goes on to reflect that everything in the world must die except 'a sweet and virtuous soul'. Percy Young commends the pentatonic opening of this setting as an example of Sullivan's original and daring approach to song composition.[5]

George Herbert was not the only clergyman whose lyrics appealed to Sullivan. In 1868, he set a poem by the Dorset vicar William Barnes (1801–86), 'The Mother's Dream' (originally 'Mater Dolorosa') about a mother mourning the death of her young son.

As in heaven high
I my child did seek,
There in train came by
Children fair and meek;
Each in lily white,
With a lamp alight;
Each was clear to sight
But they did not speak.

In fact, her own son does speak to his mother, telling her not to mourn his loss. Sullivan set this typical piece of Victorian sentiment prompted by the death of a child with an appropriately soulful and muted melody in andante time. Shortly after his own death, his tune for 'The Mother's Dream' was republished by Boosey set to words by Fred Weatherly, 'My Child and I' expressing similar sentiments to those of Barnes.

In 1872, Sullivan set a poem by a third clerical author, Henry Francis Lyte (1793–1847), the perpetual curate of Lower Brixham in Devon, best known for the hymns 'Abide with me' and 'Praise my soul, the King of Heaven'. 'The Sailor's Grave' is about the unmarked grave of a sailor, who has died at sea and whose body has been tossed into the ocean. Sullivan's setting of its bleak opening verse begins with his hallmark repeated notes and rising sixth interval. Characteristically, he superbly matches the changing mood of the song, rising up the scale after another series of repeated notes for its triumphant resurrection-centred ending:

And when the last trump shall sound,
And tombs are asunder riv'n,
Like the morning sun from the wave thou'lt bound,
To rise and shine in Heaven.

In a letter of 1876, Sullivan wrote, '"The Sailor's Grave" shortened my life. Why did I ever write that terrible ditty!' This comment, made when he had largely finished with sacred ballads, but before he had composed his masterpiece 'The Lost Chord', could, I suppose, be taken as a verdict on the quality of his work in this genre and an indication of his feelings about it. That is certainly the interpretation taken by David Eden: 'Sullivan felt that his life had been shortened by giving birth to such a terrible ditty. However, when darkly gloomed the sea and tempests rocked one's financial bark, it was sometimes necessary to pay meet adoration to the household gods of Victorian sensibility.'[6] I am not sure, however, whether we can conclude that Sullivan was simply motivated by financial considerations when he set this and other sacred verses. Their sentiments chimed in with his own feelings during this period of his life, as revealed, for example, in his comments following the death of his father and his brother. There is a delicacy and sympathy with the words revealed by his settings, which is more than mechanical and workmanlike and suggestive rather of a real empathy with these expressions of religious yearning.

Sullivan contributed two tunes to *The Sunlight of Song* published in 1875 by Routledge and Novello as 'a collection of sacred and moral poems with original music by the most eminent composers'. Only one of the texts he set, 'We've ploughed the land', which expresses the sentiments of 'All things bright and beautiful' and has the feel of a harvest hymn, really counts as a sacred song. The other, 'The River', in which a river reflects on its wayward youth as 'a mad-cap, hoyden rill' and soberly contemplates its destination in the ocean where its grave will be, comes rather into the category of an improving moral tale.

Among the poems of Gilbert set by Sullivan is one that does have some of the hallmarks of the Victorian sacred ballad. 'The Distant Shore', a sad tale of a girl who dies of a broken heart when she learns that her sailor boyfriend has died in a shipwreck, ends with the assurance that the two lovers walk hand in hand evermore 'at rest on a distant shore'. It perhaps comes as close as Gilbert ever did to an expression of religious belief, and Sullivan characteristically invested this intimation of eternal life with appropriately religious sentiment. Much more obviously religious in tone is the poem by Tennyson, 'St Agnes' Eve', which he set in 1879, eight years after the two men's collaboration on the Schubertian song cycle, 'The

Window'. First published in 1837 as 'St Agnes', the title was changed by the Poet Laureate in 1857 to bring it closer to Keats's well-known work, 'The Eve of St Agnes'. St Agnes was a 13-year-old Christian girl, who was martyred in 304 for refusing to sacrifice to pagan gods and to surrender her virginity. She became the patron saint of virgins and of those women who espoused the dedicated religious life. Tennyson's verses, which inspired several Pre-Raphaelite painters, expressed the pious sentiments of a nun who longs to be united with Christ, the heavenly bridegroom:

> Deep on the convent-roof the snows
> Are sparkling to the moon:
> My breath to heaven like vapour goes:
> May my soul follow soon!
> The shadows of the convent-towers
> Slant down the snowy sward,
> Still creeping with the creeping hours
> That lead me to my Lord:
> Make Thou my spirit pure and clear
> As are the frosty skies,
> Or this first snowdrop of the year
> That in my bosom lies.

Another classic sacred ballad text by a contemporary author, C. J. Rowe's 'The Village Chimes', looks back nostalgically on childhood memories of village church bells, ringing in 'a better life that brings a brighter morrow' and all the more poignant because of the loss of 'a mother's kiss, a mother's love'. Sullivan's 1870 setting brings out its atmosphere of yearning. Even more emotional was his tune for 'The First Departure', another tear-jerking ballad in which a mother addresses first the sea which has swept away her son and then God 'who will keep my child for me through grace unfailing given'. Written by Revd Edward Monro, the Tractarian vicar of St John the Evangelist, Leeds, and published by Cramer in 1874 in a collection of three songs entitled 'The Young Mother', it attracted little attention and Cramer, to whom Sullivan had sold his tunes for a few guineas, sold them on in 1876 to Metzler for a similarly paltry sum. Metzler sent the tune of 'The First Departure' to Fred Weatherly, the 28-year-old lawyer who was beginning to make his way as a song writer and would eventually become one of most prolific and deft of all parlour ballad lyricists, writing 'The Holy City', 'Danny Boy', 'The Old Brigade' and 'Roses of Picardy'. In his words:

Without any suggestion from Sullivan, but entirely on my own, I wrote 'The Chorister.' Madame Sterling [Antoinette Sterling, the American-born contralto who was one of the leading exponents and promoters of drawing room ballads], who was very difficult to please with words, and who would sing no song unless she honestly felt the words, took up the song, and in a very short time the receipts of the publisher were enormous.[7]

It was unusual for a Victorian poet to write verses to fit a pre-composed tune, although it is the way that Tim Rice and Andrew Lloyd Webber worked in the later twentieth century. Weatherly clearly found Sullivan's highly emotional melody affecting, and it inspired him to produce a real tear-jerker about a young orphaned chorister singing with the voice of an angel:

> His earnest eyes to heav'n were bent,
> With yearning pure and lowly,
> To follow where his singing went,
> And join the Angels holy.
> No gentle mother's love had he,
> But God had comfort giv'n,
> For he might sing on earth
> And she might hear her child from heaven.

As if it were not enough to portray this motherless child singing his pure melodies to heaven, Weatherly has the young chorister himself dying and in the last glimpse we have of him, accompanied by Sullivan's pulsating minims, he is singing among the angels, beside the crystal river, the light of God on his brow, 'for ever and for ever'.

Similar sentiments informed 'Thou art lost to me', an anonymous poem which Sullivan set in 1865 and dedicated to Mrs Freake, who would the following year lay the foundation stone for the new church of St Peter's in Cranley Gardens which her husband built and where Sullivan served as organist. It tells of two lovers living far apart and separated on earth but looking forward to their heavenly reunion:

> Time shall cease,
> And some day we shall be launched
> Into eternity:
> Then I'll meet thee,
> Fondly greet thee,
> And no more thou'lt be lost to me.

Of the 14 sacred ballads by named contemporary poets for which Sullivan supplied tunes, half were by female authors. This reflected the strong
contribution of Christian women to the writing of sacred verse, which,
in the absence of any female ordination, was often undertaken as a kind
of vocation. Every one of their poems yearned for death. In 'Longing for
home' by the popular poet Jean Ingelow, written in 1869 and probably
set around then by Sullivan, although it was not published as a song until
1904, a woman, whose husband and children have died, expresses the
hope that she will soon follow them:

> Oh, one after one they flew away
> Far up to the heavenly blue,
> To the better country, the upper day,
> And – I wish I was going too.

Felicia Hemans's 'Thou'rt passing hence' mourns the death of a much-
loved brother and expresses a longing to follow him

> Where the dirge-like tone of parting words
> Shall smite the soul no more!
> And thou wilt see our holy dead,
> The lost on earth and main:
> Into the sheaf of kindred hearts,
> Thou wilt be bound again!

Sullivan finished and wrote out this song on 22 September 1874, while
staying at Balcarres, the home of Sir Coutts and Lady Lindsay. He noted
in his diary: 'It is very curious that I should have done it just now. Time
passes very quickly. It doesn't seem eight years ago since dear father died
[on 22 September 1866].'

Almost certainly the last sacred ballad that Sullivan composed, in
1887, set lyrics by the American-born poet, Clara Bloomfield Moore, an
American-born philanthropist and poet, who lived largely in London after
the death of her husband in 1878. 'Ever' is a strange mystical effusion, in
which the singer is held 'as by a spell' by strange music, which rises and
falls in waves and leaves her glorified for ever. Predictably, this fairy-like
possession inspires a desire not to return to the mundane earth but to remain for ever among the dead in heaven:

> 'Call me not back to earth,' I said,
> Here leave me as among the dead!

Where sorrow enters never;
Through gates that music leaves ajar,
The glory streams from heav'n afar,
For ever!

The female poet whose verse seems particularly to have inspired Sullivan was Adelaide Ann Procter (1825–64). He set four of her religious
poems as sacred ballads and one ('The way is long and dreary') as a sacred
part-song in addition to composing tunes for her secular love poem 'A
shadow' and her hymn 'My God, I thank Thee, who hast made/The earth
so bright'. A convert to Roman Catholicism, Procter was a pious and
sickly spinster – she died of tuberculosis at the age of 38 – who devoted
her short life to poetry and charitable work among the poor. Charles
Dickens described her as 'a fragile and modest saint'. Her verse was admired by Queen Victoria and, according to Coventry Patmore, she was
second only to Tennyson as the most popular poet of the age.

The first of Adelaide Procter's poems that Sullivan set was 'Will he
come?' (1865), in which a dying woman senses that she can hear a horse-
man coming to rescue her. In fact, it is only the reapers carrying home
their sheaves and, by implication, bringing in the harvest of death. The
song ends with a touching invocation of the deathbed scene, so familiar
in Victorian novels:

There was only a sound of weeping
From watchers around a bed,
But rest to the weary spirit,
Peace to the quiet dead.

'Will he come?' was the first of Sullivan's songs to be published on a
royalty basis rather than being sold outright to the publisher, an arrangement which considerably enhanced his earnings. The fact that he played it
in church, when a bishop was late for a service (page 59), could be taken
to suggest that he did not take it over-seriously. However, the tune he
supplied was typically lyrical and appropriate to the sentimental words. It
almost has the quality of recitative and particularly effective is the passing
bell introduced at the end, a favourite device of Sullivan's when dealing
with the subject of death. It has been suggested that he wrote the song as
a tribute to the author who had died the previous year.

Procter's 'See the rivers flowing', which was published as a song entitled
'Give' in 1867, has an improving message about learning from nature –
notably the rivers and the flowers – and giving without expecting any

immediate reward but rather waiting on God's generous bounty. Sullivan dedicated his setting to the wife of Thomas Helmore, his mentor at the Chapel Royal, and gave it an elaborate art song treatment, reminiscent of Schubert and going through a dazzling range of keys before finally settling on the dominant on the sixth page. 'Thou art weary', which Sullivan set in 1874, conveys the heart-rending prayer of a starving and exhausted mother, convinced that 'God is good but life is dreary', for her hungry child's death:

> Better thou shouldst perish early,
> Starve so soon, my darling one,
> Than in helpless sin and sorrow
> Vainly live as I have done.
> Better that thy angel spirit
> With my joy, my peace were flown,
> Than thy heart grow cold and careless,
> Reckless, hopeless, like my own.

This desperate cry ends with a plea to God to 'take us to his heaven, where no want or pain can be'.

There is a conundrum at the heart of Sullivan's corpus of sacred songs. Why did a composer who was so much in love with life choose to set almost exclusively texts which not only dwelt on the theme of death but positively yearned for it, as a means either of being reunited with a departed loved one or of finding escape and salvation from a wretched life on earth? Was he attracted to them because he knew that he would make money out of them or because they genuinely moved him? In part, the prevalence of morbid sentiments in his sacred songs reflects their ubiquity in Victorian verse and their popularity for affecting and improving Sunday afternoon sing-songs. We are back once again to the powerful hold of Victorian sentimentalism and the central role within it of death and heaven. Sullivan's letters suggest that he shared the view that many of his contemporaries had of heaven as a warm and welcoming place where family and loved ones would be reunited. Perhaps his own particular family experiences and lack of fear of death played a part in his choice of these verses and the way that he set them to music. These factors certainly seem to have been important in attracting him to another of Adelaide Procter's poems, which he was to turn into the best-selling of all Victorian sacred ballads.

'The Lost Chord'

Adelaide Procter's poem 'A Lost Chord' first appeared in 1858 in *The English Woman's Journal*, which she and a number of feminist friends had founded to encourage women's involvement in the management of philanthropic activities such as temperance campaigns, industrial and ragged schools, cottage hospitals and local refuges. It tells of a troubled organist, 'weary and ill and ease', whose fingers 'wandered idly over the noisy keys'.

> I do not know what I was playing,
> Or what I was dreaming then;
> But I struck one chord of music,
> Like the sound of a great Amen.
>
> It flooded the crimson twilight
> Like the close of an Angel's Psalm,
> And it lay on my fevered spirit
> With a touch of infinite calm.
>
> It quieted pain and sorrow,
> Like love overcoming strife;
> It seemed the harmonious echo
> From our discordant life.
>
> It linked all perplexed meanings
> Into one perfect peace,
> And trembled away into silence
> As if it were loth to cease.
>
> I have sought, but I seek it vainly,
> That one lost chord divine,
> Which came from the soul of the organ,
> And entered into mine.
>
> It may be that Death's bright angel
> Will speak in that chord again, –
> It may be that only in Heaven
> I shall hear that grand Amen.

This is a powerful religious text at a number of levels. As David Eden has pointed out, it provides an almost classic account of a mystical experience – the initial agitation, the sudden sense of being flooded with inward light, the intense feeling of well-being and harmony and integrative sense of linking all perplexed meanings into one perfect peace, the fading of the experience and the desperate desire to repeat and recover it with the final realization that it will only come again with death.[8] There are other clear theological resonances in terms of the poem's glimpses of glory and intimations of eternity. It describes one of those moments when we experience heaven on earth, in academic theological terms an example of 'realized eschatology'. There are two interesting reference to angels, something of a hallmark of the poetry of Procter who, in the perhaps over-cynical words of Hoxie Fairchild, 'lugs in an angel whenever she wants to pluck at our heartstrings'.[9] It is highly significant that the source of the overpowering, integrative peaceful mystical experience is a musical chord which 'comes from the soul of the organ' and enters into the very being of the organist. A similar theme is found in several other poems that were to become popular sacred drawing-room ballads. There are clear echoes of it in the song 'Sometimes' written by Lady Lindsay and also set by Sullivan in 1877:

> Sometimes, when I'm sitting alone,
> Dreaming alone in the gloom,
> There comes on the wings of the twilight,
> Sweet music that fills the room.
> I know not from whence it comes,
> I know not what message it brings,
> Though my soul of its burden is lighten'd
> By the sweet voice that plaintively sings.

The notion of the music made by angels is picked up again in Fred Weatherly's 'The Holy City', written in 1892 and set to music by Stephen Adams, where, in the context of a dream about Jerusalem, the singer reflects: 'Methought the voice of Angels from Heaven in answer rang'. The idea of a stirring piece of music that will only be heard again after death resurfaces in Francis Barron's 'The Trumpeter' (1904), with its observation that although the soldiers who have fallen in battle will not be able to experience the stirring call to 'Reveille',

> They'll hear it again in a grand refrain,
> When Gabriel sounds the last 'Rally'.

With its strong tribute to the power of music, it is not surprising that 'A Lost Chord' should have appealed to composers. It seems first to have been set as a song by George Macfarren in 1866. Sullivan made an attempt to set it in 1872, but was dissatisfied with the result. He was drawn back to the text during the three-week vigil that he spent at the bedside of his brother Fred, who died on 18 January 1877 at the age of 39.

> One night – the end was not very far off then – while his sick brother had for a time fallen into a peaceful sleep, and he was sitting as usual by the bed-side, he chanced to come across some verses of Adelaide Procter's with which he had some five years previously been much struck. He had then tried to set them to music, but without satisfaction to himself. Now in the stillness of the night he read them over again, and almost as he did so, he conceived their musical equivalent. A stray sheet of music paper was at hand, and he began to write. Slowly the music grew and took shape, until, becoming quite absorbed in it, he determined to finish the song. Even if in the cold light of day it were to prove worthless, it would at least have helped to while away the hours of watching. So he worked on at it. As he progressed, he felt sure this was what he had sought for and failed to find on the occasion of his first attempt to set the words. In a short time it was complete.[10]

The accuracy of this moving account by Charles Willeby, apparently based on Sullivan's own reminiscences, is attested by Arthur Lawrence in his biography and also corroborated by Newman Flower, who adds the information that Sullivan had first come across Procter's poem in the magazine *Household Words*.[11] It is amplified by the reminiscences of Frederick's daughter, Amy, who recalled that her dying father had a hand in the construction of the melody:

> As Uncle worked on *The Lost Chord* by the bedside, Father would hum it. Once Uncle asked: 'Now I have worked out some chords for the ending – do you like it? Would you change it?' Father hummed the tune and said 'Go up, up, up'. Uncle pencilled in the changes, got up and went downstairs to the piano. I got Mother and she sang while Uncle played through the changes. We all thought it splendid, and Uncle seemed satisfied.[12]

When Sullivan's song was published a few months after his brother's death, Procter's mother objected to the use of the original title and so it was changed to 'The Lost Chord'. The song also introduced a slight change in wording: 'I know not what I was playing' in place of the poem's 'I do not know what I was playing'. Shortly before the song was published, Antoinette Sterling, the singer, who had made such a success of 'The Chorister', asked Sullivan if he might consider setting Procter's verses, which had made a profound impression on her. 'I have already set them' was his response. He agreed that Sterling should give the first performance of the song, although he was nervous about its prospects, telling her at the first rehearsal, 'It won't be a success, I'm afraid.' In fact, when 'The Lost Chord' was first performed at a ballad concert by Sterling with Sullivan at the piano and Sydney Naylor on the organ, it was greeted with thunderous and prolonged applause. Its success was both immediate and lasting. It sold an average of 20,000 copies annually for 25 years, a total of half a million copies, making it the best-selling ballad of the last quarter of the nineteenth century.

Although Sterling premiered 'The Lost Chord', the singer who became most associated with it during Sullivan's lifetime was Fanny Ronalds (1839–1916). Born and brought up in the United States, she entered into an unhappy marriage and separated from her husband, moving to London in 1871 and becoming Sullivan's lover and companion. She sang the song regularly at Sunday evening musical soirées at her house at 7 Cadogan Place. The Prince of Wales, later Edward VII, famously said that he would happily travel the length of his future kingdom to hear her sing it, and it was said to be the favourite song of his consort, Queen Alexandra. They were not the song's only royal fans. Queen Victoria is reported to have quoted it, telling her favourite prime minister, Benjamin Disraeli, 'You have struck my lost chord and sounded my great Amen.'

For Sullivan, Fanny Ronalds was the supreme exponent of 'The Lost Chord'. In the words of Newman Flower, 'She sang the song to his liking as no one else ever sang it, and of all those who rendered it during the many years when it was the most widely sung melody in the world, put into it that sorrow he knew when he composed it. He openly said that she alone brought tears to his eyes with his own notes.'[13] He gave her his original manuscript of the song, which she chose to have buried with her when she died in 1916. She passed on another manuscript copy written out in a book in Sullivan's hand to the English contralto Clara Butt (1872–1936), who herself made the song her signature piece, recording it and singing it to an audience of 10,000 in the Albert Hall to support British troops fighting in the Boer War in January 1900 and again in the same venue in August 1902 at the request of Queen Alexandra on the occasion of the postponed coronation of Edward VII. During World War One, Clara Butt famously said, 'What we need now is more songs like "The Lost Chord". There is something of the grandeur of Beethoven in it.' In 1950, her widower, Kennerley Rumford, gave her copy to the Worshipful Company of Musicians, and it remains in their possession today.

'The Lost Chord' has found a place in musical and cultural history for several reasons. A performance on cornet and piano in 1888 was almost certainly the first phonographic recording made in England. When it was played at a phonograph party on 5 October, Sullivan recorded this message to Thomas Edison:

> For myself, I can only say that I am astonished and somewhat terrified at the results of this evening's experiment: astonished at the wonderful power you have developed, and terrified at the thought that so much hideous and bad music may be put on record for ever. But all the same I think it is the most wonderful thing that I have ever experienced.[14]

Perhaps inevitably, as the most popular and iconic of all Victorian parlour ballads, 'The Lost Chord' was the subject of numerous parodies. Sullivan responded to one of the earliest, by the operetta composer, Edward Solomon, with the rebuke 'I wrote The Lost chord in sorrow at my brother Fred's death, don't burlesque it.'[15] Subsequent parodies included George Grossmith's 'The Lost Key' and Jimmy 'Schnozzle' Durante's 'The Guy Who Found the Lost Chord'. The song inspired at least three early twentieth-century films which took its title.

Critics have long mocked the excessive emotionalism of 'The Lost Chord'. The late Victorian and early twentieth-century novelist E. F. Benson described it as 'a test piece for tears', in which every female singer tried her strength as if with a punching machine at a fair which registered muscular force: 'If there were not a dry eye in the room when she had delivered her blow she was a champion.'[16] Many more recent critics have been scathing about it. Routley predictably castigates its dull and contrived religiosity, commenting that 'the atmosphere of the Victorian city church demands at once thirteen F's in a row'.[17] John Caldwell sees it as exemplifying 'the awful potential of maudlin verse combined with apposite music ... Its hymnic harmonies and its static melodic line are undoubtedly suited to the words, but the relentlessness with which they are pursued serves only to emphasize the underlying shallowness.'[18] However, others have recognized an authenticity and power in its emotional sentimentality. For Nicholas Temperley, 'The Lost Chord' is 'Sullivan's maligned masterpiece ... Sentimental this song undoubtedly is, but it is a powerful piece of work none the less. Clara Butt was not far wrong when she said "there is something of the grandeur of Beethoven in it".'[19] Meinhard Saremba compares the fortissimo setting of the line 'It may be that only in heaven I shall hear that Great Amen' to be sung 'con gran forza' with the moment in *The Dream of Gerontius* when Gerontius's soul is judged and confronted with the holy face of God, when the score indicates that 'for one moment, must every instrument exert its fullest force'. He comments: 'Elgar does not relate directly to Sullivan's musical depiction of a similar moment, but continues to lead the underlying idea of Sullivan's song to perfection.'[20]

The way that Sullivan set 'The Lost Chord' tells us much about his religious leanings as a composer and perhaps a little too about his own faith. Maurice Disher comments that Adelaide Procter 'endowed it with devotion', and 'Sullivan, in a mood of mourning, matched it with strains suited to church organs', effectively creating an anthem rather than a song.[21] The intense chromaticism gives it the feel of a high Victorian hymn tune. The scoring for harmonium as well as piano accompaniment and the use of the traditional contrapuntal texture associated with Anglican organ music further enhances its ecclesiastical atmosphere. So does the influence of plainchant, which pervades it from the string of repeated notes at the beginning which, as Arthur Jacobs points out, are very similar to those found in 'How many hired servants' in *The Prodigal Son*, 'I hear the soft note' in *Patience* and 'Now to the sunset' in *The Golden Legend*. Are they there, as he suggests, to convey 'solemn intensity' or are they rather the almost subconscious echoes of that style of church music instilled into Sullivan in his Chapel Royal days by Helmore?[22] David Owen Norris has pointed to the similarity of the opening bars: 'Seated one day at the organ, I was weary and ill at ease' with the versicle and response found in both morning prayer and evensong: 'Oh Lord, open thou our lips, and our mouths shall show forth thy praise.' He also detects other ecclesiastical and religious echoes in the way that the song is set, like the bells on the descending bass scale after 'It seemed the harmonious echo', the 'Amen' in the sub-dominant suggesting another world, and the similarity between the notes for 'I struck one chord of music' and the opening phrase of 'The day Thou gavest'.[23]

Could it be that this song had a deeper significance for Sullivan and that it was wrung not just out of his grief for his dying brother but also out of his own waning faith? Was the lost chord that he sought and came to feel that he would find again only in heaven that simple, trusting Christian faith of his youth and early adulthood? There is an extraordinary sense of wistfulness and yearning about his melody, quite apart from the way that it also reflects the mystical experience conveyed in phrases like 'it flooded the crimson twilight'. Was this song, destined to be so popular, so parodied and so pilloried, not just playing to the gallery of Victorian sentiment but also reflecting the spiritual state of its composer, seeking to link all perplexed meaning into one perfect peace and yearning in a life that was increasingly restless and ever more bent on pleasure and distraction for a sense of infinite calm? Does it represent yearning for the simpler, more trusting faith of his youth? When he wrote it, he was 34. For Derek Scott, 'the appeal of "The Lost Chord" lies not in its depiction of a numinous experience, but in conveying a feeling of loss ("I have sought but I seek it vainly") and an optimistic faith in death as the final comforter and the solver of all mysteries'.[24] Perhaps the way that he set those final lines 'It may be that only in heaven I shall hear that Great Amen' to be sung triumphantly 'con gran forza' reflected his own lack of fear of death (page 16) and takes us as near as anything that he wrote to the heart of his own faith.

6

They Sing Choruses in Public: Oratorios and Cantatas

The Victorians' passion for oratorios has already been highlighted (pages 28–9). In the words of Nigel Burton:

> The musical life of nineteenth-century Britain was governed not by opera, as in the rest of Europe, but by oratorio, a form that was sacred but not liturgical, unstaged yet dramatic ... an ideal compromise for a nation whose Established Church sought to combine and resolve both Catholic and Calvinist traditions in its worship and theology.[1]

With oratorio playing such a central role in musical culture, it was hardly surprising that as a young composer determined to make his mark nationally Sullivan should have turned his hand to this form. He wrote his first oratorio, *The Prodigal Son*, at the age of 27, when he already had a symphony and a secular cantata, *Kenilworth*, under his belt, and his second, *The Light of the World*, four years later. His other large-scale sacred work, *The Martyr of Antioch* (1880), did not conform to the strict definition of an oratorio as a work based on a story from Scripture and using only biblical words, and he described it as a 'sacred musical drama'. *The Golden Legend*, his most substantial choral work, written in 1886, although based on a secular text, has many spiritual resonances and had a significant influence on the development of the English oratorio in the twentieth century.

His commitment to this particular musical form was also very clearly demonstrated in nearly 20 years as conductor of the Leeds Festival, the biggest of the provincial festivals based around performances of oratorios, which were such an important part of Victorian musical life. In that role, he did much to encourage the performance of major sacred works.

Sullivan's first involvement in this area of music, beyond his youthful performances while a chorister in the Chapel Royal, came in February 1869, when, at the request of Joseph Barnby, he embellished the score

of Handel's *Jephtha*, based on the story of the Israelite judge, who led
his people against the Ammonites as described in chapters 11 and 12 of
the book of Judges. The addition of accompaniments to Handel's scores
to provide more colour and interest had been initiated by Mozart and
continued more recently in Britain by Michael Costa and George Macfarren. Sullivan's work on *Jephtha*, which consisted largely of adding wind
and brass accompaniment to choruses, was probably undertaken principally as a favour to Barnby and for financial reasons, but it confirms
his continuing enthusiasm for Handel's oratorios, which he had so loved
as a boy, and his determination that sacred works should be appealing
and attractive to audiences as well as faithful to their biblical roots. This
conviction was later to land him in trouble with critics who felt that his
own oratorios were altogether too easy on the ear.

The Prodigal Son (1869)

Sullivan's own first oratorio came as the result of a commission from
the Three Choirs Festival. In accepting the challenge to compose a major
sacred choral work, he was following in the wake not just of his great
heroes Handel and Mendelssohn but also of leading figures in the contemporary British musical establishment like Michael Costa (1808–84),
the Italian-born composer who had settled in Britain in 1830 and had
written *Eli* in 1855 and *Naaman* in 1864, and William Sterndale Bennett
(1816–75), Sullivan's piano teacher at the Royal Academy, who had written *The Woman of Samaria* in 1867.

  With the choice of subject matter left entirely to the composer, he decided on the well-known story of the Prodigal Son. He began his preface
to the work by reflecting how remarkable it was that this parable 'should
never before have been chosen as the text for a sacred musical composition'. In fact, it had been set both by the French composer Marc-Antoine
Charpentier (1643–1704) in 1690 as a dramatic motet, *Filius Prodigus*,
and by Samuel Arnold (1740–1802), like Sullivan a chorister in the Chapel
Royal, in 1773. Neither of these settings was well known, and Sullivan
was effectively breaking new ground in Victorian England in choosing
this parable for musical treatment. It fitted well with the general religious
ethos of the time with its message of God reaching out to the wayward
sinner and lovingly bringing him back into the fold. There is surely a clear
allusion to the story of the Prodigal as well as to the parable of the lost
sheep in the verse, which Henry Baker interpolated into his paraphrase
of Psalm 23, 'The King of Love My Shepherd Is', and which also made

its first appearance in 1869 in the appendix to the first edition of *Hymns Ancient and Modern*:

> Perverse and foolish oft I strayed,
> But yet in love he sought me,
> And on his shoulder gently laid,
> And home rejoicing brought me.

The sense of acceptance and forgiveness conveyed by Baker's verse, and enhanced by the gentle lyrical tune written specially for it by J. B. Dykes, did much to make this one of the Victorians' favourite hymns. It was these same qualities in the Prodigal's father, and by analogy in God, that appealed to Sullivan. The rest of the preface to his own work gives a revealing insight into his own religious convictions:

> The story is so natural and pathetic, and forms so complete a whole; its lesson is so thoroughly Christian; the characters, though few, are so perfectly contrasted, and the opportunity for the employment of 'local colour' is so obvious, that it is indeed astonishing to find the subject so long overlooked.
>
> The only drawback is the shortness of the narrative, and the consequent necessity for filling it out with material drawn from elsewhere.
>
> In the present case this has been done as sparingly as possible, and entirely from the Scriptures. In so doing, the Prodigal himself has been conceived, not as of a naturally brutish and depraved disposition – a view taken by many commentators with apparently little knowledge of human nature, and no recollection of their own youthful impulses; but rather as a buoyant, restless youth, tired of the monotony of home, and anxious to see what lay beyond the narrow confines of his father's farm, going forth in the confidence of his own simplicity and ardour, and led gradually away into follies and sins which, at the outset, would have been as distasteful as they were strange to him.
>
> The episode with which the parable concludes has no dramatic connection with the former and principal portion, and has therefore not been treated.

It is significant that Sullivan described the lesson of the parable of the Prodigal Son as 'so thoroughly Christian'. Perhaps more than any other passage in the Bible, it portrays God in an utterly non-judgemental light as a loving parental figure full of grace and compassion. Sullivan's conception of the character of the Prodigal Son as 'a buoyant restless youth ... going

forth in the confidence of his own simplicity and ardour' is also highly significant. It is almost impossible not to feel that the 27-year-old composer
was not in some sense describing himself here. Maybe he also had his own
grandfather in mind. According to a Leeds newspaper, Thomas Sullivan
senior was 'an Irish squire [who] spent his patrimony on riotous living'.
Arthur Sullivan himself described his grandfather as 'an impoverished
young Irish squire much given to steeplechasing', who had been pressed
into service with the British Army after a night of excessive drinking.[2] It
is significant that he left out the final part of the parable, in which the
Prodigal's brother complains to his father about the partiality and favour-
itism shown to the errant younger son 'as having no dramatic connection'
with the main story. It does have an important theological connection in
terms of confirming the theme found in so many of Jesus' parables about
God's apparent favouring of the repentant sinner over the steady faithful
servant. Sullivan was far from oblivious to that message. The themes of
repentance and of God's overflowing mercy are both prominent in the
texts that he chose to set. It was the lack of dramatic connection rather
than any theological considerations that led to the omission of this part of
the story. For Sullivan, the dramatic element was the most important in
constructing his oratorio. In this he was following Mendelssohn who had
written to a Lutheran pastor friend while working on *Elijah*, 'I would fain
see the dramatic element more predominant as well as more exuberant.'[3]
Sullivan's main focus was on the characters of the Prodigal and his father
and the relationship between them. His own father, to whom he had been
so devoted, had died less than three years earlier and was surely in the
composer's mind in the way he portrayed the Prodigal's father in such
human and loving terms.

Sullivan seems himself to have selected the texts that make up the libretto for *The Prodigal Son*. Their choice suggests an extensive, almost
encyclopaedic, knowledge of the Bible and an impressive grasp of the
theological meaning as well as the dramatic potential of this particular
parable. In addition to the story itself as recounted in Luke's Gospel, he
incorporated verses from Revelation, Proverbs, Ecclesiastes, Isaiah, 1
John, Genesis, Hebrews and especially from the Psalms, which are quoted
extensively and to particularly strong effect. I wonder, in fact, if his great
friend George Grove may have helped in identifying and selecting suitable
biblical verses, as he did subsequently for *The Light of the World*. Grove
came to Worcester for the premiere of *The Prodigal Son*, but I can find
no direct evidence that he was involved in the construction of the libretto.

Structurally, *The Prodigal Son* follows the conventions of oratorio as
established by Bach and Handel and is clearly influenced by Mendelssohn's

St Paul and *Elijah*. A mixture of choruses, solo recitatives and arias tell the story and also reflect on its wider significance and message, with every word sung being taken directly from the Bible. A full list of the musical numbers and their biblical sources can be found in Appendix 5 (pages 207–8).There are four soloists: tenor (the Prodigal), bass (the father) and soprano and alto used partly as narrators and also to provide theological commentary and moral homily.

The oratorio begins with words from Luke 15.10, which precede the story of the Prodigal Son and form the conclusion to the parable of the lost coin: 'There is joy in the presence of the angels of God over one sinner that repenteth.' Sung first by the sopranos alone and then picked up by the whole chorus, this immediately establishes one of the central themes of the story, and of Jesus' parables and teaching as a whole, that of repentance and of the joy in heaven over one sinner who turns to God. The message is reinforced by a quotation from Psalm 103: 'Like as a father pitieth his own children, even so is the Lord merciful to them that fear him' and somewhat more surprisingly, though by no means incongruously in the context of the story of the Prodigal, from Revelation 7.16 and 17: 'They shall hunger no more, neither thirst any more; and God shall wipe away all tears from their eyes.' Sullivan was clearly drawn to that text; he set it again in *The Light of the World*.

The tenor enters to tell the story of the Prodigal straight from Luke's Gospel, with the bass coming in as the father to tell his son to attend to his words and, in what is perhaps a reflection of an emphasis already noted in Sullivan's own faith, to 'Trust in the Lord with all thine heart' (Prov. 3.6). The soprano then takes up the story and the chorus joins the Prodigal in a lively Bacchanalian number, entitled 'The Revel', which sets words from Isaiah: 'Let us eat and drink, for tomorrow we die. Fetch wine and we will fill ourselves with strong drink.' It expresses the philosophy of 'Carpe diem' which undoubtedly reflected Sullivan's own attitude to life and is eloquently expounded in the quintet 'Try we lifelong' in *The Gondoliers*. Some critics regarded the style and sentiments of this chorus as being not altogether seemly for an oratorio: not for the last time Sullivan seemed to be sympathizing with the sinners more than with the righteous. The contralto responds with the admonition, again from Isaiah, 'Woe unto them that rise up early in the morning that they may follow strong drink, that continue until night till wine inflame them' and an aria expressing the distinctly un-Sullivan like sentiment: 'Love not the world, nor the things that are in the world' culled from 1 John 2.15 and 17. While it undoubtedly shows the composer's skill in amplifying and enhancing the story of the Prodigal with material from very different sources, this aria is generally adjudged one of the weakest numbers in the piece with a bland and restricted vocal line and an unadventurous and predictable accompaniment. This is surely because its message is so far from the world-loving, life affirming Sullivan's own philosophy of life. By contrast, the father's 'Trust in the Lord', which is set in the same three-four time, is altogether more adventurous, unexpected and inventive.

Following a Handel-like soprano aria, 'O that thou hadst hearkened to my commandments', the central section of the oratorio focuses on the story as told by Luke. The tenor aria, 'How many hired servants', marks the Prodigal's moment of realization and repentance when, starving and humiliated, he resolves to go back to his father as a penitent confessing his sin. Beginning with the characteristic Sullivan device of 11 repeated notes, it is operatic in its passion and intensity, the anguish being conveyed by the pulsating triplets in the accompaniment. With the tenors carrying the melody, the chorus repeat the opening refrain, 'There is joy in the presence of the angels of God over one sinner that repenteth', to which is added the line: 'The sacrifices of God are a broken spirit; a broken and contrite heart, O God, Thou wilt not despise' (Psalm 61.17), a text set by Sullivan with particular feeling and sensitivity that further reinforces the theological message about repentance and God's reaction to it. The son returns, and his father runs out and kisses him while he is still far off. Their reconciliation is represented by a touching duet in which the father is given Jacob's words from the Old Testament story of Joseph: 'My son is yet alive! Now let me die, since I have seen thy face, and thou art yet alive' (Gen. 45.28; 46.30). This is a daring and inspired piece of biblical transposition, which again points to a considerable knowledge of the Scriptures. There is no suggestion in the parable of the Prodigal Son of the father feeling that he can now die having seen his son return. By putting into his mouth the words said by Jacob to Joseph, Sullivan enhances the dramatic element in the story without substantially distorting it. The father goes on to call for the best robe to be brought and the fatted calf to be killed and sings an aria which picks up again the words from the opening chorus: 'Like as a father pitieth his own children, even so is the Lord merciful to them that fear him' and blesses God for hearing his prayer.

Sullivan could well have ended his oratorio at this point. Without the elder brother's reaction, there is nothing further to quote from Luke's narrative of the parable. However, he chose to have four more numbers, an overlong chorus of praise to God drawn from Psalm 107, a tenor aria on the theme that 'whom the Lord loveth He chasteneth' from Hebrews 12, an unaccompanied quartet singing about the Lord being nigh those that are of a contrite heart (Psalm 34.18) and a final triumphant, somewhat

over the top chorus acknowledging the Lord as 'our Father and our Redeemer'.

The Prodigal Son, which Sullivan took only three weeks to compose,
was first performed in Worcester Cathedral on 8 September 1869 and repeated the following year in Hereford Cathedral. Performances conducted
by the composer followed in the Crystal Palace, London, in December
1869 and in Edinburgh in 1870. Charles Hallé conducted the first Manchester performance in 1870. Perhaps inevitably, given the haste of its
composition, it is somewhat uneven in quality. The Prodigal's main aria
and the duet between father and son have considerable pathos and drama,
but the concluding numbers are dull and suggest padding. The story that
Gilbert fell asleep near the beginning of the work and remained in this
state for the rest of the London performance to which he was taken by
Richard D'Oyly Carte is probably apocryphal, although it is worth recording simply for the response that he supposedly uttered when the anxious
impresario asked him what he would say to Sullivan about the work: 'I
shall tell him that it has transported me to another world.' More flatter-
ing was the verdict of Rachel Scott Russell, with whom Sullivan had his
first serious love affair. After attending the first performance, she wrote to
him: 'The *divinity* of your gift of God breathes through the whole work
and it is a glory to have written a thing which will stir men's souls to their
depths, as it does, and make them feel better and nobler.'[4]

Fellow composers, including those generally well-disposed towards
Sullivan's work, acknowledged the curate's egg quality of *The Prodigal
Son*. J. B. Dykes noted that 'the first part is very interesting and beautiful
... it falls off in interest towards the end'. John Goss praised his former
pupil but felt that he could do better:

> All you have done is most masterly – your orchestrations superb, and
> your efforts many of them original and first rate. Some day you will
> I hope try at another oratorio, putting out all your strength – not the
> strength of a few weeks or months. Show yourself the best man in
> Europe! Don't do anything so pretentious as an oratorio or even a sym-
> phony without all your power, which seldom comes in one fit. Handel's
> two or three weeks for the *Messiah* may be a fact, but he was not al-
> ways successful, and was not so young a chap as you.[5]

John Stainer, writing to Frederick Bridge, expressed similar sentiments:

> I heard the Prodigal Son at Worcester – the instrumentation throughout
> is <u>charming –</u> but as a whole the work lacks 'bottom' – you under-
> stand me. The melodies are graceful but not always original. It will keep

afloat until the publishers have made a good thing of it, then ___! It is as good as the Woman of Samaria – and very much in the same sugar candy style.

I do wish dear Sullivan would put his thumb to his nose – to the public and critics, – and write for 'the <u>future</u>'.

The later works of Mendelssohn and Beethoven, and all works of poor neglected Schubert and tardily acknowledged Schumann – all point to the future of music. Sullivan ought (I feel that he is a great man and could do so) to begin where they left off – regardless of encores and banknotes.[6]

Despite these candid comments by friends and supporters, the overall critical verdict was overhelmingly positive. The view of the *Musical Times* was typical:

The Prodigal Son is a thoughtful, conscientious work; and although unequal in merit, there can be no question that it will take rank far above any previous composition of its author. It is deeply sympathetic with the subject, betrays throughout not the slightest sign of haste or carelessness, and may be at once accepted as the latest proof of the development of a mind which has been steadily and diligently trained in that legitimate school of writing which has produced the really great artists of the world. In constructing the libretto much skill has been shown, the parable itself being accompanied with suitable portions selected from the scriptures, which are woven in so as to form rather an Oratorio than a Sacred Cantata; the composition indeed being of sufficiently ample portion to justify this more important name.[7]

Reviews of *The Prodigal Son* generally concurred that it elevated Sullivan to a whole new level. The *Pall Mall Gazette* reflected that 'Mr Sullivan now occupies a very different position from that in which he stood before the production of his oratorio', and the *Musical Standard* opined that it allowed him to enter the ranks of 'those who have achieved'.[8] The oratorio went into the standard choral repertoire for the next 40 years. 'There is joy in the presence of the angels of God' found its way into several church anthem books and the arias 'How many hired servants' and 'Love not the world' were popular in church concerts.

Like the rest of Sullivan's serious work, *The Prodigal Son* effectively disappeared through most of the twentieth century. The few performances which were given tended to provoke a distinctly lukewarm response even from Sullivan's supporters. Nigel Burton observed in 1981 that 'Sullivan seemed to have taken greater trouble over the construction of the libretto than over the music', and a review by David Eden of a 1991 concert at Woodford Green, Essex, when it was coupled with Elgar's *The Light of Life*, brought out the old canard about Sullivan's lack of faith:

> As one might expect, *The Light of Life* emerges as a better work, but the difference is more one of commitment than ability. Elgar, a man of faith, was emotionally involved in his text in a way that Sullivan, a very perfunctory Anglican, was not. As a result, the conviction of Elgar (on the way to *The Dream of Gerontius*) emerges throughout, whereas Sullivan (on his way to *The Mikado*) was only intermittently engaged.[9]

The early years of the present century have seen the work's rehabilitation and reappreciation. Since being professionally recorded in 2003, there have been a number of amateur performances, including in St Anne's Lutheran Church in Münster, Germany (October 2011), by the North-ampton-based A La Carte group in St John's Church, Buxton, in August 2012 and by the 150-strong St Andrews Chorus and 37-piece Heisenberg Ensemble in the Younger Hall, St Andrews, in November 2012. Academics have been more inclined to take it seriously. In a recent scholarly article about the evolution of oratorio in nineteenth-century Britain, the theologian David Brown gives it an honourable mention and singles out its theological emphasis, arguing that 'Sullivan sees his role as essentially to reinforce the message of the parable rather than in any sense to tell the story anew. Musically, the main focus lies in reflection on the general character of God, and that is why the story comes across as but a staging post on the way to the oratorio's grandiose conclusion.'[10] This interpretation directly conflicts with David Eden's statement in the sleeve notes for the 2003 recording that Sullivan approached *The Prodigal Son* 'not as a musical theologian but as a composer of opera looking for human emotion and local colour'. It seems to me that in fact Sullivan provides both a dramatic retelling of the story and a substantial amount of theological and moral reflection. He is perhaps more at ease with the human emotion and drama, which are enhanced by inventive orchestration, but there is no doubt at all, from the extensive range of extraneous texts that he selects and sets, that he is also concerned from the opening chorus onwards to reinforce and reflect on the theological themes of repentance, God's pity for his erring children and the overwhelming and overflowing character of divine forgiveness and love.

Appropriately, perhaps, given Sullivan's indebtedness to Mendelssohn and the oratorio's origins with Bach, the most perceptive and appreciative recent analysis of *The Prodigal Son* has come from Germany. The summer 2012 issue of the journal of the Deutsche Sullivan Gesellschaft was largely devoted to it and included a detailed musicological study by Richard Silverman, which points to the care which Sullivan took to craft the music to enhance the meaning of the text and shows how, for all the haste of composition, he clearly conceived of the work as an integrated structure, with repeated and interweaved themes, rather than just a series of discrete and unrelated choruses and solos. Silverman's overall verdict is overwhelmingly positive:

> *The Prodigal Son* is a satisfying, uplifting work, full of youthful vitality, with many memorable arias and choruses. That Sullivan composed it in a mere three weeks and orchestrated it so finely in the same brief period is a manifestation of the genius with which he was blessed.
>
> Granted that it has its less than inspired passages, the score still amply displays Sullivan's special gift of immediately capturing the listener's attention by the freshness and vitality of his musical ideas.[11]

The Light of the World (1873)

Sullivan's second oratorio was the result of a commission from the Birmingham Musical Festival, which had an impressive record in this sphere, having hosted the first performances of Mendelssohn's *Elijah*, Costa's *Eli* and *Naaman* and, more recently, Julius Benedict's *St Peter* in 1870.

Several theories have been put forward as to where Sullivan got the inspiration for *The Light of the World*. Newman Flower suggested that it was from an Irish lady with whom he was in love.[12] Michael Ainger has speculated that it might have come to him while staying at Costessy Hall near Norwich, the home of the Staffords, an old Catholic family, in September 1872. He wrote to his mother, 'there is a fine chapel which Lord Stafford took me to see in the moonlight and a dim lamp was burning in front of the altar'.[13] This sounds to me more like an allusion to the second line of James Drummond Burns's 'Hushed was the evening hymn' – 'the lamp was burning dim beneath the sacred ark' – which he must have been setting around this time, rather than a reference to *The Light of the World*. It is more commonly suggested that the inspiration for the oratorio came from the painting of the same name by William Holman Hunt showing Jesus with a lantern in his hand knocking at a door overgrown with brambles. The Pre-Raphaelite artist produced the original version of the painting between 1851 and 1853 following a religious conversion. A smaller version, probably painted by a friend of Hunt's, was exhibited around the United Kingdom and the United States and an engraving made in 1860 sold widely and boosted the painting's iconic status. Its popularity may have been a factor in determining the title and theme of Sullivan's work, although I can find no mention of its influence in his letters or diary. The standard modern work on the painting traces its influence on numerous hymns in the 1860s, and even on a 1980s' pop group, but makes no mention at all of Sullivan's oratorio, and it is perhaps significant that neither Jesus' description of himself as the Light of the World (John 8.12; 12.46) nor the specific verse that inspired Holman Hunt's painting, 'Behold, I stand at the door and knock' (Rev. 3.20), appear in the libretto.[14] This suggests to me that while the painting may possibly have been in Sullivan's mind when he selected the title of his work, it was certainly not a major influence in terms of its theme.

Although Flower states that the entire work occupied Sullivan 'less than a month', it seems clear that he worked on it for longer than on most of his sacred works. He told his friend J. W. Davison, music critic of *The Times*, in May 1873, 'I never go out in the world as my oratorio takes all my time and thought ... I have stuck to my work since last Michaelmas without faltering.' Another common misconception springs from a comment in *The Times* review of the first performance that 'Sullivan is alone answerable for the book'. Arthur Jacobs states in similar terms that '[i]ts words, directly from the Bible without additions, were selected by the composer himself'. In fact, the letter to Davison makes clear that Sullivan was not solely responsible for the libretto: 'The words are all compiled from the Bible by Grove and myself. I think the book is really beautiful thanks to dear old "G".'[15]

This last remark suggests that George Grove had a major hand in choosing the text for *The Light of the World*. He was certainly well qualified to do so, being a serious biblical scholar as well as a writer on music (page 61). It may well be Grove's hand that is behind the extraordinarily eclectic and diverse range of texts that make up the rather diffuse and overlong libretto. A list of the musical numbers and their biblical sources is provided in Appendix 6 (pages 209–11).

Sullivan set out clearly the purpose of the work in an 'opening argument' printed as a preface in the vocal score:

> In this oratorio the intention has not been to convey the spiritual idea of the Saviour, as in the *Messiah*, or to recount the sufferings of Christ, as in the 'Passionsmusik,' but to set forth the human aspect of the life

of our Lord on earth, exemplifying it by some of the actual incidents in His career, which bear specially upon His attributes of Preacher, Healer, and Prophet.

This is an interesting statement making exactly the same point that Tim Rice and Andrew Lloyd Webber made about *Jesus Christ Superstar*, namely that the intention is to focus on the human rather than the divine or supernatural aspects of Jesus and treat him as a man in terms of his life as preacher, healer and prophet rather than as the Son of God.[16]

In fact, although *The Light of the World* hardly touches on the passion or crucifixion, it is not simply a portrait of a human Jesus devoid of supernatural or Christological trappings. It is true that in a daring departure from the convention established by Handel in English-language oratorio, Sullivan does make Jesus a character, portrayed by the baritone soloist and singing in the first person. In other respects, however, Jesus is not really portrayed as 'just a man', to quote Mary Magdalen's song in *Jesus Christ Superstar*. Sullivan's Jesus is largely devoid of human feelings and emotions. There is a strong emphasis on the resurrection in the last scene, in marked contrast to *Jesus Christ Superstar*, which ends with the crucifixion. As the use of the terms 'Christ' and 'our Lord' in the opening apology suggests, Sullivan's is a very orthodox portrayal of Jesus as the Son of God and not calculated to ruffle any feathers in the Victorian Church.

The oratorio, which runs in its original version to two and three-quarter hours, is divided into two parts and begins with a prologue sung by the chorus setting verses from Isaiah about the coming Messiah. The first and longest scene, which contains 11 musical numbers, is set in Bethlehem and tells the story of the Nativity, based largely on the account in Luke's Gospel. An Andante Pastorale somewhat reminiscent of Handel's Pastoral Symphony in *Messiah* introduces the shepherds, to one of whom Elizabeth's words to Mary, 'Blessed art thou among women', are given as a solo. A truncated Magnificat is sung by the soprano soloist as Mary, and two moving numbers follow based on Jeremiah's account of Rachel weeping in Rama, as picked up in Matthew's account of Herod's slaughter of the innocents.

The second scene, entitled Nazareth, is set in the synagogue. Jesus makes his first appearance with a long and complex song, 'The spirit of the Lord is upon me', which lasts 13 minutes and includes material from Luke, Matthew and John. Identifying himself as the object of Isaiah's prophecies, he is expelled by the crowd and left alone with his disciples to whom he sings an amalgam of the Beatitudes and other key sayings that could perhaps be said to sum up Sullivan's own generous and liberal faith, which was also shared by Grove:

> Blessed are they that are persecuted for righteousness' sake, for theirs is the kingdom of heaven. Judge not that ye be not judged. Condemn not and ye shall not be condemned. Forgive and ye shall be forgiven, that ye may be the children of your Father which is in heaven.

The third scene features Jesus' raising of Lazarus and is a fairly straight retelling of this miracle story from John's Gospel with some rather unexpected interpolations from Jeremiah and Isaiah. It seems curious to include in a work supposedly focused on Jesus' humanity what is arguably the most supernatural of all his miracles, bringing someone back from the dead. Presumably it is there because of its dramatic potential, but this does not really seem to be exploited. Instead the scene moves to Bethany and to a sustained focus on the theme of resurrection. The fourth and final scene in the first part covers Jesus' entry into Jerusalem on the first Palm Sunday. There are solos for a Pharisee, a deep bass rather in the mould of one of the high priests in *Superstar*, a disciple and Jesus. A soprano solo provides one of the few moments of real drama in the treatment of the verse from Isaiah 'Behold, thy salvation cometh' and a chorus of children sing 'Hosanna to the Son of David'.

The second part is set entirely in Jerusalem and begins with an overture which, in the words of the composer's apology, 'is intended to indicate the angry feelings and dissension caused by our Lord's presence in the city'. Jesus has a solo telling the story of the sheep and the goats, again perhaps reflecting Sullivan's own credo of practical good works and helping others. There then follows an unnecessarily complicated sequence, fairly described by the late nineteenth-century American music critic, George Upton, as 'a somewhat tedious scene', in which a ruler argues with the people, contemptuously asking if Christ shall come out of Galilee.[17] Nicodemus strives to reason with the ruler, and the women of Jerusalem sing a lugubrious chorus, 'The hour is come', to which Jesus responds with a solo addressed to the daughters of Jerusalem assuring them that he will overcome the world. His trial and crucifixion are barely covered – instead an unaccompanied quartet sing 'Yea though I walk through the valley of the shadow of death' from Psalm 23 set with all the hushed piety of the Victorian sacred ballad at its most sentimental.

The final scene is set in the sepulchre. After an opening recitative quoting from Samuel and Jeremiah, Mary Magdalen sings an aria drawing on imagery in the psalms about the Lord hiding himself. It would be interesting to know whether it was Grove or Sullivan who was responsible for this imaginative and highly original interpolation of Old Testament material, which is somewhat reminiscent of the Prodigal's father quoting Jacob, although on a much bigger scale, and quite unparalleled in any other oratorio that I know of about Jesus. The angel tells Mary not to weep as Jesus is risen and the concluding numbers draw on the Pauline epistles and Revelation to meditate on the resurrection and its significance. In the pious words of the Apology (and if they were written by Sullivan rather than Grove, he was certainly putting on his Sunday best at this point):

> The disciples acknowledge that Christ has risen, and that God has caused the light to shine in their hearts, making all things new; and after an earnest exhortation from one of them to follow in their Master's steps and fight the good fight of faith, they glorify God for the triumphant close of their Lord and Master's earthly labours.

The Light of the World was given its first performance in Birmingham on 27 August 1873 in the presence of Sullivan's close friend, the Duke of Edinburgh, to whose Russian bride the work was dedicated. It was received with enormous enthusiasm by the audience: three pieces were encored, and there were requests for more. The Duke of Edinburgh, to whom the composer left the score in his will 'in remembrance of the many happy hours which he spent with his Royal Highness while he was writing it', contented himself by repeating again and again to the composer, 'a triumph'.[18] The critics were broadly enthusiastic and commended the fact that the work did not seem too derivative of the predecessors with which it would inevitably be compared. The *Observer* concluded: 'The oratorio is one of imagination, of not only clever ideas but of really devotional religious thought', and *The Standard* noted approvingly: 'The Light of the World has nothing in common with the *Messiah*; it borrows neither style nor ideas from the *Passion Music*; and it even steers clear of that magnetic rock, Mendelssohn, upon which so many fair and well-freighted barks have been lured to their doom.'[19] *The Times* critic, having expressed the view that 'To the profound feeling of reverence with which Mr Sullivan has musically illustrated all the passages relating to the Saviour, and in which the Saviour is supposed to hold forth, no intelligent listener can be insensible', rated the work as 'the best oratorio for which we are indebted to an English musician'.[20] Reviewing a performance in the Albert Hall five years later, it adopted a slightly more critical tone, identifying the difficulties inherent in realizing 'the human presence of the Saviour without touching upon those divine qualities which, in this country at least, are not considered the subject for dramatic treatment, however reverential'. This constraint had weakened the impact and interest of Sullivan's work:

> Christ is conceived by him as the Divine teacher and admonisher, free from suffering and fear, and inapproachable to those human passions which play so conspicuous a part in Mendelssohn's *St Paul* or *Elijah*. Such a conception is sublime, but it cannot be made the centre figure of a dramatic action. Hence the feeling of monotony attaching to the long and measured utterances of the baritone solo.[21]

The oratorio was performed in an abridged version in London, Liverpool, Bootle, Norwich and Manchester in 1874 and in Glasgow in 1876. Gounod came specially to hear it in London and declared it 'a masterpiece', and Queen Victoria said that it was 'destined to uplift British music'.[22] 'Yea, though I walk through the valley of the shadow of death' was taken up as an anthem in churches, and the contralto aria 'The Lord is risen' from the final scene was issued by J. B. Cramer as a sacred parlour ballad under the title 'God Shall Wipe Away All Tears' and recorded by Clara Butt. Sullivan's admirer, Frederick Bridge, organist of Westminster Abbey, adapted the concluding part of the chorus 'Men and Brethren' from the first scene of the Second Part for use as an Introit in the coronation service of Edward VII in 1902.

As with other Sullivan works, *The Light of the World* dropped out of the repertoire in the twentieth century, as the critical climate changed. The *Westminster Gazette* described it in 1903 as 'the dullest and flattest oratorio in existence', and Ernest Walker dismissed it in 1907 as having 'hardly enough vitality even to be vulgar'.[23] It was only at the end of the twentieth century that it came to be revived, and then rarely in its entirety. It was performed in Southwark in 1982, Oldham in 1988 and the Isle of Man in 1991. The last three scenes were performed in All Saints Church, Purleigh, Essex, on Palm Sunday 1991 and Scenes 1, 4, 5 and 6 in the Chapel of Keble College, Oxford, where the original version of Holman Hunt's painting of *The Light of the World* is hung in a side chapel, during the Sullivan Society Festival in 1996. The last complete performances of the work that I am aware of were in 2000, one in Bromley and the other in the Anglican Cathedral in Liverpool. The Liverpool performance, with organ accompaniment and professional soloists, was recorded on the initiative of Ray Walker and issued on CD. Substantial excerpts were performed in June 2012 in St Laurentii-Kirche, Itzehoe, near Hamburg, providing a further indication of the growing interest in Sullivan's sacred music in Germany.

Recent critical comment has tended to focus on the dullness of the music given to Jesus. Richard Silverman sees this as the work's main weakness but is complimentary about the rest of the oratorio in which he finds 'many fine choruses, brilliant solos and beautiful pastoral passages'.[24] More damning is Paul Ensell's verdict, occasioned by the 2000 recording:

> Many of the problems of the piece can be laid at Sullivan's door. This is probably one of the worst pieces that he wrote. I think much of the problem may have been the libretto which Sullivan chose from the Bible himself. If he had persuaded someone else to do this, things might have improved.[25]

In fact, as we have seen, Sullivan was not solely responsible for the libretto, and George Grove may well have chosen the considerable amount of text interpolated from non-Gospel sources, which is employed with less obvious purpose and effect than it is in *The Prodigal Son*. The overall effect of all this extraneous material is to produce a rather uneven, unwieldy and unnecessarily complex treatment of Jesus' life and significance. Jesus himself is given substantial passages to sing, which by their nature have to be set in the style of recitative rather than in a more lyrical way. For me, far from being among the duller parts of the work, they have an appealing clarity and measured restraint.

It is interesting to compare *The Light of the World* with *The Crucifixion*, written by Sullivan's great friend and contemporary John Stainer as 'A Meditation on the Sacred Passion of the Holy Redeemer' in 1887. Stainer's is a more obviously devotional work. It is also much shorter and more manageable, being written for a church choir with organ accompaniment and not for the massive resources gathered at music festivals. It is much simpler and more straightforward theologically. Apart from the Christological hymn in Philippians 2.7–8, its libretto, selected by W. J. Sparrow-Simpson, rector of a London parish church, is taken entirely from the Gospels. There is a much clearer theological focus on the atonement, expressed in the chorus 'God so loved the world', which unsurprisingly remains such a popular church anthem. The way that Stainer sets this text, and especially the words 'God came not into the world to condemn the world' show him to be a much more theologically nuanced composer than Sullivan, albeit one with a similar broad liberal faith.

The Light of the World has no comparable central number setting out a theory of atonement. Nor, rather surprisingly perhaps given Sullivan's huge enthusiasm for hearty hymn singing, does it provide hymns in which the audience or congregation could join. This, of course, is one of the distinguishing features of *The Crucifixion* with its five congregational hymns including the immortal 'Cross of Jesus' and 'All for Jesus'. Sullivan had no qualms about bringing hymn tunes into his two big Te Deums, but he obviously felt them to be inappropriate for an oratorio. Is this another example of his natural impulses being stifled by the canons of Victorian good taste and religiosity? *The Light of the World* has a very churchy feel. It exudes the atmosphere of the Anglican cathedral rather than the Nonconformist chapel. Of all Sullivan's major choral works, it shows most clearly the lingering influence of the Chapel Royal – there are lots of high floaty soprano lines, better suited for boys' than women's voices, and he wrote in a special chorus part for male altos. The overall effect is ethereal and restrained, less lively than *The Prodigal Son*, yet undeniably consoling, moving and in parts deeply devotional. It deserves a proper professional performance and recording with full orchestra.

The Martyr of Antioch (1880)

In January 1878, Sullivan was approached by the committee of the Leeds Musical Festival for an oratorio for the 1880 Festival. He received the invitation when he was ill in Nice and turned the offer down, but on his return to London and to better health he reconsidered it and told the committee that while unable to 'undertake the composition of an oratorio which should occupy the whole of the concert ... I should not be unwilling to write a work of the same length and character as the "Prodigal Son" – a work of about an hour or an hour and a half, and forming one part of a concert'.[26] He was duly commissioned to write a piece of the kind he proposed for a fee of 100 guineas, to include all his personal expenses and the provision of band and chorus copies.

He decided to base the new work around the biblical story of David and Jonathan and to prepare the libretto himself. 'I search the Scriptures daily,' he told the festival secretary Fred Spark, 'only to find that the best verses for filling up in the orthodox fashion have been used by oratorio writers before me. If I take these, there will be always comparisons drawn as to the setting. One will say, "Oh, Handel's music to those words is much better," or "Mendelssohn's ideas are far superior to Sullivan's".'[27] In fact, although Handel had incorporated the figures of David and Jonathan in *Saul*, Mendelssohn had not set this particular story. Perhaps the truth was that Sullivan, mindful of the constraints that he had faced when writing *The Light of the World*, went off the idea of setting another libretto based on biblical texts. This is certainly the impression given by a report in the *Leeds Express* in June 1880, which noted that after wrestling with the story of David and Jonathan for some time, he had abandoned it as the basis for a libretto because of his realization 'that words from the Sacred Book required a certain amount of conventional treatment, somewhat limiting the composer's ideas'.[28]

Sullivan turned instead to a legend from early Christian history and a long poem written in 1822 about St Margaret of Antioch by Henry Hart Milman (1791–1868), a distinguished church historian and writer, who had been professor of poetry at Oxford and dean of St Paul's Cathedral. It recounted the story of Margarita (as Milman called her), the daughter of Callias, a pagan priest in Antioch, during the period of Christian persecution in the reign of the Roman emperor Diocletian at the beginning of the fourth century AD. Although herself a pagan priestess, she converted to Christianity, leading her to reject the advances of her former lover, Olybius, a Roman prefect, who thereupon denounced her and condemned her to torture and death. Sullivan saw the dramatic possibilities inherent in the poem's contrast between pagan and Christian worship and in Margarita's heroic sacrificial death for her faith. There was the added attraction that she was portrayed as the principal musician of the pagan temple, and the theme of religious music was at the core of the poem's dramatic and philosophical interest. A central dilemma for Margarita, expressed in a soliloquy in which she apostrophized her lyre, incorporated by Sullivan in his work, was whether she should take into her new faith the musical gifts that were previously 'hallow'd to an impious service'. It has recently been convincingly argued that Milman, who himself contributed several verses, including the Palm Sunday hymn 'Ride on! Ride on in majesty!', to one of the earliest hymn books produced in the Church of England, which met with episcopal condemnation, used *The Martyr of Antioch* to explore the vexed question of whether hymnody, with its sensuous and heretical connotations and 'perilous pleasures', was suitable for Christian worship.[29]

Sullivan struggled to condense Milman's lengthy poem into a manageable libretto. To help him out, he turned to W. S. Gilbert, with whom he had recently and successfully collaborated on *The Pirates of Penzance*. In what his biographer Jane Stedman describes as 'a labour of friendship', Gilbert took time off from working on the libretto of *Patience* to arrange the material and turn some of Milman's blank verse into rhyme. In his preface to the finished work, which he called a 'sacred musical drama', Sullivan wrote that 'the responsibility of the selection rests with the composer' and credited Gilbert with 'the change which in one or two cases (marked with an asterisk) has been necessary from blank verse to rhyme'. There are, in fact, four numbers so marked in the libretto, and there is one other passage which is Gilbert's work. He is also thanked for 'many valuable suggestions'. Arthur Jacobs states that Sullivan also consulted George Grove on textual matters and musical settings although he received no acknowledgement in the preface.[30]

As honed by Gilbert, Sullivan and Grove, *The Martyr of Antioch* runs to an hour and twenty minutes and has four scenes. The first, set in the Temple of Apollo, opens with a lengthy chorus of sun-worshipping youths and maids, transferred virtually uncut from Milman's original. In its review of the first performance, the *Musical Standard* critic rightly described this as 'a complete scene in itself of Pagan rites and idolatrous worship' and went on to praise it as 'one of the most extraordinary pieces of workmanship that any composer, of any land, has ever produced'.[31] In his opening song, 'Come, Margarita come', one of Gilbert's versifications which could do duty as a pagan parlour ballad and bears more than a passing resemblance to 'Come into the garden, Maud', Olybius calls on the priestess to take her appointed place and preside over the sacrificial rituals. When she fails to appear, Callias charges Olybius with being lukewarm towards the cult of Apollo, but the prefect responds with a clear statement of his determination to put Christians to death.

The second scene is set in a Christian cemetery at night where the funeral hymn 'Brother, thou art gone before us', taken straight from Milman's original, is being intoned as one of the persecuted Christian community is buried. Margarita stays behind alone after the ceremony to sing of her new faith in the hymn 'Thou didst die for me, O Son of God!', which is taken straight from Milman's poem and provides both a much more detailed and harrowing account of Jesus' crucifixion and a much clearer statement of its salvific and atoning purpose ('To wash our souls from sin's infecting stain, To avert the Father's wrathful vengeance flame') than is found anywhere in *The Light of the World*. Her father enters and discovers for the first time her conversion from paganism. They sing a duet extolling their respective gods. The third and briefest scene, set in the palace of the prefect, begins with the chorus of maidens singing their evening song to Apollo, 'Come away with willing feet', and sounding somewhere between the fairies in *Iolanthe* and the lovesick maidens in *Patience*. Olybius and Margarita sing a duet in which she attempts vainly to win his soul for Christ. He curses her faith, and she leaves him for her prison cell.

The fourth and last scene takes place outside the prison where Christians are kept. Heathen maidens on their way to the temple chant the glories of Apollo, while the Christian prisoners hymn their God. Julia, one of the pagan sun worshippers, sings a frenzied chant to Apollo, 'Io Paean!' Margarita prepares to go to her funeral pyre – Sullivan had changed her manner of death from Milman's poem, where it was execution. In a quartet, which, although not marked with an asterisk in the libretto, was written by Gilbert and is slightly reminiscent of the early part to the finale of Act II of *Princess Ida*, Margarita, Olybius, Callias and Julia all cry for mercy but the crowd bay for the Christian's blood. In her final aria, as the flames lick around her, Margarita has a vision of heaven, the great victorious train of martyrs and the Son of Man appearing:

> The Christ, the Christ, commands me to His home,
> Jesus! Redeemer! Lord! I come, I come, I come.

The piece ends with the chorus of Christians rejoicing that 'The Lord almighty reigneth' and that 'He who forfeits earthly life a life celestial gaineth'.

Although Christians get the last word, there is no doubt that taken overall *The Martyr of Antioch* focuses as much if not more on pagan beliefs and ritual. In terms of choruses, three times as much music is given to the pagans as to the Christians. This is in marked contrast to Milman's original poem, where five pagan chants and seven Christian hymns punctuate the blank verse. There is certainly no doubt that the heathens get the best tunes. This is particularly striking in the double chorus which opens the fourth scene, where the Christian prisoners' slow, dull dirge, 'Now glory to the God whose throne', contrasts with the lively brightness of the pagan maidens' 'Now glory to the god who breaks' with its thrilling trumpet accompaniment. Frederick Ouseley had done something similar in his *Martyrdom of St Polycarp*, in the premiere of which the young Sullivan had sung in 1854 (page 45), where the Christian disciples of St Polycarp sang a 'grave and solemn' chorale in the key of C, which gave way to a lively march heralding the arrival of the heathen Roman soldiers. Perhaps Sullivan still remembered it 26 years later.

The contrast in the music given to the pagans and Christians was remarked on by several of the reviewers of the first performance in Leeds on 15 October 1880, when *The Martyr of Antioch* formed the first part of a programme, which also included Beethoven's Mass in C and Schubert's *Song of Miriam*. The *Musical Times* noted that it was a sensible move of Sullivan's to call it 'a Sacred Musical Drama' as in that way 'no objection can be raised to a preponderance of music which, from the Christian point of view, is not sacred at all' and went on to observe:

Comparatively speaking, the poor Christians are nowhere. We hear them singing a funeral hymn, and presently their voices reach us from the dungeons where they await their death. But Mr Sullivan is not happy in their company, and slips away at the earliest opportunity to the joyous flower-crowned votaries who worship the Lord of the lyre. I cannot find it in my heart to blame him.[32]

Joseph Bennett, writing in the *Daily Telegraph*, took a similar view:

Mr Sullivan is most charming when represented by the incense, flowers and songs of Apollo's maidens. With these are all his sympathies, and he invests them with so much musical beauty of form and colour that they command our sympathies likewise, and make the poor Christians and their lugubrious strains appear as uninteresting as they are sombre.[33]

More recent writers have made the same point. Percy Young comments that while the 'heathen maidens' show characteristics of both Major General Stanley's daughters and the lovelorn girls of *Patience*, the Christians' 'song of faith' is 'so dull that one is inclined to hope for the continued incarceration of the singers'. He even suggests that it may have been a parody in which 'Sullivan drew the face of Anglicanism as he knew it'.[34] Is this fair? It is certainly true that the brightest and liveliest music is given to the worshippers of Apollo. The most vigorous song in the whole piece is the contralto aria, 'Io Paean!', which excitedly calls on the pagan maidens to swing their smoking censers. However, I am not sure that we can deduce from this, as some have, that Sullivan's sympathies were with the pagans or that he felt he had to portray Christian worshippers in a restrained, sober, reverential way, whereas he could let himself go and express his natural love of life when writing for the heathens. It was not so much the sense of inhibition, so often detected by critics in his sacred music, nor the stifling effect of Victorian religiosity which dictated Sullivan's music in *The Martyr of Antioch* but rather his desire to be faithful to the text that he was setting. The music that he writes for the Christians is restrained and serious, because that is the condition in which they are portrayed in Milman's poem and in the drama that he, Gilbert and Grove constructed out of it. The two main Christian choruses are respectively a funeral anthem, 'Brother, thou art gone before us', a deeply affecting and pastorally very sensitive setting, which rightly found its way into several church anthem books (and was sung at Sullivan's own funeral), and a prisoners' hymn. Both called for restrained and solemn setting. By contrast, the pagan choruses cried out for bright, lively treatment. Milman himself wrote in the preface to his original poem: 'I have opposed to

Christianity the most beautiful and natural of heathen superstitions – the worship of the Sun.'[35]

Ironically, and typically, while some critics felt that Sullivan had produced too much dull and lugubrious music for the Christians, others complained that the overall feeling of the work was lightweight and not serious enough. For the *Daily Telegraph*, 'criticism will always point to the fact that the drama is treated substantially as a pretext for charming choruses and airs', while *The Athenaeum* declared: 'It might be wished that in some portions Mr Sullivan had taken a loftier view of his theme, but, at any rate, he has written some most charming music.' Overall, however, there was general enthusiasm and the *Guardian* was by no means alone in its verdict: 'Sullivan has risen in this work to a height which has astonished those who prophesied that he would never step out of the chains of comic opera.'[36]

The Martyr of Antioch was widely taken up on the concert circuit. Sullivan conducted its first London performance at the Crystal Palace in December 1880 with further performances the following year at St James's Hall and the Albert Hall. He also took it to Norwich in October 1881 and again in October 1890, Brighton in November 1882 and Nottingham in March 1886. A performance in Bradford was conducted by Charles Hallé in December 1893 and one in Leeds by Hubert Parry in 1896.

Perhaps taking their cue from the fact that Sullivan had called it a sacred drama, and following their successful staging of a biblical cantata entitled *The Sign of the Cross*, the management of the Carl Rosa Opera Company decided to put *The Martyr of Antioch* on stage. It opened at the Lyceum Theatre, Edinburgh on 25 February 1898 in a double bill with *Cavalleria Rusticana*. For this staged version, Sullivan made certain changes, the most notable of which was substituting his recent funeral anthem 'Wreaths for our Graves' (page 146) for 'Brother, Thou art gone before us' at the start of the second scene. Elaborate sets and costumes were provided. Noting the enthusiastic response from the audience, the *Scotsman* commented that 'if one might judge from its reception it might be said that as an opera "The Martyr" is a distinct success'. While acknowledging the excellence of the music, however, the paper's critic felt that 'as drama it is indifferent. There is a lack of action and passion that is ordinarily fatal to stage productions.' However, he was prepared to give the piece the benefit of the doubt for the improving effect it might have on the theatre-going public:

If *The Martyr of Antioch* in its stage setting prove interesting, entertaining, and elevating to those who hear it, if it helps to bring home to an audience the bitter trials of the early converts to the Christian religion and at the same time to make them acquainted with a noble work by the greatest of English composers, the experiment has its justification.[37]

The stage production played with reasonable success in several venues and in its more conventional concert hall form Sullivan's musical drama continued to be performed throughout the Edwardian era before going into oblivion for most of the twentieth century. No known performance took place between March 1911, when it was given by Huddersfield Choral Society, and March 1983 when it was revived by Imperial Opera and Imperial College Operatic Society under the auspices of the Sullivan Society at the church of St Mary-le-Bow in London. New band parts had to be copied from the autograph full score bequeathed by Sullivan to the Royal Academy of Music as the orchestral parts had been destroyed in a fire at Chappell & Co. in 1965. Since this first modern revival there have been several performances, most notably with professional soloists and orchestra under the baton of Richard Balcombe in the Buxton Octagon, which was recorded in 2000.

As with so much of Sullivan's output, modern musicologists have been more complimentary about *The Martyr of Antioch* than many of their predecessors. Writing in 1999, John Caldwell described it as 'the most interesting oratorio in dramatic form before *Gerontius*'.[38] Of all Sullivan's sacred works it is the most G & S-like, more lyrical and noticeably lighter in tone than his two earlier biblical oratorios. By the time he wrote it he was in full comic opera mode, having already produced *Trial By Jury*, *H.M.S. Pinafore* and the *The Pirates of Penzance*. It is perhaps significant that it was the one and only sacred work on which he collaborated with Gilbert, who appears to have been genuinely touched, when Sullivan gave him an engraved silver chalice as a thank you present:

> It most certainly never occurred to me to look for any other reward than the honour of being associated, however remotely and unworthily, in a success which, I suppose, will endure until music itself shall die. Pray believe that of the many substantial advantages that have resulted to me from our association, this last is, and always will be, the most highly prized.[39]

As so often with Gilbert, it is difficult to know whether to take that statement at face value or not. Arthur Jacobs is probably right to see it as a sign of the formality of their relationship, 'never to ripen into intimacy', but it could equally be taken as indicating the librettist's genuine enthusiasm for this new and loftier joint project.[40] Their collaboration led to predictions that there would be more Gilbert and Sullivan oratorios. It also inspired a piece in *Punch*, almost certainly written by F. C. Burnand, who claimed to have heard the opening performance on a telephone line from Leeds (in fact it was relayed in this way to a number of Yorkshire towns).

> The great song rather reminded me of something in *Trial by Jury* and *Pinafore*; it is called *I'll tell you how I came to be a martyr*, with chorus. The refrain of the next most popular number is
>
> > In spite of all temptations
> > From some denominations,
> > I remained a Christian.
> > I remained a Christian.[41]

The implication of this spoof, and the complaint of critics, was that Sullivan had been too much in the G & S mode when he wrote *The Martyr*, not sufficiently grave and serious. Those who wanted more 'aspect stern and gloomy eye' were missing the point, however. Sullivan was not seeking to bring the levity of comic opera into his sacred musical drama. He was, as always, seeking to be accessible and to represent the text as faithfully as he could.

The Leeds Festival

Aside from his own compositions, Sullivan played an important role in promoting oratorios and other large-scale sacred works through his long association with the Leeds Musical Festival. From 1880 to 1898, he conducted seven successive festivals, which were held every three years and stretched over four days in October, involving a specially selected choir of over 300 and an orchestra of around 112 players. He initially came in as a compromise candidate. Michael Costa, his predecessor as conductor, and Charles Hallé both had more support in the committee but laid down conditions, Costa refusing to do anything by Bach and Hallé insisting on using his own Manchester-based orchestra. Sullivan proved much more accommodating and also had the distinct advantage in terms of popular appeal of being English (Costa was Italian and Hallé German). When his appointment was confirmed in March 1880, a local newspaper columnist could not resist quoting a slightly amended version of one of Gilbert's best known songs:

We might have had a Russian – a French, or Turk, or Prussian,
Or else I-ta-li-an.
But in spite of all temptations to go to other nations
We select an Englishman!

Sullivan's contribution to the Leeds Festival extended well beyond his role
as conductor. He prevailed on his close friend the Duke of Edinburgh
to be president, thereby considerably boosting the Festival's kudos and
prestige. He took a keen interest in the repertoire, working closely and
harmoniously with the committee to ensure a good balance of new and
well-established works, both sacred and secular. He was particularly keen
to promote British composers and was responsible for the first performances of George Macfarren's *King David* and Edward Elgar's *Caractacus*.
The major sacred choral works from the classical European repertoire that
he conducted included Mendelssohn's *Elijah* (programmed as the opening
item in five of his seven festivals) and *St Paul*; Handel's *Messiah*, *Samson*
(twice) and *Israel in Egypt*; Palestrina's *Stabat Mater*; Mozart's *Requiem
Mass*; Haydn's *Creation* (twice); Schubert's *Mass in E Flat*; Beethoven's
Mass in C (twice) and *Grand Mass in D* (twice); Brahms's *Requiem*; and
Spohr's *Last Judgement*.

   He also made an important contribution to the Bach revival in Victorian
Britain, conducting the first complete British performance of the B Minor
Mass in 1886. An earlier performance in London in 1876 had involved
an abridged score and modified orchestration. Sullivan was adamant that
the Mass should be performed as Bach wrote it and took considerable
trouble to ensure authenticity, personally supervising the arrangement of
the organ part and having trumpets specially made to reproduce what he
believed to be the pitch and tone quality of the instrument in Bach's time.
Reviewers were unanimous in their praise for his performance, which was
reprised in the 1892 and 1898 Festivals. He also introduced several Bach
cantatas into the Festival programme, giving the first British performance
of *Thou Guide of Israel* in 1883, and conducted the first two parts of the
Christmas Oratorio in 1895.

   Characteristically, Sullivan had a passion for connecting with the audience. He was initially uneasy about including *The World's End*, a work by
the contemporary German composer, Joachim Raff, on the grounds that
'it is not sufficiently effective to suit the British audience. It is wanting in
character and brightness.'[42] Persuaded to put this rather forbidding piece
in the programme, Sullivan sought to make it more appealing by visually
dividing the double chorus, in which one group expressed the anguish and
dismay of lost souls and the other the joy of the saved. He caused much

merriment among the Leeds choristers by announcing in rehearsal, 'Now ladies and gentlemen, I want a clear division in this chorus, and in order to get it I must ask the "righteous" to keep their seats and the "wicked" to stand up.'[43] He was always looking for 'bright' works to balance a programme which would otherwise be rather heavy. In 1886, he felt it important to pair Bach's B Minor Mass with something lighter to avoid 'a want of brightness', and for the same festival he chose the first part of Mendelssohn's *St Paul* to follow his own *Golden Legend* on the grounds that it was 'bright, dramatic and full of interesting and beautiful music'.[44]

It was no doubt partly this desire to brighten things up that caused Sullivan to fall foul of the musical establishment. A group of influential critics poisoned the Leeds Festival committee against him and suggested bringing in Stanford in his place. He was unceremoniously ousted as conductor in December 1899, receiving no official thanks or public recognition for all his work.

The Golden Legend (1886)

Following the success of *The Martyr of Antioch*, the Leeds committee approached Sullivan in 1884 for a new work for the 1886 festival. Initially, they suggested an orchestral piece, but he responded that he would prefer to write 'a short choral work, not necessarily sacred, but of an earnest character'. Newspaper reports in 1885 suggested that 'Sir Arthur Sullivan has undertaken to compose a new sacred oratorio expressly for the Leeds Musical Festival.'[45] He informed the committee in December that he was considering three subjects none of which seemed wholly right. According to Joseph Bennett, it was Flora Chappell, daughter of Tom Chappell, the music publisher, who suggested that he look at Henry Longfellow's poem *The Golden Legend*. They worked on it together for some time before bringing in Bennett who fashioned it into a satisfactory libretto.[46] Sullivan spent the summer of 1886 composing *The Golden Legend* side by side with *Ruddigore*.

Strictly speaking, *The Golden Legend* does not come within the scope of this book, as it is a secular cantata. However, it has a strongly religious theme and atmosphere. Longfellow's poem, written in 1852, was based on a medieval German legend and also influenced by Goethe's *Faust*. It tells of a prince, Henry, who can only be cured of leprosy by a maiden giving up her life. Elsie, a pious farmer's daughter, resolves to make this sacrifice and Henry, under the influence of Lucifer, accepts it. As she is about to surrender her life, he is struck with remorse and saves her, whereupon he is cured by the relics of St Matthew. In 1872, Longfellow incorporated his poem into a trilogy entitled *Christus* dealing with the three great Christian virtues of faith, hope and charity. Within the trilogy, *The Golden Legend* stood for the faith of the Middle Ages. In the preface, he wrote that 'it exhibits, among the corruptions of the Middle Ages, the virtues of disinterestedness and self-sacrifice'. Longfellow's story of sacrifice and redemption offered a theme of strong dramatic appeal in religious guise and as such was, in Arthur Jacobs's words, 'the very essence of the Victorian "sacred" choral work'.[47] Indeed, four composers before Sullivan set it as a cantata in the early 1880s: Dudley Buck, Henry Hodson, George Carter and William Creser, organist at Leeds Parish Church, who submitted his work for the 1886 Leeds Festival, only to have it rejected in favour of Sullivan's.

More than half of the words and music in Bennett and Sullivan's *The Golden Legend*, which runs to an hour and a half, could be categorized as religious in theme and tone. It begins with a prologue in which Lucifer is thwarted in his attempts to tear down the cross on the spire of Strasbourg Cathedral by its saints and guardian angels and by the bells, represented by the male chorus singing in unison to the praise of God with organ accompaniment. In the first scene, Prince Henry is corrupted by Lucifer through the medium of alcohol despite the repeated warnings of a chorus of angels. The second scene contains an evening hymn, 'O gladsome Light', sung a capella by the villagers, and an extraordinary invocation of Christ by Elsie who has a vision of him standing at the door of his Father's mansion and beckoning to her from afar. This leads her to sing a heartfelt prayer, 'My Redeemer and my Lord' asking that she may resemble Jesus by dying sacrificially. There is another choral hymn, this time sung in Latin by pilgrims, in the third scene, which ends with Elsie's aria 'The night is calm and cloudless' in which she hears snow white choirs singing 'Christe eleison!'

The fourth scene focuses on Elsie, as she prepares to lay down her life as a choir of attendants reflect that the lilies, which will spring from the dust of her body, will have 'Ave Maria' written on their petals. In a brief fifth scene, her mother, Ursula, is told that her daughter has not died and sings a hymn of thanksgiving to the Virgin Mary. The sixth and last scene sees Elsie and Henry married and reflecting on their eternal love. A concluding choral epilogue, memorably characterized by Gervase Hughes as showing 'Berlioz shaking hands with Mendelssohn in a hearty atmosphere of muscular Christianity', describes her as a messenger of faith sent to scatter God's freshness on the barren sands and solitudes of death with her unselfish hands in the same way that rain is sent by God to water the arid plains.[48]

Although Lucifer has a prominent role in *The Golden Legend*, it is most definitely not a work where the Devil has the best tunes. The music given to the hymns, prayers and other statements of Christian belief is sincere and affecting without being cloying. The strong religious overtones of the score, and their source in Sullivan's own musical upbringing, were not lost on the critics. The *Leeds Mercury* hailed 'O gladsome Light' as

> a massive example of simple diatonic harmony, such as might have been written by Tallis or Farrant. Here Sir Arthur's church training serves him well, and, in estimating pieces of this kind, we must not forget that the composer was a chorister of the Chapel Royal, St James's, where he made a part of himself the best traditions of English church music, and steeped his whole being in the classics of our ecclesiastical art.[49]

The Golden Legend's unashamed sentimentality and religiosity made it hugely popular with the public, especially the Nonconformist-dominated choral societies and chapel choirs up and down the land. It was effectively treated as a sacred work. My own copy of the score in Novello's Original Octavo Edition was awarded as the first prize for musical composition in the Liverpool Sunday School Union Eistedfodd of 1896. Modern musicologists have emphasized its religious aspects, perhaps none more so than Nigel Burton, who located it in a mystical but non-Tractarian Anglican tradition:

> It was a late florescence of the Handelian school, which was based on the visible and demonstrative aspects of Christianity and rooted in one of the two authentic national religious traditions. Its high-church counterpart had been assiduously fostered by the Oxford movement. By contrast, it emphasized the contemplative and devotional virtues and expressed the subjective mysticism inherent in Arminian Anglicanism and Roman Catholicism.[50]

With 17 performances within a year of its triumphant premiere in Leeds Town Hall on 16 October 1886, *The Golden Legend* ousted Mendelssohn's *Elijah* as the second most performed work in Britain after Handel's *Messiah*, a position which it continued to occupy for around 25 years. Critics rightly hailed it as Sullivan's greatest choral work and for once found themselves in harmony with popular opinion. *The Times* critic, noting how pleasant it was to be 'in full accord with the *vox populi*', delivered a very fair verdict which could stand for much of Sullivan's sacred music:

Sir Arthur Sullivan has had the good sense to make no attempt at being what he is not; he has simply put on paper what he felt and how he felt it; hence his success. Popularity, in the true meaning of the word, which is a very different thing from vulgarity and by no means incompatible with refinement of form, is this composer's birthright.[51]

Almost inevitably, there was a sting in the tail. Good though it was, this was still not quite what the musical establishment had hoped for from Sullivan, the Leipzig-educated Mendelssohn scholar and *wunderkind* of British music. *The Times* reviewer concluded that *The Golden Legend* was 'a work which, if not one of genius in the strict sense of the word, is at least likely to survive till our long-expected English Beethoven appears on the scene'.

Why did Sullivan fail to produce the big sacred choral work that, in the eyes of critics, stood on a par with those of Mendelssohn and Brahms? Was it lack of talent or lack of commitment? Was his heart just not in it? Did he lack the soul, the seriousness and the religious gravitas for a work comparable to *Elijah* or the *German Requiem*? Some of his friends felt that oratorio was not where his gifts really lay. The composer Ethel Smyth had the courage to tell him so:

> One day he presented me with a copy of the full score of the *Golden Legend*, adding: 'I think this is the best thing I've done, don't you?' and when truth compelled me to say that in my opinion *The Mikado* is his masterpiece, he cried out: 'O you wretch!' But though he laughed I could see he was disappointed.[52]

Others took the contrary view and felt that he should have written more oratorios. Joseph Bennett was perhaps the supreme exponent of this position. In his memoirs, he noted that his friendship with Sullivan reached its climax with the production of *The Golden Legend* in 1886. From then on, it declined.

> As far as I was responsible for the state of things, I attributed it in part to disappointment naturally felt at Sullivan's failure to go on to 'higher things' ... I saw him immersed in West End life, which is never healthy for an artist; I saw him, as I thought striving for such poor honours as the Turf can bestow; in these pursuits wasting time which was precious not only to himself, but to the nation. Moreover, I felt that gifts so exalted as his were not turned to best account in the writing of comic operas, however popular and charming.[53]

In fact, Sullivan did come close to writing another major choral work for the 1898 Leeds Festival. He wrestled with a libretto by the music critic Paul England, the subject of which is not known, but found it impossible to set at a time when he was suffering acute pain and distress from the kidney affliction that would kill him two years later. He wrote presciently in April 1898 'I fear I can't retain the conductorship of the festival if I don't write a work.'[54] Six months later the *Musical Times* reported that he was 'unable to fulfil his promise of a choral composition' for Leeds. This failure was undoubtedly a factor in precipitating his enforced and reluctant resignation from the conductorship of the festival in December 1899. A draft of a letter to Spark from around this time suggests that he had one last project in mind for the 1901 Festival which he was sorry he would not now be able to fulfil:

> In 1901, I shall have been 40 years before the public (as I date my career from the time I returned from Leipzig in 1861) and I intended making the festival an occasion of publicly retiring from the active pursuit of my profession, and to do this with éclat I meant to produce a work (which I am engaged on now) which would I hope be a worthy successor to *The Golden Legend* and form a dignified close to my personal public appearances. The words are from one of the (in my humble opinion) finest poems in the English language, and it has taken a strong hold upon me. This was my project and I confess to feeling some disappointment that it is not to be carried through.[55]

In the event, Sullivan did not live to see 1901. It is fascinating to speculate on the identity and nature of the (presumably lengthy) poem he was hoping to set as his swansong. Was it a sacred work, perhaps coming from the pen of either Milton or Tennyson, maybe even *Paradise Lost* or *In Memoriam*, both of which might reasonably qualify for the accolade that Sullivan accords? There is some evidence that he also contemplated another oratorio. In her reminiscences following his death, Mary Carr indicated that he showed interest in a libretto about Daniel which she sent him.[56]

As it was, Sullivan never returned to the oratorio form in which he had shown such interest and talent in his early years as a composer. He almost certainly found its particular constraints too restrictive, a view that was shared by many of his contemporaries. When Joseph Barnby composed *Rebekah* in 1870, he forsook a libretto based solely on biblical texts for one made up of new words specially written for the purpose, with the result that he had to call his work a 'Biblical idyll' rather than an oratorio. Even those composers generally regarded as much more serious than Sullivan found oratorio little to their taste. When the Birmingham Festival commissioned Hubert Parry to produce a major choral work for their 1888 festival, he feared that what was wanted was a traditional biblical oratorio: 'I don't like the Oratorio notion – though of course one can make a work on Oratorio lines which shall be perfectly independent of ecclesiastical or so-called religious conventions.'⁵⁷ He flirted with the idea of something based on Parsifal or the Albigensian heresy, but the Birmingham committee were adamant that they wanted a biblical subject. Eventually he relented, coming up with *Judith* and telling his piano teacher Edward Dannreuther,

> The Birmingham people stood out for a regular Oratorio. I hope you won't swear! After some correspondence in which they declined my alternative proposals, I caved in. But with a mental reservation that there shouldn't be much of religion or biblical oratorio beyond the name.⁵⁸

Elgar felt similar constraints, complaining to Delius that writing oratorios was 'the penalty of my English environment' and noting of the fugue, with which he ended his own first oratorio, *The Light of Life* (1896), 'I hope there's enough counterpoint to give the real British religious respectability.'⁵⁹

The combination of religious respectability and sentimentality, which underlay the Victorians' love of oratorios, did not just make composers uneasy. It also perplexed sensitive Christian souls such as George Tatham, the Quaker mayor of Leeds, who felt unable to occupy the position of chairman of the festival committee because of his religious scruples:

> Musical festivals and oratorios seem to me to be the incongruous combination of divine worship with amusement – the most solemn act of the soul with an evening's entertainment – where the most awful and sacred themes and events are rehearsed, the highest and holiest names familiarly used, often addressed to many who may be in no way in accord with the subject, and by those whose outward daily lives afford little evidence of the sacredness of their offerings. It seems to me like drawing near with the mouth and the lip, whilst the heart is far off.⁶⁰

Sullivan did not share these high-minded objections to treating solemn and sacred themes in the concert hall before a paying audience, who might not all subscribe to the highest Christian principles. He related to the religious texts that he set primarily as stories, for their dramatic possibilities and their moral messages. He is credited by several music historians as having been instrumental in liberating oratorio from its tight religious bands. Percy Young comments that the two works he wrote for the Leeds Festival 'stand away from the general run of oratorio as it was understood in the Victorian age, and on the edge of opera ... In the general context of choral music of that era both works represented a departure from the overriding convention of religiosity, and by doing so helped to emancipate such music from the shackles by which it was bound.'[61]

There is no doubt that Sullivan's work had a particular influence on Edward Elgar. It is highly likely that the 12-year-old Elgar attended the first performance of *The Prodigal Son* in Worcester, in which both his father and uncle were playing in the orchestra. He later himself played in performances of *The Prodigal Son*, *The Light of the World* and *The Golden Legend* in Worcester, Birmingham and Hereford. Elgar's admiration of *The Golden Legend* is well documented, as is Sullivan's support and help for the young British composer to whom he perhaps felt closest and admired most. David Russell Hulme has pointed to the striking similarity of the opening tenor phrases in *The Golden Legend* and *The Dream of Gerontius*, and Meinhard Saremba sees the lament of the dying Gerontius as recalling the sufferings of Prince Henry. Saremba, indeed, argues that Sullivan's sacred work exercised a broader influence on Elgar and suggests that the prologue to *The Prodigal Son* may have paved the way for the younger composer's involvement in biblical subjects. For Nigel Burton, who sees *The Dream of Gerontius* as the apogee of the tradition represented by *The Golden Legend*, 'Elgar was Sullivan's spiritual successor rather than a man of the academically respectable "renaissance".'[62]

How do we sum up Sullivan's large-scale sacred choral music? There is no doubt at all that it was an area of his work to which he felt committed throughout his life. While his two oratorios, understood in the strict meaning of the word, were the work of his youth, both *The Martyr of Antioch* and *The Golden Legend* belonged to his maturer years and, as we have noted, he was hoping to write another such work at the end of his life. Perhaps the clearest evidence for his commitment is in the way he went on making time to conduct his oratorios and sacred cantatas, even when he became frantically busy with other things. It was certainly not for money. On several occasions, he broke off work on the Savoy operas to conduct a sacred piece. Soon after arriving in the United States in November 1879 to supervise the first authorized performance of *H.M.S. Pinafore* and to premiere *The Pirates of Penzance*, he took off for Boston to conduct *The Prodigal Son* there. In September 1889, he broke off from composing *The Gondoliers* for two days to rehearse and conduct *The*

Prodigal Son and *The Golden Legend* at Gloucester Cathedral. Perhaps the clearest example of his dedication was shown on 10 and 11 October 1881. After rehearsing all day from 11 a.m. to 4.30 p.m., he conducted the first performance of *Patience* in the newly opened Savoy Theatre, attended a reception afterwards, and then went on to supper with Gilbert. His diary notes: 'returned home at 3 am, changed my clothes, had coffee and then drove to Liverpool Street station to take the 5.10 am train to Norwich'. He arrived in Norwich at 9 a.m. and after a quick breakfast went straight into rehearsing *The Martyr of Antioch* for a performance the following evening.

These are not just the actions of a man who can't say no and who crams far too much into each day and night for his own health – although there were undoubtedly elements of both of those traits in Sullivan's make-up. They also show the continuing dedication of the former Chapel Royal choirboy to religious music long after he had found fame and fortune in the sphere of comic opera. There will always be those who feel that Sullivan's oratorios and sacred works have too much of the comic opera style about them, being overdramatic, sentimental, secular and showy. In this respect, he is in good company. The German poet Heinrich Heine criticized Rossini's *Stabat Mater* as 'too worldly, sensuous and playful for a religious subject', and Hans von Bülow famously described Verdi's *Requiem* as opera dressed up in a cassock. Sullivan was to some extent constrained, like all Victorian composers, by the prevailing religiosity which demanded a grave treatment of sacred themes and perhaps made some of his religious music a touch dull. But he also 'burst the bonds of art' by putting more drama and life into religious scenes and themes than his contemporaries did. In this, he was not pandering to conventional taste – indeed, in many ways he was going against it, although it won him huge popular if not critical acclaim – but rather being true to himself, his love of life, his humanity and his own simple trusting faith.

7

For All Our Faults, We Love Our Queen: Anthems and Other Liturgical Pieces

Although Arthur Sullivan's direct contribution to church music in the composition of anthems and liturgical settings was less extensive and significant than his work in the field of hymnody, it was by no means negligible. He composed 19 anthems, wrote a psalm chant, arranged two pieces of Russian church music and produced three settings of the great Christian hymn of praise, the Te Deum. A full list of these works, with date of composition, can be found in Appendix 7.

Anthems

The use of anthems in services of worship soared through the latter half of the nineteenth century as a result of the choral revival and the introduction into many churches and chapels of robed choirs singing in four-part harmony. In order to cater for this booming new market, publishers commissioned anthems from contemporary composers and issued them on a regular basis in cheap and accessible editions. The *Musical Times* began an anthem supplement in 1844, and Novello launched a new series entitled the *Parish Choir Book* in 1866. The success of these and similar publications greatly increased the use of anthems written by contemporary composers, which were generally more popular with organists, choir members and churchgoers than the Tudor anthems favoured in cathedrals and by the ecclesiastical and musical establishment. A survey of the anthems sung in a representative group of parish churches has revealed that between 1850 and 1900 the proportion which had been composed in the nineteenth century rose from 25% to 73%.[1]

The new anthems published by Novello and others were aimed not at cathedral choirs but rather at those in parish churches and Nonconformist chapels. They tended to be short, relatively simple and similar in style to the Victorian hymn tune and sacred part-song in being more obviously sentimental and bolder in their expression of emotions than the classic English anthems of the sixteenth and eighteenth centuries. The most popular and prolific composers of these anthems included many of the same names who dominated the indices of later Victorian hymn books: John Goss, George Elvey, Frederick Ouseley, S. S. Wesley, John Stainer, Joseph Barnby and Arthur Sullivan. Sullivan's output was small compared with that of most of the others – his 16 published anthems compare with Barnby's 53, Goss's 46, Stainer's 44, Elvey's 42 and Wesley's 37 – but it was significant enough to put him consistently around halfway down the list of the top ten Victorian anthem composers in terms of representation in the anthem books published between the mid 1860s and the mid 1880s.

The majority of Sullivan's anthems were written during his first three decades, although the proportion is not quite so marked as with his hymn tunes. His first known composition was an anthem, 'By the waters of Babylon', written at the age of eight in 1850. Like two anthems composed while he was a chorister at the Chapel Royal, 'Sing unto the Lord' (1855) and 'Bless the Lord, O my soul' (1856), it was never published. Nine of his anthems were written during his time as a church organist in London, and a further six were written between 1875 and 1883, when his collaboration with W. S. Gilbert was at its height. He wrote his last anthem, 'Wreaths for our graves' in 1898, less than two years before his death.

In common with his contemporaries, Sullivan based most of his anthems on texts from the psalms. Of his 19 anthems, 13 were settings of verses from the psalms. Only two did not have biblical sources. 'The Strain Upraise' (1869), which is often classified as a hymn tune, perhaps because it was commissioned by Robert Brown-Borthwick for his *Supplemental Hymn and Tune Book*, but has the structure and complexity of an anthem, was a setting of a devotional poem by Balbulus Notker, a ninth-century Benedictine monk at the Abbey of Saint Gall in Switzerland, in a translation by J. M. Neale. 'Wreaths for our graves' was written by command of Queen Victoria for the service at the Royal Mausoleum at Frogmore on 14 December 1898 to commemorate the twenty-seventh anniversary of the death of Prince Albert. The text, by Mrs L. F. Massey, is a classic example of Victorian funerary verse. It was used in place of the funeral anthem, 'Brother, thou art gone before us', when *The Martyr of Antioch* was staged by the Carl Rosa Opera Company (page 133).

Sullivan departed from psalm texts for four of his later anthems. 'I will mention the loving-kindnesses of the Lord' (1875) and 'Hearken Unto Me, My People' (1877) both set words from Isaiah. 'There is none like unto the God of Jeshurun' (1882) completed an anthem, which John Goss had begun based on the song of Moses in Deuteronomy 33.26. 'Who is like unto Thee?' (1883), Sullivan's last biblically based anthem, took its text from Exodus 15. This move away from exclusive reliance on the psalms conforms to a trend noted recently by Peter Horton in respect of all English anthems in the second half of the nineteenth century.[2]

Sullivan's anthems display a variety of styles. The early 'O Love the Lord', 'O taste and see', 'Rejoice in the Lord' and 'I will lay me down in peace', all written in the 1860s, are relatively short and simple, although not without their daring harmonies and dissonances, which perhaps show the influence of S. S. Wesley. They are the closest to the part-song idiom and tended to be criticized as such. The review of 'O taste and see' in the *Musical Times*, while acknowledging 'some excellent vocal part writing and some graceful melodic phrases', found the work as a whole 'rather secular in style, perhaps, considering the purpose of the composition'.[3] Also in a strongly romantic and emotional idiom is the longer 'Sing, O Heavens', which uniquely combines texts from two psalms and from Isaiah. The influence of Mendelssohn is clear in the haunting solo in the middle: 'For his salvation is nigh them that fear him, that glory may dwell in our land'. The overwhelming impression conveyed by this anthem through its emphasis on the message that 'the Lord hath comforted His people and will have mercy upon His afflicted' is a sense of calm reassurance reminiscent of that found in his early song, 'O Israel' (page 47).

The later anthems are more complex, in several cases conforming to a pattern of a full choir introduction, an SATB quartet and a full choir conclusion with fugal treatment. This sequence is followed in 'O God, Thou art worthy' and 'Who is like unto Thee?' It is first displayed in the earlier 'We have heard with our ears', which Sullivan originally wrote in 1860 and then revised for publication by Novello five years later. Dedicated to Thomas Helmore, this anthem shows Sullivan's love of plainchant. It begins with an intonation by the men's voices of the eighth Gregorian tone. Castigated by the *Musical Times* for harmonic infelicities, which were mercilessly exposed and dissected, it found a supporter in John Stainer, who, in a lecture in 1875 on church music through the ages, singled it out for praise alongside works by Handel and Bach, Mozart's 'Ave Verum Corpus', Crotch's 'Holy, holy, holy', Goss's 'O Saviour of the World' and Gounod's 'Jesu, our Lord'. In many ways, it harked back to an earlier age. Percy Young describes it as 'Sullivan's nearest approach to the authentic tradition of English church music', and Nicholas Temperley comments that it 'still belongs to the antiquarian phase'.[4] Sullivan's love of plainchant is also very evident in 'The Strain Upraise', which is perhaps best described as a mixture of hymn, anthem and chant.

A striking feature of Sullivan's anthems is how many were dedicated to his mentors and friends in the world of church music. 'We have heard with our ears' actually had two dedications; when originally written and performed at the Chapel Royal in 1860 to Sir George Smart, and when revised and published in 1865 to Thomas Helmore. 'O Love the Lord', Sullivan's first published anthem, was dedicated to 'his esteemed master and friend' John Goss; 'O Taste and See' to Hugh Haweis, the clerical author of *Music and Morals*; 'Rejoice in the Lord' to Robert Brown-Borthwick, editor of *The Supplemental Hymn and Tune Book*; and 'Sing, O Heavens' to Francis Byng, the aristocratic vicar of St Peter's, Cranley Gardens. 'I will worship towards thy holy temple' was composed for the twelfth anniversary of the foundation of St Michael's College, Tenbury Wells and dedicated to Frederick Ouseley. 'I Will Mention The Loving-kindnesses' was dedicated to John Stainer and 'Who is Like unto Thee' to Walter Parratt on the occasion of his appointment as organist at St George's Chapel, Windsor. This list of dedicatees reads like a roll-call of the great and the good in Victorian church music and also serves as a re-minder of whom Sullivan considered as his friends and mentors. In other respects, too, his anthems served as tokens of friendship and esteem: 'O God, Thou art Worthy to be praised' was composed for the wedding of his friend Adrian Hope and Lady Ida Duff on 3 June 1867 and 'Rejoice in the Lord' for the Brown-Borthwick wedding in Westminster Abbey on 16 April 1868.

These dedications could be taken as signs that Sullivan was proud of his anthems and felt that they were worthy of association with the names of the best church musicians of the day, although the more cynical might suggest that they were a good means of promotion. It is difficult to be certain how seriously Sullivan took his anthems and how important this sphere of composition was to him. In the case of those that were written during the period of his collaboration with Gilbert, there is sometimes a sense that they were squeezed in amid the main work on the Savoy operas. Sullivan's diary reveals that 'Who is like unto thee' was written over four days in August 1883 in the middle of the composition of the Act 2 finale to *Princess Ida*. He broke off after setting Hilarion's aria 'Whom thou hast chained must wear his chain', wrote the anthem and then resumed his main task. Perhaps the composition of liturgical music provided welcome rest and balm from the relentless demands and topsy-turvydom of the comic operas. In the midst of his frenzied last-minute work on the score of *The Pirates of Penzance* in New York in December 1879 to prepare for its premiere, he took time off on a Sunday morning to visit Grace Church on Broadway to hear his Jubilate, Te Deum and Kyrie in D being performed. He made a similar visit to Westminster Abbey in February 1886 in the midst of composing the first act of *Ruddigore* in order to hear the choir sing 'Who is like unto Thee?'

Sullivan's anthems, like his hymns, enjoyed their heyday in the early years of the twentieth century, when they found their way into most church anthem books, albeit in considerably smaller numbers than those of other Victorian church composers. The 1905 *Anthem Book of the United Free Church of Scotland*, for example, contains two Sullivan anthems, 'O Love the Lord' and 'Turn thy face from my sins' alongside eleven by Stainer, six each by Goss and Elvey, four by Hopkins and three each by Wesley and Gauntlett. A leaflet that has recently come into my possession indicates that 'The strain upraise' was sung in the Jubilee celebration of Mount Pleasant Wesleyan Church, Chapeltown, Sheffield, in 1916, confirming its position as a favourite with Nonconformist chapel choirs. On the evidence of their appearance in church hymnals, choruses from Sullivan's oratorios and cantatas were more often sung by church choirs than his anthems explicitly written for church use. 'There is joy in the presence of the angels of the Lord' from *The Prodigal Son* and 'Brother, Thou art gone before us' from *The Martyr of Antioch*, which were both regularly sung at St Paul's Cathedral during Stainer's time as organist there, were especially popular. The melody of 'The Long Day Closes' was reused for an anthem for use at evening services, 'Saviour, thy children keep', shortly after Sullivan's death and appeared in several early twentieth-century anthem books.

Like so much of his sacred work, Sullivan's anthems largely disappeared from use during the twentieth century. The disapproving reception which greeted them from the musical establishment when they first appeared has largely continued, even from those generally sympathetic to his music. Percy Young sums up the prevailing view, putting the blame on Sullivan's contemporary critics as much as on the composer himself:

> His contribution to the repertoire of the anthem was slender, but one or two items suggest what Sullivan might have done had his ideals not been subjected to such unfriendly scrutiny. The difficulty was that there was a frontier between 'secular' and 'sacred' which was not to be crossed. On the few occasions when he did appear to cross this frontier, he was recalled and reminded of his proper duty.[5]

Arthur Jacobs has virtually nothing to say about Sullivan's anthems, and Nicholas Temperley restricts himself to noting that 'Sullivan followed the trend of the times', although he does criticize those who have 'unfairly combed his cathedral music for echoes of the Savoy operas'.[6] Several of the best Sullivan anthems have been sensitively recorded by the choir of Keble College, Oxford, but they remain largely shunned by cathedral choirs and the organists of those churches which still maintain a choral tradition. This is a pity – their atmosphere of calm reassurance and emphasis on the gracious forgiveness and mercy of God is much needed in our disturbed times and divided Church.

Other Liturgical Settings

Sullivan wrote relatively little liturgical music for use in church services aside from his anthems. His first work in this area, the Te Deum in D, was one of 46 settings of the early Christian hymn of praise commissioned by Novello from contemporary composers in 1866 for *The Church Anthem Book*. Contrasting with the austere chants produced by Ouseley and W. C. Macfarren and the chromatic harmonies favoured by Barnby, Sullivan composed an elaborate and ambitious setting described by Nicholas Temperley as 'boldly original, demanding and dissonant'.[7] Sullivan supplemented the Te Deum with a sprightly Jubilate Deo ('O be joyful in the Lord') and Kyrie ('Lord, have mercy') also in D.

In 1874, Sullivan adapted and arranged two hymns from the Russian church, 'Mercy and truth are met together' and 'Turn thee again, O Lord'. Published by Novello, they are cast in the form of short anthems. It is not clear exactly how much original work by Sullivan went into these compositions. On a subsequent visit to Russia, as part of his Baltic cruise with the Duke of Edinburgh in 1881, he was profoundly moved by hearing the Imperial Chapel Choir, whose red and gold uniforms reminded him of his days in the Chapel Royal, performing at the Winter Palace in St Petersburg:

> There were about 80 and, blasé as I am with music, I confess to a new sensation at hearing them. It was like nothing else. They have basses with the most wonderful voices going down to the low A and the effect of their singing their church music was thrilling. Sometimes it was exactly like an organ, only more beautiful. They sang for an hour and I could have heard them for a couple of hours more.[8]

Despite the impact of this experience, Sullivan did not make any further forays into Russian liturgical music, although an unpublished autograph manuscript of an orchestral arrangement of a Russian hymn was sold at Sotheby's in 1965. Herbert Sullivan and Newman Flower suggested in their biography that the music that he heard sung by the Imperial Chapel Choir in St Petersburg in 1881 was a major influence on the unaccompanied quartets and ensembles in the Savoy operas (see page 172).

A manuscript in the Pierpont Morgan Library in New York carries Sullivan's signature and note: 'My first and only chant! For the 150th Psalm'. Recent detective work by Andrew Sims reveals that the psalm chant was written in 1887 for St George's Anglican Church in Berlin, possibly at the request of Victoria, Crown Princess of Prussia, for use at a service to be attended by her mother, Queen Victoria. Sullivan was in Berlin in March 1887 for the performance of *The Golden Legend* as part of the ninetieth-birthday celebrations for the Emperor Wilhelm I. He spent much time there with Crown Princess Victoria, who posed as Yum-Yum at two private parties, while he played 'The moon and I' from *The Mikado*. He found her 'fascinating' and subsequently referred to her in his diary as 'Princess Yum-Yum'. If the psalm chant was in part the product of this infatuation, it does not seem to have been a labour of love in other respects. Andrew Sims describes it as 'a pastiche of a typical nineteenth-century chant; not what someone of Sullivan's abilities and imagination might have been expected to provide. It seems to me that Sullivan did not really wish to write it, but felt he had little choice!'[9]

Not long after his return from Berlin, Sullivan was asked by John Stainer for settings of the Magnificat and Nunc Dimittis for the 1887 Festival of the Sons of the Clergy in St Paul's Cathedral. In the event, these were not forthcoming for reasons indicated in two revealing letters to his old friend written at the Athenaeum Club on the same day. In the first he wrote:

> It is a shame and humiliation to confess it, but I cannot set the Magnificat. I tried it before, years ago when I wrote my little service in D, but I broke down and only set the Morning Service. I have covered pages with sketches but I hate them all. If I could have got anything satisfactory I would have had it ready for you as I am, as you know, very quick in scoring and writing out. But my endeavours are fruitless. Pray forgive me. I can't help it.

Why did Sullivan find it so hard to set Mary's song in Luke's Gospel with its powerful words about God's work in putting down the mighty from their seat, exalting the humble and meek, filling the hungry with good things and sending the rich empty away? Was it that his standards were too high? In his second letter to Stainer he wrote: 'I have been working at it since I returned from Berlin, but all my efforts are weak and unworthy of the object ... I worked up to the last hour, hoping against hope. You cannot be so vexed as I am myself'.[10] Or was it rather that the text intimidated him with its disturbing expression of the radical heart of the Christian social (and socialist) gospel? He had set the opening verses of the Magnificat as a soprano solo in *The Light of the World*, but had stopped short before the scattering of the proud in the imaginations of their hearts. The God who showed strength with his arm and forcibly overturned the social order was not the kind of divine being with whom the staunchly Tory Sullivan found particularly easy to identify.

In the event, Sullivan was represented at the 1887 Sons of the Clergy Festival in St Paul's by his *In Memoriam* overture, which was played at the beginning of the service. The strong filial affection and family piety which had inspired it seemed to touch Sullivan's spiritual side in a way which the Magnificat with its propositions about God's saving work did not. Yet other biblical texts clearly moved him and seemed to present little difficulty in setting.

Overall, it is difficult to avoid the conclusion that Sullivan found composing liturgical music for direct use in services of worship uncongenial and that this area of church music had little appeal or interest for him. Without the High Church background and sensibilities of many of his contemporaries, he perhaps lacked both the commitment and the quality of reserve and restraint necessary for liturgical music. One wonders what he would have made of the adaptation more than 100 years after his death of some of his most ebullient secular tunes for liturgical purposes. The 2006 Pirate Eucharist contains a very effective Gloria, 'Hurrah for the King of Kings!', which begins 'All glory be to God on high', written by Hayden Konig to the tune of the Pirate King's song from *The Pirates of Penzance*. In 2012, John Hartley, vicar of St Luke's Church, Eccleshill, near Bradford, responded to an Internet appeal for a Gloria set to a well-known tune by providing one based on 'When Britain Really Ruled the Waves' from *Iolanthe*. An oratorio on the prophet Jonah by Leland Ross, a North American Baptist, reuses the march of the peers from *Iolanthe* for the chorus, 'Bow, bow, ye Ninevitic masses/Bow, bow in sackcloth, bow in ashes' and 'Tit-Willow' from *The Mikado* for a song which begins: 'Neath a tree by a river a prophet of God/Cries, 'Kill me, so kill me, just kill me!'

Maybe Sullivan would have approved of these crossovers from the stage to the sanctuary and attempts to find the sacred in the midst of the secular. His own natural preferences when it came to setting liturgical texts are perhaps most clearly displayed in the flamboyant and dramatic style of the two Te Deums that he wrote for massed choirs and orchestra for occasions of royal and national celebration in 1872 and 1900. They could hardly be more different in character from his initial 1866 version which, however harmonically bold, seems very restrained and conservative in comparison. They are not really liturgical pieces at all, being written for large national celebrations rather than for use in church services. Indeed, in form and character they are much closer to the oratorios and sacred cantatas discussed in Chapter 5, but they find a place in this chapter because they are settings of liturgical texts.

The *Festival Te Deum*

Towards the end of 1871 Queen Victoria's eldest son, Albert Edward, the Prince of Wales, fell ill with typhoid fever, the disease which had killed his father, Prince Albert, ten years earlier, leading his mother to withdraw almost completely from public life. Daily reports of his condition were carried in the press, and more than once the end was thought to be near. However, he rallied in the New Year and, following a Thanksgiving Service in St Paul's Cathedral, the directors of the Crystal Palace Company decided to mount a large fête to celebrate his recovery and reflect the mood of deliverance and thanksgiving felt across the nation. They commissioned Sullivan to provide a grand *Festival Te Deum*, which would be performed in the presence of the Queen at the Crystal Palace on 1 May 1872.

This commission confirmed Sullivan's position as composer laureate to both the Crown and the nation. In accepting it, he was standing in the tradition of Handel, who had composed similar celebratory Te Deums to mark the end of the War of Spanish Succession with the signing of the Treaty of Utrecht in 1713 and the British victory over the French at the battle of Dettingen in 1743. These works established a precedent for using this particular liturgical text for what were effectively secular purposes, extolling the United Kingdom and its monarchy in particular and expressing national pride.

As a strong monarchist and patriot, Sullivan warmed to his task and resolved to set the Te Deum for soprano soloist, massed choirs – the chorus numbered around 2,000 at the first performance – orchestra, organ and military band. He obtained Queen Victoria's permission to dedicate the work to her and for the opening performance, one of the first occasions in which she appeared in public following her long period of seclusion after her husband's death, he changed the penultimate line from 'O Lord, have mercy upon us' to 'O Lord, save the Queen'.

Sullivan divided his *Festival Te Deum*, which lasts for around 33 minutes, into seven discrete movements. The first opens with brass and organ and offers a hint of the hymn tune ST ANN, which comes in again much more prominently in the final movement. The choir sings 'We praise Thee, O God' in a strong chordal setting before breaking into an elaborate fugue at the line 'To Thee all angels cry aloud'. The second movement, which is much more gentle and stately, introduces the soloist repeatedly singing the refrain 'To Thee Cherubin and Seraphin continually do cry' and soaring, angel-like, up to a high B flat over the chorus's 'Holy, holy, holy'. The next movement begins with the choir singing 'The glorious company of the Apostles' as a plainchant melody over a rich and fast moving orchestral accompaniment before breaking into another fugue on 'Thou art the King of glory'. The fourth movement seems to belong to the opera house with a lyrical oboe solo introducing a brisk soprano aria 'When Thou tookest upon Thee to deliver Israel', which modulates from the minor to the major and becomes even more up-beat on the line 'Thou sittest at the right hand of God'.

The last three movements are characterized by a juxtaposition of the seemingly secular and sacred. The fifth begins with the chorus solemnly intoning 'We believe that Thou shalt come to be our judge', before the orchestra plays a lilting waltz-like siciliano tune which is taken up for 'We therefore pray Thee, help thy servants'. The sixth movement, which starts with the soloist singing 'O Lord, save Thy people' to organ accompaniment, has a more measured and ecclesiastical feel but is not without its lighter touches in the almost skittish setting of 'Day by day we magnify Thee' in the middle. The final movement begins with a reprise of the opening statement by brass and organ following which the soprano chorus sing 'Vouchsafe, O Lord' to the hymn tune ST ANN, which is then taken up by the whole chorus, building up to a spectacular fugue on the line 'O Lord, let thy mercy lighten upon us'. At the end of the fugue, the military band enters with an apparently utterly incongruous jaunty march tune which sounds as though it belongs to *The Marriage of Figaro*, if not even *H.M.S. Pinafore*. This tune is carried on as an accompaniment to the chorus's continuing singing of ST ANN and finally blends into a great unison finale.

The first performance on 1 May 1872 met with a hugely positive reception. As Roderick Swanston writes in his excellent sleeve notes for the CD recording issued in 2001: 'the effect on the audience of 26,000 in the Crystal Palace as the military band joined the choir, orchestra and organ must have been overwhelming. It is no wonder Sullivan was "uproariously cheered" as the last triumphant chords of C major rolled round the vast expanses of glass and iron.'[11] For once, the critical musical establishment was in agreement with the public. An almost uniformly positive review of the published score in the *Musical Times* drew comparisons with Handel's *Dettingen Te Deum* and concluded:

> With much of the breadth of Handel, some of the grace of Mozart, and an orchestral colouring almost unique in its masterly handling, this Te Deum ought to serve as a gratifying promise that English music is blos-

soming into a Spring to be succeeded by a Summer, such as this land has not experienced since the death of Purcell.[12]

Inevitably, the *Musical Times* reviewer drew attention to the seeming incongruity of the melange of musical styles in the closing movement. Far from finding it clashing and vulgar, however, he praised the way that it worked:

> Surely nothing could be more glaringly in contrast than the chorale with which the movement commenced (known to everyone as the common measure tune St Anne's) and the gay and even sprightly march immediately following it. Yet it is not long before we find the tenors and basses leading off with the first phrase of the psalm tune, with the march STILL GOING ON, soon to be joined by the organ, which taking the fugal subject previously heard for its share, forthwith proceeds SIMULTANEOUSLY to work its way without the slightest reference to the march or the chorale; and yet there is no discord. Each of these three subjects – apparently divided in feeling wide as the poles asunder – retaining its marked characteristics, merges with the others into a unity of effect as musically harmonious as it is grandiose.

In a detailed musical analysis of the *Festival Te Deum*, Benedict Taylor concludes that the device of pairing the jaunty march with the stately hymn tune is not only highly effective but also part of a deliberate design to link the sacred and the secular. For him, the *Te Deum* is a highly complex and carefully crafted piece which uses well established musical ideas with clear sacred connotations, notably the 'Credo' motif from Mozart's *Missa Brevis* in F repeated at the beginning of Mendelssohn's Fifth Symphony. He argues that the seemingly incongruous pairing of the military march with the hymn tune parallels what Beethoven does in the choral finale of his Ninth Symphony, where, after the grandiose climax on 'der Cherub steht vor Gott', a banal version of the 'Joy' theme is played as a Turkish march.

> The effect is incongruous, and perplexed many listeners in the nineteenth century. Towards the end of the movement, the 'Joy' theme (in a different variant) and a second idea ('Seid umschlungen') are combined in a double fugue, analogous to Sullivan's double chorus of his two themes. Many different readings have been given in account for Beethoven's strange decision; what they nearly all seem to have in common is the idea of the (dialectical) synthesis of opposing worlds into one, of ultimate equality of brotherhood.[13]

Taylor concludes: 'There is therefore absolutely no need to make an apologia for Sullivan's finale. To put it simply, anyone who accepts Beethoven's decision but not Sullivan's finds themselves open to quite justifiable charges of hypocrisy.'[14]

Both Roderick Swanston and Benedict Taylor argue in their analysis of the *Te Deum* that what Sullivan was seeking to do in the finale was to combine the sacred and the secular into one. In Taylor's words: 'Sullivan is fusing two opposing worlds – the "high", sacred, official style suitable for the national celebration of the recovery of the Prince of Wales, and the everyday, common, secular, style of the people who were the subject of their Prince, and after all, Sullivan's public.'[15]

It seems to me that the *Festival Te Deum* and especially its final movement, can be taken and interpreted at a number of levels. As Percy Young remarks, 'in its conclusion (with military band added to the orchestra) the work is probably to be included among those defined by under-nourished pedants as vulgar. Whether it is vulgar (in this sense) is, of course, a matter of opinion.'[16] Like so much of Sullivan's religious work, it is vulgar in the best sense of the word, in being accessible, stirring and written for the people rather than the critics. The prominent use of the hymn tune ST ANN, probably composed in the early eighteenth century by William Croft, organist at the Chapel Royal, and indissolubly linked in the public mind with Isaac Watts's great paraphrase of Psalm 90, 'O God our help in ages past', introduces what is almost a second national anthem, still sung today on Remembrance Sunday and at great state occasions. It testifies to Sullivan's love of hymn tunes and his sense of their deep popular appeal and significance; one is reminded of his remark in connection with Queen Victoria's Diamond Jubilee 'I think I should reach the hearts of the people best in a hymn tune' (page 91). Fifty years later, Ralph Vaughan Williams used ST ANN in a somewhat similar way in his anthem 'Lord, Thou hast been our refuge' although in his case it was accompanying Watts's familiar words and counterposed with the chanting of Psalm 90.

The patriotic element is hugely important in this piece. Kenneth Long was right to suggest that 'it would make a marvellous item for the Last Night of the Proms', and, as Jeffrey Richards writes, '[i]t somehow encapsulates the Victorian age musically: the devotion of a Protestant church interwoven with the military swagger of imperial pomp, all in a work dedicated to the recovery of the Prince of Wales'.[17] The context is important. The *Te Deum* expresses public relief at the recovery of the heir to the throne from a near-fatal illness but perhaps even more it expresses public joy at the emergence of a beloved Queen out of purdah (it is significant that the words inserted by Sullivan for the first performance were 'O Lord save the Queen' rather than 'God bless the Prince of Wales' which might have been more appropriate given the circumstances) and more broadly a sense of national thanksgiving and well-being. It is by no means the only liturgical work by a Victorian composer to be given an added patriotic flavour. Stainer incorporated the national anthem into his anthem 'Lord, Thou art God' for the Festival of the Sons of the Clergy service in St Paul's Cathedral in 1887, the year of the Queen's Golden Jubilee.

Percy Young is right to say that the *Festival Te Deum* 'as well as presenting the hungry ear with sonorous splendours of Berlioz proportions, has the ring of truth: this is the English people in the high summer of Victorian optimism'.[18] Sullivan did not just catch the national zeitgeist – he felt it deeply himself. Like all his work, it is sincere and from the heart. He was himself full of optimism when he wrote it. He was also genuinely full of gratitude to God for giving Britain such a wonderful Queen, to whom he was devoted, as well as for sparing her somewhat dissolute son.

Is there perhaps also a deeper theme in this work, hinted at by Swanston and Taylor and illuminated by the comparison with Beethoven's Ninth Symphony? Was Sullivan seeking to make a point about the juxtaposition, the interweaving and the ultimate fusion of the sacred and the secular? The remarks quoted above about 'the synthesis of opposing worlds into one, of ultimate equality of brotherhood' bring to mind the tenets of Freemasonry. Is this, in fact, one of Sullivan's more explicitly Masonic musical statements? Is he, indeed, returning to the motif that runs through 'The Lost Chord' and seeking to link all perplexed meaning into one perfect peace? Can the *Te Deum* be taken as an expression of his own religious faith, inclusive, eirenic and yearning for peace and reconciliation? Maybe this is to read too much into what is first and foremost a work of patriotic sentiment and civic religion. Yet Sullivan's character was one, as we have already observed, in which the sacred and the secular jostled together and in which, in William Parry's words, 'inner seriousness and spirituality and outer joie de vivre are delightfully juxtaposed' (page 10). There are perhaps few places where that juxtaposition is more evident than in the finale to the *Festival Te Deum*.

Before moving on from this work, it is worth noting that it did not disappear when the immediate celebrations of which it was part were over. It received two further performances in the Crystal Palace on 18 July 1872 and 1 March 1873 and an early provincial performance in Norwich on 16 September 1872. It remained in the repertoire of local choral societies and chapel choirs well into the twentieth century. On the wall of the museum in Great Malvern, Worcestershire, there is an advertisement for a concert by the North Malvern Choral Society on 21 March 1893, in which the

Festival Te Deum featured alongside Mendelssohn's *Hymn of Praise*. It was still being sung by the choir of the Methodist New Connexion Chapel in Barrow-in-Furness in 1917, when a new 15-year-old recruit found that it was the first work he had to learn.[19]

The *Boer War Te Deum*

On 26 May 1900, Sir George Martin, who had succeeded Stainer as organist of St Paul's Cathedral in 1888, approached Sullivan on behalf of the cathedral's dean and chapter and asked him to consider writing a thanksgiving Te Deum for use at a future service to celebrate the conclusion of the South African War, which had begun six months earlier and which everyone hoped would soon come to an end. Sullivan readily accepted and set to the task with unusual speed, perhaps because he, too, hoped the bitter and bloody conflict with the Boers would soon end – in fact, it was to drag on for another 18 months – and also because of his own poor health and sense that his composing days were limited. Putting to one side *The Emerald Isle*, the operetta on which he was working for the D'Oyly Cartes in collaboration with the librettist Basil Hood, he concentrated on the sacred rather than the secular commission, and by the end of July he had completed what would become known as the *Boer War Te Deum*. Less than fourth months later, he was dead and with the Boer War still raging, it was left to Martin to announce the work to the world in a letter to *The Times*:

> Some time ago, with the sanction of the Dean and Chapter of St Paul's Cathedral, I approached the late Sir Arthur Sullivan on the subject of a Thanksgiving Te Deum suitable for performance in St Paul's and other churches in the event of a successful termination of the war in South Africa. I am glad to say that he took the matter up warmly, and as I well know, he worked devotedly and conscientiously on this composition. A little more than a month ago (he was very ill then) he played this short work to me on the piano, and we discussed with great minuteness the exact strength he required as to instruments, chorus &c. I am happy to say that he has left in my hands the score, which is finished to the smallest detail. This was his last completed work. Thus the lad who received most of his early musical education in the Church, and who afterwards won such phenomenal popularity, not only where the English language is spoken, but in other countries, devoted his last effort to his Queen, to his Church, and to his country.[20]

The *Boer War Te Deum* is a much more restrained and dignified work than the *Festival Te Deum* without its florid and frequent fugues and operatic echoes. Less than half the length, it is through composed rather than divided into separate movements giving it a much less disjointed quality and a strong forward drive. Set for chorus, orchestra and organ, there is no soloist or military band, although there is plenty of use of bright brass. There are several moments of considerable pathos such as the hushed unison chant of 'Holy, holy, holy, Lord God of Sabaoth' and the setting of 'When Thou tookest upon Thee to deliver Israel' as a funeral march. What the two works do have in common is the prominent use of a hymn tune. In the case of the *Boer War Te Deum*, this is Sullivan's own ST GERTRUDE, which is introduced subtly in the opening bars and then employed to considerable effect towards the end, when it is played by the orchestra with increasing volume as the choir sings 'O Lord, in Thee have I trusted, let me never be confounded' and finally returns to the opening verse 'We praise Thee, O God'.

The first performance of the *Boer War Te Deum* took place in the context of a national service of thanksgiving attended by King Edward VII in St Paul's on 8 June 1902, just a week after the Boer War had finally ended with the signing of the Peace of Vereeniging. The service began with the processional hymn 'Onward, Christian Soldiers' sung to ST GERTRUDE. *The Times* enthused: 'Nothing more stately can well be imagined than the Royal procession advancing to the inspiring hymn, which so stirringly gives voice to the faith and enthusiasm of the Church militant and the Church triumphant. It seemed as if here, as indeed, was the case, one was in the presence of the most supreme act of acknowledgement of the Divine favour and mercy which the nation could perform.'[21]

Reviewers were united in praising the work's simplicity, directness and reverence. Many pointed to the way in which its largely diatonic rather than chromatic harmonies harked back to an earlier age and placed it firmly in the great tradition of English church music. The *Yorkshire Daily Post* noted that 'it is easy to recognise the influence on the composer of his early grounding in Anglican Church music at the Chapel Royal', and the *Daily Telegraph* rejoiced that 'the Te Deum honours the traditions of English church music. It is grave, restrained, solid, with enough of sentiment to satisfy modern taste. The work is everywhere pervaded by the refinement and distinction never absent from the composer's productions.'[22]

Modern critics have generally echoed these sentiments. Richard Silverman has pointed to an unprecedented use of dissonance in the work and described its finale as 'not bold and exhilarating as in the Festival Te Deum but resolute and sombre'.[23] Benedict Taylor sees its most characteristic feature as being the subtle use of tonality and harmony combined with the overriding diatonicism which gives an 'imposing, monumental simplicity'. For him, as for virtually all other critics and commentators, the most intriguing feature is Sullivan's quotation of his own tune ST GERTRUDE, which would, of course, have immediately brought to mind the hymn 'Onward, Christian soldiers' to all who heard it, both subtly and in fragmentary form at the beginning of the work and then at full throttle in its closing moments.

> The effect of this closing section is majestic but not remotely bombastic, the sense of control and quiet dignity continually present. There is a lyricism and sweep to this conjunction of fugal working-out and chorale-like hymn tune which is quite moving, leading to the final merging of opening chorus and hymn as the work's culmination. ST GERTRUDE has remained outside the choral parts to the end, present only in the extraneous orchestral voices. The programmatic implications of this particular feature are well worth consideration. Though Sullivan could not have realized just how long and protracted the Boer war conflict was to prove, the fact that the triumphal sounds of the hymn are always outside the consciousness of the vocal parts – are never actually 'spoken' by the human participants in the performance – could suggest that victory is perhaps not yet won. The two spaces – vocal and instrumental – are separate, and remain so, though they exist alongside each other in counterpoint. Alternatively, one could interpret the chorus as voicing the concerns and prayers of the public back home, in relation to the separateness of the soldiers fighting far away in a foreign land, whose efforts can be heard but not joined in.[24]

For Taylor, this is why 'the work is far from seeming jingoistic or triumphant'. He rightly points out that 'though the hymn "Onward Christian Soldiers" has been described as envoicing what could be termed as "the church militant" the words are pointedly (but often mistakenly overlooked) "marching as to war", not "off to war" – the struggle metaphorical and as much spiritual as physical. The regaining of peace is the ultimate prize, not military glory.' Jeffrey Richards takes a contrary view, writing that in building the *Te Deum* around the tune of 'Onward, Christian soldiers', Sullivan was 'imbuing the Boer war with the idea of a Christian struggle against the infidel'.[25] It is true that any congregation or audience hearing those familiar repeated notes would instantly think of Christian soldiers marching onwards and would be unlikely to have the distinction between 'as to' and 'off to' war uppermost in their minds. Inserting ST GERTRUDE undoubtedly gave the *Te Deum* a more martial theme and evoked the sense of the church militant. Yet the atmosphere that it evokes is ultimately not one of Christian imperialism or jingoism. Even in its closing moments the work manages to remain devotional, restrained and above all calmly reassuring.

It is intriguing to speculate why Sullivan so prominently quoted one of his own tunes in this his last ever work. Was he setting his seal on his life's work in an explicitly autobiographical manner, rather as Richard Strauss did in 'Im Abendrot' from his *Four Last Songs*? William Parry has speculated whether 'he was making a proud and deliberate statement – at what he felt to be the end of his career – to all his critics with an unusually effusive self-quotation (he knew what people loved, and what choirs, even at St Paul's, liked to sing)'.[26] It is tempting to suggest that this might have been a final cock of the snook to the musical establishment, deliberately ending a sacred work with his most popular hymn tune, which had been so roundly castigated for its vulgarity and poor construction. Yet I am not sure that this was Sullivan's style. Rather, I think that his sincerity and desire to connect with the public may have been to the fore, leading him, as in the 1872 *Te Deum*, to have recourse to an iconic hymn tune to express the national mood of thanksgiving and deliverance. That it was one of his own tunes was perhaps almost incidental.

What was surely not coincidental was that the hymn in question was especially associated with the church militant and the church triumphant. Maybe as his strength ebbed away Sullivan's thoughts were turning towards death and what lay beyond it; and maybe the message of Christian hope and victory over the powers of Satan, the images of singing with the angels and blending our voices in the triumph song in 'Onward, Christian soldiers' resonated with him, as he set the great words of the Te Deum, which clearly moved him so much more than those of the Magnificat.

It was originally intended that the *Boer War Te Deum* be performed again on 3 July 1902, when Edward VII was expected to visit St Paul's Cathedral for a thanksgiving service after his coronation at Westminster Abbey. In the event, his coronation was postponed because of an emergency appendectomy and did not take place until 9 August. A thanksgiving service the following day in St Paul's, which the king did not attend, featured a Te Deum by Charles Stanford, and at the official thanksgiving service attended by Edward VII on 26 October one of George Martin's own compositions was used. Sullivan's last work fell into oblivion, published in both full score and vocal score versions, but largely unperformed until its revival in recent years thanks largely to the activities of the Sullivan Society. There have, in fact, been three recent professional recordings of it

– by chamber choir and brass ensemble in Ely Cathedral in 1992, a group of Oxford musicians in 1999 and the London Chorus and New London Orchestra in 2003.

Although Sullivan's music did not feature in the post-coronation thanksgiving services held at St Paul's Cathedral in the summer of 1902, it was heard at the coronation itself in Westminster Abbey. Frederick Bridge, the Abbey organist and, like Martin at St Paul's, an enthusiast for Sullivan's music, set words from Psalm 5, 'O hearken Thou unto the voice of my calling, my King and my God' to the concluding part of the chorus 'Men and Brethren' from *The Light of the World* for the Introit, which began the Communion service and followed the processional anthem 'I was glad' specially written for the coronation by Sir Hubert Parry. A piece of purple journalistic prose quoted in the *Musical Times* enthused about its effect: 'The silver throats of the trumpets were lifted into the air and a wild blast from them rang across the choir, while, out of its echoes, followed, softly, as if it had fallen from them, Sir Arthur Sullivan's tender little introit.'[27] A form and order of service published by Novello for use in Church of England churches throughout the Empire on Coronation Day included the Sullivan introit as well as two specially written hymns by Mary Bradford Whiting to his tunes BISHOPGARTH and BOLWELL. BISHOPGARTH, which had, of course, originally been written for a royal celebration (pages 90–3) was pressed into similar service for 'O God, the Ruler of our race'. BOLWELL, hitherto unpublished, accompanied another stirring song of patriotic sentiment:

> Lord of might, our land's Defender,
> God of Hosts, our Strength and Stay,
> Thanks and praise to Thee we render
> On this Coronation Day;
> While our prayer to Thee we bring –
> Guard our land and shield our King!

Sullivan would undoubtedly have relished the use of his music in the celebration of the coronation of Edward VII in 1902. Had he been alive, he would certainly have wanted and been expected to contribute more to what was by general consent the most splendid such ceremony ever carried out in the United Kingdom. As it was, the use around the time of the coronation, and just 18 months after his own death, of the *Boer War Te Deum*, the adapted chorus from the *Light of the World* and his two hymn tunes with their new patriotic verses attached provided a fitting epitaph to one who had devoted so much of his effort to extolling the causes of monarchy, Church and country.

8

I Hear the Soft Note:
Spiritual Echoes in Sullivan's
Secular Works

This book has now covered all of Sullivan's church music and his settings of sacred texts. There is much of the rest of his output, made up of supposedly secular compositions, which also has a profoundly spiritual quality.

Perhaps the most obviously spiritual of Sullivan's orchestral works is the *In Memoriam* overture. Like 'The Lost Chord', it was written at a time of intense grief. In the summer of 1866, Sullivan was having great difficulty in coming up with a composition for the Norwich Festival, which had commissioned a work from him. Just a month before the Festival, he told his father that he would have to concede defeat. 'No, you mustn't give it up,' his father counselled, 'you will succeed if you stick to it. Something will probably occur which will put new vigour and fresh thought into you. Don't give it up.' Three days after uttering these words, on 22 September, Thomas Sullivan died suddenly and unexpectedly. On the evening of his funeral, his distraught son told his mother, 'I can't bear it. I must cry out my grief in music.'[1] On the envelope of a letter of condolence from George Grove, he sketched the solemn hymn-like theme which opens and closes the work and marked it 'In Memoriam'. There have been suggestions that the overture was also inspired by Tennyson's poem of the same title written after the death of his great friend Arthur Hallam and completed in 1849, but I can find no evidence of this. Sullivan worked intensively on the overture for the next ten days and it was performed on 30 October 1866 in St Andrew's Hall, Norwich, under the baton of Sir Julius Benedict.

The *In Memoriam* overture became a favourite piece in the Victorian concert repertoire. Its religious connotations were not lost on John Stainer, who often used it as the opening item in the Festival for the Sons of the Clergy Service at St Paul's Cathedral. Its solemn opening theme, which begins with the characteristic device of repeated notes found at the beginning of 'The Lost Chord' and in several of his best-known hymn tunes, was adopted as a hymn tune shortly after Sullivan's death. The 1904 *Methodist Hymn Book* used it to accompany Isaac Watts's hymn 'Not all the blood of beasts/On Jewish altars slain', and it was taken up for several other hymns in early twentieth-century hymnals (page 81). In October 1930, the BBC broadcast the *In Memoriam* overture as a tribute to those who had lost their lives in the crash of the R101 airship over France during its maiden voyage.

Herbert Sullivan and Newman Flower wrote somewhat gushingly of this work that 'In the grandeur of its theme, in its simplicity, was all the majesty of Death's farewell. *In Memoriam* is the cry of a man in sorrow translated into Art and beauty as the best votive offering.'[2] Later critics have been less fulsome. Gervase Hughes, while conceding that the work taken as a whole 'has a solid dignity that is quite impressive', felt that it was too lightweight to sound a universal note of mourning:

> The music is purely subjective; Sullivan might be able to convey his mental reaction in terms of crotchets and quavers but it was beyond his powers to project an emotional experience into the consciousness of a detached audience. After all, he was only twenty-four, and if the opening melody strikes a sophisticated ear as being inadequately expressive of even personal grief, there is no need to laugh at those who find its obvious sincerity rather touching.[3]

Judged in the context and by the canons of Victorian sentimentality, Sullivan's *In Memoriam* overture is an affecting expression of grief and compares favourably with other more maudlin works inspired by the experience of the deathbed. If the youthful Sullivan's optimism and zest for life shines through in its tuneful lyricism, this does not make it a secular or shallow composition but rather one that emphasizes his essential humanity and empathy.

At several points, the lyrics of Sullivan's dramatic cantata *On Shore and Sea*, written for the International Exhibition of 1871 and the first work to be performed in the newly opened Albert Hall, take on a character that effectively makes them religious texts, and they were set by the composer appropriately. The libretto by Thomas Taylor, a dramatist and future editor of *Punch*, tells of sea battles between North African Moors and Italian Christians in the Mediterranean in the sixteenth century. The Christian hero, Il Marinajo, a Genoese sailor, has arias invoking the protection of the Virgin Mary, Star of the Sea, and asserting that 'They chain

not Christian souls that chain their limbs', for both of which Sullivan supplied suitably soaring tunes. Rather more daringly, he deployed Arabian
musical motifs and techniques, including the use of Turkish bells, for the
'Moresque', a chorus of triumph and a Muslim call to prayer sung by the
victorious Moors. A more staid melody accompanied the response of the
Genoese sailors as they found themselves chained in slave galleys. The
words of their chorus echo the sentiments of Norman Macleod's 'Courage, brother, do not stumble', which Sullivan was also setting at around
this time, but he gave them less rumbustious treatment:

Hold to Christian manhood, firm in Christian faith
Faithful hearts make fearless hands, and faithful hearts have we
The Christians 'gainst the infidel, chained though we be.

On Shore and Sea ended with a stirring chorus, 'Sink and Scatter, Clouds
of War', which was later detached from the cantata and inserted into the
concert repertoire as 'The Song of Peace'. It has been described by Selwyn
Tillett as 'Sullivan's *Land of Hope and Glory*', and it has some affinities
with that great musical statement of British imperialism although without
the spacious simplicity and dignity.[4] Altogether too martial to carry com-
fortably the message of the blessings and benefits of peace that the text
proclaims, Sullivan's tune does have a distinct anthem-like quality, and in
its middle passage for sopranos there are distinct echoes of George Elvey's
hymn tune ST GEORGE, which had been published in 1858 and later taken
up for the harvest hymn 'Come, ye thankful people, come', for which it is
still almost universally used.

There is more of 'Land of Hope and Glory' in Sullivan's most imperial-
istic work, the Ode for the laying of the foundation stone of the Imperial
Institute in South Kensington by Queen Victoria as part of her Golden
Jubilee celebrations in July 1887. This was, in fact, the second imperial
Ode that Sullivan composed. The first, a collaboration with Tennyson
commissioned for the opening of the Colonial and Indian Exhibition in
Hyde Park the previous year, made no mention of the Almighty and was
content to proclaim the essentially secular, if ultra-patriotic message:
'One life, one flag, one fleet, one throne! Britons, hold your own!' The
religious element on this occasion was supplied by a spirited rendering
of the Hallelujah Chorus from *Messiah* and a prayer by the Archbishop
of Canterbury. The 1887 Imperial Institute Ode was a more elaborate
work, which introduced a distinctly metaphysical note, even if it was Fate
rather than God that it directly invoked. It was written by Lewis Morris
(1833–1907), the Welsh-born poet, who penned several fulsome paeans

of praise to Britishness and might well have become Poet Laureate, were it not for his association with Oscar Wilde. Jeffrey Richards suggests that he rather than William Morris is the poet referred to alongside Swinburne in Robin Oakapple's song 'My boy, you take it from me' in *Ruddigore*.[5]

Early on, the 1887 Ode invoked the idea of Britain as a chosen nation. Sullivan, who shortened and altered Morris's words at several points, substituted 'England' for 'Britain' at this point, presumably for reasons of stress rather than out of animus against the other three nations of the United Kingdom:

> Our England at the call of Fate
> Left her lone islets in the sea,
> Donned her Imperial robe and state,
> Took the sole sceptre of the Free!

At Sullivan's suggestion, a verse encouraging emigration to the colonies was cut from the Ode and more focus was put on Queen Victoria, hailed as 'First Lady of our English race'. The composer ramped up the patriotic sentiment with plenty of brass and martial chords before moving into more spacious Elgarian mode, reminiscent of the closing chorus from *The Golden Legend*, for the final stanza:

> Oh, may the Hand which rules our Fate,
> Keep this our Britain great!
> We cannot tell, we can but pray
> Heaven's blessing on our work today.
> Rise, palace fair, where all may see
> This proud embodied unity!
> For Britain and Queen one voice we raise,
> Laud them, rejoice, peal forth; worthy are they of praise!

Sullivan was supremely happy setting texts such as these, and it is tempting to suggest that their combination of monarch worship and ultra-patriotism expressed his real religion. Fervent monarchist and staunch patriot that he undoubtedly was, however, it would be wrong to see him simply as a tub-thumping secular imperialist, whose only objects of devotion were Queen, country and Empire. As we have already noted, he had a deep spiritual sensitivity allied to a simple, trusting Christian faith and a love of the Church in which he had been brought up and nurtured. These qualities come over in his operas, not least those for which he is most famous.

Sullivan's spiritual side is very clearly evident in his one and only grand opera, *Ivanhoe*, based on Walter Scott's famous novel and first performed in D'Oyly Carte's Royal English Opera House (now the Palace Theatre) in January 1891. The libretto by Julian Sturgis put religious themes at the centre of the opera, most notably the contrast between the pure and trusting faith of Rebecca, the Jewish heroine, and the casual and coarse Christianity of her seducer Sir Brian de Bois-Guilbert, a Norman knight and the Commander of the Order of Knights Templar. More broadly, there is an underlying emphasis on religious tolerance, displayed in the attitude towards Jews on the part of the English Saxons, the importance of forgiveness, and the triumph of good over evil which is given a patriotic twist in terms of the struggle between Saxons and Normans – all themes calculated to appeal to Sullivan and elicit sensitive and appropriate musical treatment.

From a religious point of view, the most interesting scene is the final act where Rebecca prays to Jehovah and then engages in a powerful duet with the Templar knight, in which she resists his wooing and chastises him for his blasphemy in appealing to the Christian cross to aid him in his sins. Rebecca's aria 'Lord of our chosen race' could have come straight out of *The Martyr of Antioch*; indeed it bears many similarities in terms of both words and music to what Margarita sings as she prepares to face the funeral pyre. Prefaced by the invocation 'O Lord Jehovah, aid me in this hour', it is a haunting statement of deep religious faith with the wide intervals in the melodic line producing an atmosphere of melancholy and longing. Hermann Klein, the Jewish music critic of the *Sunday Times*, told Sullivan that he was particularly struck by the oriental character of the harmonies and intervals in the aria and 'thought nothing could be more distinctively eastern or Hebraic in type'. Sullivan told him that for the phrase 'Guard me, Jehovah, guard me', which serves as a refrain at the end of each verse, he had borrowed a melody, which he had heard chanted in the synagogue in Leipzig when he was the Mendelssohn scholar there and in which 'this quaint progression in the minor occurred so frequently that I have never forgotten it'.[6]

The subsequent duet between Rebecca and the Templar commander, which is among the most dramatic that Sullivan ever wrote, has distinct echoes of the exchange between Margarita and Olybius in the third scene of *The Martyr of Antioch*. The key difference is that instead of trying to win her wooer's soul for Christ, Rebecca chastises him for his failure to live up to Christian standards and the blasphemous way in which he invokes the cross while behaving in a wholly selfish and repellent way:

I hold my father's faith, and if I err,
May God forgive me – and He will forgive.
But thou, a Christian knight, wilt thou appeal
To thine own Cross to aid thee in thy sins?

Sullivan set those lines, which speak so eloquently of Jewish faith, forgiveness and Christian hypocrisy, in a way that is as spiritually sensitive and powerful as anything in his sacred oratorios and cantatas. There is a further parallel here with *The Martyr of Antioch* in terms of which religion is accorded the most sympathetic and moving music. Here it is not that Judaism, like paganism in the earlier work, gets the best tunes and Christianity is made to seem rather dull in comparison. Rather the music that underscores Rebecca's faith and her utter trust in 'the God of Abraham' is much more powerful and expressive than anything that is given to the Christian characters.

It is perhaps hardly surprising given this very favourable treatment of Judaism that *Ivanhoe* led to a revival of the suggestion that Sullivan himself had Jewish ancestry (see page 39). In its review of the opera the *Jewish Chronicle* noted that:

Three of the most popular musicians in England, including the musician who has been invited by Mr. D'Oyly Carte to create English opera, are Jews, or of Jewish origin – Cowen, Solomon, and Sullivan … A large number of Jewish faces were to be seen both at the dress rehearsal and at the premiere last Saturday of *Ivanhoe*. Jewish interest in the experiment is undoubtedly stimulated by the accident of the first English opera being devoted to the story of the Jewish heroine whom the genius of Scott has made immortal.[7]

In fact, as we have already noted, there is no evidence that Sullivan did have Jewish ancestry. The fact remains, however, that he did display considerable sensitivity in his setting of Rebecca's expressions of her faith. His musical treatment of the most obviously Christian character, the genial Friar Tuck, is by contrast humorous and light-hearted although never disrespectful. The friar's first entrance is accompanied by a motif with an ecclesiastical feel and a hint of medieval plainchant which is reintroduced for his subsequent appearances. Arthur Lawrence took this as an example of the church music in which Sullivan had been steeped in his youth and which 'even in his operas we find sprouting forth, sometimes with a peculiarly touching effect and at others with that subtle strain of humour that is ever enchanting without being offensive':

No better example of this latter can be found than in the ecclesiastical accompaniment which attends the presence of Friar Tuck through *Ivanhoe*. Here the broad harmonies and cadences of the church are employed with such refined taste, with such dramatic appropriateness, that it is impossible for the most fastidious to take offence.[8]

If the musical emphases in *Ivanhoe* suggest empathy and admiration for Judaism and genial affection for Christianity, more intriguing and ambiguous is the treatment accorded to the Knights Templar. One might expect that as a Freemason himself, Sullivan would have been highly sympathetic in his portrayal of them. The problem for him is that Sturgis's libretto casts the Order, and especially its Commander, de Bois-Guilbert, in a thoroughly bad light. It is the Jewess Rebecca who has to remind him that the Order was formed for poverty and chastity and not for the purposes of self-aggrandisement. When the Templar first enters in the opening scene of the opera, Sullivan delineates his character with a menacing passage in A flat major. The composer is finally allowed to give vent to what were perhaps his true feelings about the Knights Templar in the chorus 'Fremeure principes', with which they make their entrance in the closing scene. As Martin Yates writes in his sleeve notes to the recent CD recording of *Ivanhoe*, in this chorus 'Sullivan depicts not the mysterious dark side of the Order but the glory and pomp befitting their calling'.[9] There are surely echoes of the composer's own Freemasonry in the way that he sets this chorus, which is robust, clean-limbed and masculine. There is also more than a hint of the sonority of Sarastro, the distinctly Masonic high priest of the Temple of Wisdom in *The Magic Flute* in the music that Sullivan gives to Lucas de Beaumanoir, the Master of the Knights Templar.

There are several interesting religious resonances in the lighter operas on which Sullivan collaborated with librettists other than Gilbert. Perhaps the most intriguing is the portrayal of Islam in *The Rose of Persia* (1899), where Basil Hood put this uncompromising exposition of the Muslim faith into the mouth of the high priest Abdallah:

> When Islam first arose,
>   A tower upon a rock,
>   Beneath her haughty battlements
>   Were ranged around the jealous tents
> Of swift-encircling foes!
>   Then all her gates did Islam lock,
> As every Muslim knows;
>   And through those gates of Right and Wrong
> No traitor comes or goes!

For Islam's gates are strong against a friend or foe;
Her gates of Right and Wrong none passeth to and fro;
For foes are they without and friends are they within;
The postern-gate's the Gate of Doubt, that leads to the Camp of Sin!

It is difficult to know exactly what to make of this song. Abdallah is in many ways the villain of the piece and is here chastising the wealthy philanthropist Abu-el-Hassan for consorting with riff-raff and preferring 'the society of beggars to the beggars of society'. Sullivan gives it a rousing tune, in some ways reminiscent of the ultra-patriotic 'There's a little group of isles beyond the waves' which ends *Utopia Limited*. He also introduces unmistakable echoes of the opening line of ST GERTRUDE into both the orchestral accompaniment and the chorus refrain. Was this another musical joke and an affectionate nod towards the Church of England, as with the plainchant melody, which accompanied Friar Tuck's appearances in *Ivanhoe*, or was it a more subtle reference to the intransigence of Islam and its similarity to the Church militant?

Another of Sullivan's late works, *The Beauty Stone*, a 'romantic musical drama' in three acts with a libretto by Arthur Wing Pinero and J. Comyns Carr, which opened at the Savoy Theatre in May 1898, involves a Faustian compact with the Devil, who arrives in a fifteenth-century Flemish village bearing a magic stone, which confers perfect beauty on any girl who wears it around her neck. He first appears in the guise of a friar to an ugly, crippled girl, Laine, apparently in response to her prayer to the Virgin Mary that she might be allowed to die, as she is never to attain beauty or love. Derrick McClure has observed of Sullivan's exquisite setting of Laine's aria to the Virgin, 'Dear, Mother Mary':

> This alone, I suspect, would have raised a few eyebrows among the solid Church of England citizens in the Savoy stalls; but when the immediate result of a prayer to Mary turns out to be the appearance of Satan, the shock is much more profound. Shortly afterwards, the devil goes on to attribute the magic power of the stone to Mary. Is Mariolatry being equated with diabolism? Carr and Pinero, no doubt unthinkingly, have got themselves into very dangerous territory indeed here.[10]

Sullivan can hardly be accused of Mariolatry because of the sympathetic way that he set Laine's prayer, any more than he can be blamed for any subsequent suggestion in the plot that appeared to suggest that it was diabolical. He was, however, criticized for the rather low-key and bloodless music that he gave to the Devil, played in the opening production by the

D'Oyly Carte principal comedian and patter man, Walter Passmore. *The Times* review commented:

> It would not hurt the effect of the production in the least if the part were to be recast, and musically the opera would gain enormously if Sir Arthur Sullivan would treat the character with some of the *diablerie* exhibited so happily in the Lucifer of *The Golden Legend*. It is, perhaps, the greatest disappointment in the new production that there should be so little of the supernatural element conveyed in the music, and more particularly so when Sir Arthur Sullivan is the composer.[11]

There is also a clear religious theme in *Haddon Hall*, on which Sullivan collaborated with Sydney Grundy in 1892. Set on the eve of the restoration of the monarchy in 1660, it contrasts the lifestyle and attitudes of the Puritan Roundheads and Royalist Cavaliers. As one might expect, the music leaves no doubt as to which side had Sullivan's sympathies – there are echoes once again of the respective treatment of pagans and Christians in *The Martyr of Antioch*. Perhaps more significant and indicative in spiritual terms is the loving way in which he set the madrigal which begins:

> When the budding bloom of May
>   Paints the hedgerows red and white,
> Gather then your garlands gay;
>   Earth was made for man's delight!

Percy Young has written: 'It is possible that the words of that last line are a fair indication of Sullivan's philosophy.'[12]

We come finally to the works for which Sullivan will always be remembered best. On the face of it, there is little or no religion in the Savoy operas. Their themes and message are distinctly secular. The characters seldom if ever invoke God or manifest religious belief or faith. The fickle hand of fate rather than any benevolent deity seems to rule over human lives. Gilbert felt that the world was arbitrary and unfair, his own outlook on life perhaps being best expressed in Dick Deadeye's sentiment that 'it's a cruel world' and the Mikado's observation, before singing 'See how the fates their gifts allot' that 'it's an unjust world and virtue is triumphant only in theatrical performances'.

Yet if the lyrics of the Savoy operas reflect Gilbert's cynicism, pessimism and biting wit, as well as his sympathy for the underdog and delight in topsy-turvydom, the music often has a spiritual quality. It certainly has a distinctly 'churchy' feel, as noted by George Bernard Shaw, who found the Savoy operas 'most unexpectedly churchy after Offenbach' and, indeed, Gilbert who reproached his collaborator for the seriousness of his music, 'fitted more for the Cathedral than the Comic opera stage'.[13] Sullivan could never get away, even had he wanted to, from his upbringing in and deep love of church music. Several of the most characteristic musical features of the Savoy operas derive from the conventions of sacred music. Benedict Taylor has convincingly argued that the contrapuntal double choruses found in so many of the operas have their origins in the world of church counterpoint.[14] Herbert Sullivan and Newman Flower assert, presumably on the basis of what the composer told his nephew, that 'many of the unaccompanied quartets, etc., in his Savoy operas' were directly influenced by the church music that he heard in Russia during his visit there in 1881.[15] The madrigals that feature so prominently have something of the character of Tudor church anthems. Perhaps even that most characteristic device, the patter song, with its frequent repeated notes and careful attention to words owes something to the tradition of plainchant in which Sullivan was so thoroughly schooled.

More broadly, much of the writing for the chorus in the Savoy operas is highly suggestive of church music. This is perhaps particularly evident in the a capella choruses 'Hail, Poetry!' in *The Pirates of Penzance* and 'Eagle high' in *Utopia Limited*, both of which could, at least in musical terms if not in respect of their lyrics, pass muster as Victorian parish church anthems. Arthur Jacobs felt that 'Hail, Poetry!' was in fact a parody of a certain kind of religious sentiment:

> It is, in miniature, a burlesque of an operatic prayer scene, such as was liable to intrude with breathtaking irrelevance into a serious operatic plot: that in Balfe's *The Bohemian Girl* is famously ridiculous, and that in Verdi's *La forza del destino* only just escapes the charge. But the words of prayer could not be burlesqued, nor could the Deity be invoked in satire. So the abstraction of 'Poetry' takes its place, an awkward substitute.[16]

Gervase Hughes wrote in somewhat similar vein:

> The words are a lampoon (Poetry is apostrophized as a Divine emollient) and dramatically it is indefensible ... Sullivan's share has been decried as a lapse into 'churchiness', and he may or may not have had his tongue in his cheek, but he knew that his audience, steeped like himself in the tradition of English choral singing, would applaud it to the

echo. Here, to use modern jargon, he proved himself a 'listener-reaction expert'.[17]

I do not agree with these analyses, and I am not sure that either librettist or composer had their tongues in their cheek when they wrote 'Hail, Poetry!' It seems to me to be one of the relatively few songs in which Gilbert expressed a philosophy of life that chimed exactly with that of Sullivan. Another is the quintet 'Try we lifelong' in *The Gondoliers* with its injunction to 'string the lyre and fill the cup lest on sorrow we should sup' and to take life as it comes. Both librettist and composer shared the Pirate King's sentiment: 'What we ask is life without a touch of poetry in it?' I believe that Gilbert was being sincere in his tribute to poetry as 'a heaven born maid' and indeed as 'Divine emollient', which is perhaps as near as he gets to directly invoking the Deity, apart from the appeal of Josephine in *H.M.S. Pinafore* to the God of Love and the God of Reason. Sullivan was equally sincere in providing an anthem-like setting for this hymn to the flowing fount of poetic sentiment.

There are also certain chordal sequences in the big accompanied choruses in the first act finales which have an unmistakably ecclesiastical ring. An obvious example is the passage beginning 'Oh mercy, thou whose smile has shone so many a captive heart upon' in *The Yeomen of the Guard*. In this particular opera, there are also two very churchy sounding passages in the second act: the brief choral coda following the quick-fire duet, where Wilfred Shadbolt and Jack Point vie to give every detail of the shooting of Colonel Fairfax, which begins 'Hail the valiant fellow who did this deed of derring do!' and the 'Day of terror, day of tears' sequence in the Act II finale, which seems modelled on the Dies Irae. The intervals and progressions in these choruses belong to the sanctuary as much as the stage.

The key role given to the chorus was one of the most important innovations made by the Savoy operas in the world of musical theatre. I have suggested elsewhere that its roots lie less in the classical Greek chorus acting as narrator and the voice of public opinion, although there are elements of that, than in the Victorian Protestant world of church and chapel choirs singing hymns and anthems in four-part harmony.[18] It is no coincidence that the Savoy operas emerge on the back of the great choral revival in mid nineteenth-century Britain, which saw thousands of people attending classes in tonic sol-fa and part singing and the emergence of hundreds of choral societies up and down the country whose repertoire centred around such works as Mendelssohn's *Elijah* and Stainer's *Crucifixion*. Sullivan was himself steeped in this world, and he wrote for his stage choruses as if he were writing for church choirs.

The fact that so much of the four-part writing for the chorus in the Savoy operas has obvious similarities with Victorian anthems and other church music is, of course, one of the reasons why they were so avidly and widely taken up by church and chapel choirs. Many of the earliest amateur G & S performing societies on both sides of the Atlantic began as offshoots of churches and chapels, often with choir members forming the nucleus. Several of those that are still going strong retain their original church and denominational ties, and it remains the case today that there are a disproportionate number of regular churchgoers among amateur G & S performers as well as among fans. Another reason for the popularity of the Savoy operas among churchgoers, of course, was and is their wholesome, respectable character. This, together with the affectionate portrayal of clerical characters such as the saintly Dr Daly in *The Sorcerer*, is also doubtless why they have always attracted a considerable following among the clergy. This fact was made much of in the early promotion of the Savoy operas. A flyer issued by Richard D'Oyly Carte to advertise a provincial tour of *H.M.S. Pinafore* in 1879 boasted 'My theatre in London is visited largely by the clergy, who have given to it a support which they withhold from many others.' Following the success of the same show in the United States, the *American Review* expressed the hope that the work of Gilbert and Sullivan 'might be the means of starting the great work of regeneration of the modern stage in our native land' and approvingly cited wide ecclesiastical endorsement: 'Clergyman have approved it. Church choirs have sung it. Church members have gone to see it and have been conscious of no moral degradation in the act.'[19]

If the 'churchy' nature of the music provides one religious dimension to the Savoy operas, there is another of a more subtle and nuanced kind. It is found in the way that the music is always subordinate to the lyrics. In my book *You've Got to Have a Dream: The Message of the Musical*, I argued that the word-led nature of Gilbert and Sullivan's collaboration, which became the model for virtually all twentieth-century musical theatre, is in many ways a reflection of the emphasis on narrative, story and the primacy of words found in both Judaism and Protestant Christianity. It is striking, and surely not coincidental, that virtually all the main lyricists and composers responsible for the great Broadway and West End musicals, who continued the tradition begun by Gilbert and Sullivan of letting the words dictate the form of the melodies, have come from Jewish or Protestant backgrounds and that musical theatre as a genre has been most popular in the United States, the United Kingdom and Protestant Northern Europe, while the very different and much less word-led genre of operetta has thrived in the Catholic cultures of Central, Eastern and

Southern Europe. As I wrote, 'Sullivan establishes a paradigm for the role of the composer in musical theatre which might be said to be that of the sacrificial calling of the music man as the one who basically subordinates himself and his melodies to the lyricist/librettist and the words.'[20]

A more evidently spiritual quality in the Savoy operas comes out of Sullivan's innate humanity and sensitivity. Where Gilbert often seeks to caricature his characters and take them down, Sullivan instinctively wants to build them up and give them a certain nobility and dignity. This is evident in the respective treatment by librettist and composer of the unfortunate 'elderly, ugly daughters' like Katisha and Lady Jane whose music redeems and softens their often rather unappealing portrayal in terms of words, as demonstrated in their respective arias 'Hearts do not break' and 'Silver'd is the raven hair'. The way in which Sullivan softens Gilbert's lyrics is particularly evident in the quartet 'The world is but a broken toy' in *Princess Ida*. As written on the page, the words are clearly meant to be satirical and not taken too seriously, with Princess Ida's lofty and disdainful renunciation of the world and its ways being mocked and parodied by Hilarion, Cyril and Florian. Sullivan transforms their meaning by his serene and sublime lyrical setting into a poignant statement of the reality of pain and sorrow. In a rather different way, he softens the opening female chorus in *The Mikado* 'Comes a train of little ladies', giving it a much more appealing and positive message than lines like 'Is it but a world of sorrow, sadness set to song?' would suggest.

Sullivan's personality and outlook on life was radically different from Gilbert's. He was by nature much more optimistic, much more trusting, much more generous in his assessment of people's motives and character and much less curmudgeonly. It is impossible to imagine anyone writing of him, as the actor and playwright Seymour Hicks did about Gilbert, that 'he always gave the impression that he got up in the morning to see with whom he could have a quarrel'. Nor did he remotely share Gilbert's view that 'Man was sent into the world to contend with man, and to get the advantage of him in every possible way.'[21] Sullivan was incapable of writing music that expressed a depressing and misanthropic outlook on life. This meant that he nearly always softened and brightened the message conveyed in Gilbert's lyrics. If it made for a generally more optimistic and upbeat atmosphere, this 'gilding of the philosophic pill' did not lead to a uniform anodyne sweetness. Sullivan could write deeply haunting and wistful melodies just as he could supply endless tuneful marches and expressions of patriotic sentiment and brilliantly set the patter songs so that their words always came out crystal clear.

Again and again, Sullivan's music has the effect of humanizing the message and impact of Gilbert's lyrics. It also sometimes does more than this, spiritualizing the rather bleak and overwhelmingly secular outlook of his collaborator. Every year, I see university students new to the works of Gilbert and Sullivan falling under their spell. In Gilbert's case, the attraction is with the wit, the brilliant wordplay and the inventive, erudite and zany turns of phrase that provide an alternative language and means of communication for the initiated. The nature of the love affair with Sullivan is more difficult to define – it is not just a matter of the catchiness and accessibility of those unfailingly singable and hummable tunes which never fail to lift the spirits and put a spring into the step. Somehow, singing or listening to Sullivan melodies makes you feel better about yourself and about the world. They are transformative, often deeply therapeutic and also in some mysterious way transfiguring. I do not think it is too much to describe this as a spiritual quality.

There are certainly moments of deep spirituality in the Savoy operas, and they achieve that quality very largely through the contribution of Sullivan. Those who know and love the operas will each have their own favourites. I wish to single out just three in chronological order of composition. The first is another of those anthem-like choruses from Act 1 finales that have already been mentioned: 'I hear the soft note of the echoing voice of an old, old love, long dead' from *Patience* (1881). In its poignancy and its immediacy it is somehow more spiritually powerful than several of Sullivan's actual anthems. Gervase Hughes typically describes it as 'a quasi-religious effusion' and Arthur Jacobs brackets it with 'The Lost Chord', the aria 'How many hired servants' from *The Prodigal Son* and the evening hymn from *The Golden Legend* in respect of its 'obsessive repeated notes at the opening' which 'no doubt conveyed solemn intensity then as surely as they seem now to be a cliché of such emotion'.[22] It certainly has very close affinities with these much more obviously sacred pieces and, for those of us who do not share the view that Sullivan's repeated notes in these numbers now sound clichéd, it works a similar magic in terms of weaving what can only be described as a spiritual aura which is at once both calming and haunting.

The second scene, which I wish to single out for its spiritual power, is that between the Lord Chancellor and Iolanthe towards the end of *Iolanthe* (1882), which begins with the recitative 'My Lord, a suppliant at your feet I kneel' and leads into the ballad 'He loves!' Here, as he occasionally did, Gilbert provided lyrics of unaffected pathos and genuine feeling, untempered by any satirical jibes or topsy-turvy touches. Sullivan responded with a beautifully poignant yet utterly simple setting. Some have described it as Wagnerian and others have sought to find echoes of Weber, but in truth I think it is Sullivan being utterly true to himself. He began working on *Iolanthe* just three days after the death of his beloved mother. He must often have thought of her, as he set this particular number with its references to 'Tears – bitter unavailing tears, for one untimely dead' and its line 'sad thoughts of her arise'. I wonder, indeed, if he may even have written this song in some sense as a memorial to her in much the same way as the *In Memoriam* overture was a memorial to his father.[23]

My third and final scene of spiritual power from the Savoy operas is one that strikes a chord with many people; the ending of *The Yeomen of the Guard*. It is perhaps difficult to pick a particular musical moment in this finale – the effect is produced as much by how the character of Jack Point plays it and is directed as by what he sings – although his final rendering of the shanty-like 'I have a song to sing, O!' is a key element. A fellow Church of Scotland minister, who is himself devoted to the work of Bach and the great choral classics, commented to me after watching a recent production by the University of St Andrews Gilbert and Sullivan Society that he felt this scene has something of the spiritual power of *Messiah*: 'People often say they are moved to tears by "I know that my Redeemer liveth". Well, I was more moved to tears by "I have a song to sing, O!".'

Nigel Burton is absolutely right to say that Sullivan's operettas (as he calls them), 'if performed sympathetically, are not only delightful and amusing but also profoundly moving, because they are imbued with a deep and enduring sense of humanity'. He goes on:

> This is their source of life, their vital force; it reaches out to reality by means of apparent absurdity, and it should remind us, if there was ever the need, that our most popular composer was also a truly great one.[24]

The Savoy operas are not just moving; they also have a magical quality that is very hard to define. It is why both theatrical impresarios and tele-vision and radio schedulers put on Gilbert and Sullivan at Christmas time. They are quite rightly seen as appropriate companions to other staples of the festive season like carol services and the Queen's Christmas Day broadcast. This is partly because of their pantomime-like fairy tale quality, their nostalgic appeal and their atmosphere of undemanding, innocent amusement and escapism. But there is something more that links them to the celebration of the incarnation and God become flesh. Like carols and the Queen's Christmas broadcast, the Savoy operas have an unmistakably spiritual dimension which is expressed in terms of the redemptive, transforming and ultimately transfiguring effect of Sullivan's music.

9

Conclusion:
All Hail, All Hail, Divine Emollient

The floral tributes which filled four carriages of Sullivan's funeral cortege, as it made its way through the streets of London on 27 November 1900, showed the extent to which he was remembered and revered for his sacred music. They included a banner of white chrysanthemums with the first two bars of 'Onward Christian soldiers' picked out in violets, a white cushion of chrysanthemums decorated with the notes of 'I shall hear that grand Amen' and a Bible of white chrysanthemums and violets with rosebud clasps, purple ribbons and bouquets inscribed 'O Gladsome Light'. The tribute from Fanny Ronalds consisted of a large heart of white lilies with branches of pink roses inscribed 'that one lost chord divine, 1870–1900'.

The funeral obsequies further confirmed Sullivan's standing as a church musician. The pall-bearers who bore his coffin first into the Chapel Royal at St James's Palace and then into St Paul's Cathedral included Sir John Stainer, Sir George Martin, the organist at St Paul's, who had commissioned the *Boer War Te Deum*, and Sir Frederick Bridge, the organist at Westminster Abbey. Sullivan's own music featured prominently in the services at both venues. In the Chapel Royal, the choristers sang 'Yea, though I walk through the valley of the shadow of death' from *The Light of the World* and the funeral anthem 'Wreaths for our graves'. The service there concluded with the organist playing 'In Bethany' from *The Light of the World*. At St Paul's 'Yea though I walk through the valley of the shadow of death' was sung again shortly before the coffin was lowered into its resting place under the floor of the crypt. For the *Daily Telegraph* reporter, the supreme moment came at the very end:

> Never, surely, with more absolute fitness was a tribute rendered to a dead man than the singing without instrumental accompaniment of the beautiful anthem from *The Martyr of Antioch* by the chorus of the Savoy Theatre, 'Brother, thou art gone before us – where the wicked

cease from troubling, and the weary are at rest.' In much that was solemn and impressive, this, perhaps formed the most effective act of homage, the choicest and most eloquent prayer. For we seemed to real-ise the two sides of Sir Arthur Sullivan's brilliant nature, the two Sister Muses by whose inspiration he wrote. There was not so much contrast or discord between them as some have been in haste to imagine. In the lighter music of opera and burlesque there was the touch of noble and masterful purpose; in the solemn chant or anthem there was a feel-ing for melody and tune, serving to link the religious mood with the hours of everyday. Here at least, as the well-trained chorus of the Savoy Theatre, the female voices almost choked with emotion, sang the sweet words of sorrow and faith and hope, there was a complete fusion of brightness and gloom, of the grave and the gay, of the happy and the solemn. It was right that this should be the last chaplet laid on the musi-cian's bier, harmoniously welding together the varied triumphs of the operatic composer with the strains of religious feeling and awe.[1]

Of all that was written in the aftermath of Sullivan's death, those words were among the most perceptive and fitting. They encapsulated the two sides of his personality and his artistry which were complementary rather than at variance, the spiritual yearning that infused his comic operas and the feeling for melody and tune which characterized his sacred work.

Inevitably, not all the tributes to Sullivan following his death showed such perspicuity or generosity. In its leading article, *The Times*, doubtless under the influence of its chief music critic Fuller Maitland, raised the all too familiar gripe:

Many who are able to appreciate classical music regret that Sir Arthur Sullivan did not aim consistently at higher things, that he set himself to rival Offenbach and Lecocq instead of competing on a level of high seriousness with such musicians as Sir Hubert Parry and Professor Stanford.[2]

This snide jibe aroused the ire of Frederick Bridge, who wrote from West-minster Abbey to protest that neither Parry nor Stanford would surely 'claim to have produced work which will rank higher or live longer than *The Golden Legend*, the *In Memoriam*, and other overtures, the Shake-speare music and his many beautiful songs'. Bridge went on to say that 'Sir Arthur Sullivan's church music is a worthy continuance of the best Cathedral traditions.'[3]

Bridge's verdict, which would have been echoed by Stainer and Martin, has sadly not been the dominant one in the musical establishment, including the church music establishment, in the century or more since Sullivan's death. Rather, he remains condemned as secular, second-rate and guilty of all the crimes of which the English Musical Renaissance accused him. His sacred music has been dismissed and if musical snobs can allow themselves to praise anything in his output, and then usually only with a grudging and condescending manner, it is just the Savoy operas.

The fact is that Sullivan did not set out to rival Offenbach and Lecocq. He saw himself, as the quotation which stands at the head of this book makes clear, first and foremost as a serious composer of sacred music. Offenbach, Lecocq and other Continental masters of operetta like Johann Strauss and the later Franz Lehár wrote not a bar of sacred music between them. The closest that Offenbach came to the genre was when he disguised his operetta numbers as liturgical pieces during a North American tour in 1876 in order to circumvent a Philadelphia by-law forbidding entertainment on Sundays. The collected works and the musical milieu of these composers were wholly secular and in this respect, if in no other, they inhabited a totally different world from Sullivan.

Arthur Sullivan's considerable corpus of sacred music has been ignored and dismissed by the musical establishment and musical historians, because he has been seen either as having prostituted his talents in lighter works or as being out of sympathy and out of his depth with serious compositions. Both judgements are equally fallacious, as is the tendency on the part of critics and biographers to divide and partition his work. In marked contrast to the *Daily Telegraph* reporter who rightly saw it all as being of a piece, with the spiritual pervading the worldly and the lyrical infusing the serious, many commentators have wanted to distinguish different Sullivans and not to see a unity and wholeness in his work. An early example of this damaging process is the comment of the German pianist and composer Jacques Blumenthal (1829–1908) in the aftermath of *Ivanhoe*: 'You are most generous towards the English nation for giving it three composers by the name of Sullivan: the comic, the sacred and the highly dramatic.'[4] Sullivan's first biographer Arthur Lawrence compounded this mistake by suggesting that his subject's work could be reviewed in three categories: the sacred, the secular and the dramatic.[5]

This is to make far too hard and fast a distinction. As we have seen, Sullivan's oratorios and sacred cantatas are highly dramatic and his comic operas are full of spiritual moments. He did undoubtedly have two sides to his personality but as displayed in his music they were not rigidly segregated and separated but rather integrated and intertwined. Common characteristics run through everything that he wrote: the fusion of brightness and gloom, of the grave and the gay, of the happy and the solemn noted by the *Daily Telegraph* and expressed through the sweet notes of sorrow and faith and hope.

Unfortunately, nearly all of Sullivan's subsequent biographers have followed Lawrence and presented him as a somewhat bifurcated and split personality. They have also often dismissed and played down the significance of his sacred work, following the lead of the proponents of the English Musical Renaissance. This has led to several serious distortions. The first is the almost universal portrayal of Arthur Sullivan as a person without religious faith, essentially if not exclusively secular and worldly in outlook as well as lifestyle. I hope that the evidence presented in this book both from his own letters and diaries and from his works has gone some way towards dispelling that misconception. The letters and diaries point to a simple, trusting faith, at least in the first three decades of his life. The biblical texts, which he himself selected for use in *The Prodigal Son*, and the other texts which he chose to set, with their very strong emphasis on God's overwhelming forgiveness, grace and mercy suggest a clear identification with a broad liberal theology.

It is important not to overstate Sullivan's religiosity just because it has been so understated, if not wholly ignored, by his biographers. He was emphatically not an evangelical Christian, the product of a dramatic conversion experience and imbued with the savings tenets of vital religion, a personal relationship with his Saviour and a focus on the atoning power of the cross of Christ. Nor did he share the Tractarian outlook and sympathies of most of his fellow mid-Victorian church musicians, who espoused with differing levels of enthusiasm the Anglo-Catholic doctrines of reserve and sacramentalism.[6] After leaving his organist's posts, Sullivan was more disconnected from the Church than most of those who wrote hymn tunes and anthems although even in the latter part of his life there is no direct evidence that he lost the simple trusting faith of his youth. On the evidence of the biblical texts that he chose to set and the way that he set them, I am inclined to locate him at the liberal end of the Broad Church movement alongside his great friend George Grove, who perhaps had a strong influence on the direction of his faith as well as on the choice of texts for his major sacred choral works. But this is almost certainly to make him too theological – and Sullivan was emphatically not a theologian nor someone with much in the way of theological antennae. Gervase Hughes is right to say that 'he never filled his head with metaphysical speculations, but was content to take life as it came and happily encouraged others to do the same'.[7] His Freemasonry may be indicative of a broad, benevolent inclusive deism. Here again, however, that is probably too definite and dry and rational a definition of his faith. Sullivan's statement that 'music should speak to the heart, and not to the head' could equally have applied to his religion. He was more than most a child of Victorian sentimentalism, whose religious sympathies and spiritual yearnings were felt emotionally rather than articulated intellectually, not least in respect of his very characteristically Victorian approach to death and heaven.

There is a sense in which Sullivan's true religion was music. His friend Edward Dicey noted that 'he worshipped his art with the reverence of an ardent believer, if not a fanatic'.[8] Sullivan himself wrote that 'music has been my incessant occupation since I was eight years old. All my energies, all my affections, have been bestowed upon it, and it has for long been to me a second nature ... Music is to me a mistress in every sense of the word.'[9] Several times during his life, he expressed the view that music was divine. Significantly, the first occasion which prompted this reflection was when as a boy in the Chapel Royal he first heard the singing of Jenny Lind. 'She it was', he later recalled, 'who made me think that music was divine.'[10] Later he was moved to similar thoughts by the singing of Fanny Ronalds. He explored this divine aspect of his art most fully in the address 'About Music' given in Birmingham Town Hall in October 1888, where he said that 'music is co-extensive with human life. From the soft lullaby of the mother that soothes our cradle-life to the dirge that is sung over the grave, music enters into our existence. It marks periods and epochs of our life, stimulates our exertions, strengthens our faith, speaks both words of peace and war, and exercises over us a charm and indefinite power which we can all feel, though we cannot explain.'[11] It is highly significant that the examples he gave here involved the human voice in a homely and sentimental setting: the mother's lullaby to the newborn baby and the funeral dirge sung over the grave.

The Birmingham address included a good deal of reflection on the religious power of music, with observations on the fact that the Israelites dug their great wells to the sound of solemn music while wandering in the wilderness and on how 'the Reformation in Germany was powerfully advanced by Luther's famous hymn, "*Ein feste Burg*," and by his other chorales, which are well known to have precipitated the conversion of whole towns to the reformed faith'.[12] The fact was that, within his overall devotion to his muse, the specific genres of church and sacred music were the objects of Sullivan's particular and abiding affection from the time of his boyhood days in Sandhurst Parish Church and in the choir stalls of the Chapel Royal.

Just as mistaken as the idea that he was not a religious or spiritual person is the equally widespread view that his heart was not in sacred music and that his work in this area was regarded as a chore and a drudge and abandoned as soon as he was making money through other more congenial types of composition. It is true that he wrote much more church music in his twenties and early thirties than in the last two decades of his life. This was by no means an uncommon pattern of work among classical composers – indeed Mozart wrote only one piece of church music, his *Ave Verum Corpus*, after the age of 26. However, Sullivan did not cease from sacred composition during his years of collaboration with Gilbert and other lyricists on comic operas. He went on writing hymn tunes, anthems and liturgical pieces and was indeed planning another oratorio at the time of his untimely death at the age of 58.

There is an equally widespread and more insidious misconception, which this book has also sought to dispel; that Sullivan's sacred music is irredeemably second-rate if not actually beneath contempt. The accusations that have been made against it have been many and often contradictory, even when coming from the same critic, as in the case of Erik Routley. Serious sacred compositions have been seen as being beyond his capabilities and alien to his nature, while at the same time he is held to have felt a calling to such work but to have invested it with a false religiosity and piety that was fatal to its quality. His hymn tunes, anthems, sacred songs and oratorios have been attacked for vulgar, shallow secularism on the one hand and dull, sanctimonious religiosity on the other.

Few other composers have been subjected to such a barrage of criticism either during or after their lifetime. Much of this was simply sour grapes from fellow composers jealous of Sullivan's huge popularity with the public and of the money that he made. He was the victim of musical snobbery and elitism, worse in Britain than in most other countries which acknowledge musical theatre, operetta and so-called light music as just as worthy of serious appreciation and commendation as supposedly loftier and more serious genres. As I have already suggested, I think there are many similarities in the treatment meted out to Sullivan and to Andrew Lloyd Webber in our own age, as there are, indeed, in their personalities and musical talents.

There is also a deeper common bond between these two phenomenally popular British composers who lived almost exactly 100 years apart. Lloyd Webber's biographer Michael Coveney writes: 'If there is any one theme running through all of Lloyd Webber's works, it is a quest and a yearning for the spiritual dimension in life. I hear church bells in the rock and roll, the liturgy in the levity and the agony in the ecstasy.'[13] There is a similar strain in Sullivan's music. A profound sense of spiritual yearning is most obviously present in works like 'The Lost Chord' and the *In Memoriam* overture, which were wrung out of personal grief and sorrow, but it is also there unmistakably in much of his sacred music and in the note of wistfulness that so often creeps into the Savoy operas.

In part, this yearning was an expression of Sullivan's own personality. For all the love of life and genial optimism, there was an unfulfilled side to his character which expressed itself in searching and striving. He revealed it most clearly in the letter of thanks that he wrote to Thomas Helmore in 1889 for his Christmas present of a new translation of Thomas à Kempis's *Imitation of Christ*. In a rare digression into abstract philosophy, he mused: 'It sounds paradoxical, but there are times to me when the music would be more beautiful and complete without notes ... How often have I felt myself hampered by having to express all I wanted to say by voice and instruments of limited means, and definite, unchangeable quality. After all, it is only human to be longing and striving for something more than we have got.'[14]

Those elements of longing and striving lift Sullivan's music out of the merely sentimental and keep it from being complacent and shallow as well as giving a quality of wistfulness. Do they also provide its moments of passion? The criticism that his compositions, not least his sacred pieces, lack passion is often made. It is put succinctly by the authors of a book about Franz Lehár, who write of 'Sullivan, in whose enchanting scores there may be moments of melancholy, and even hymnody, but never any disturbing hints of passion'.[15] This is unjust. There are moments of passion in Sullivan's music, but they are overlaid by the lyricism of his melodies which so beautifully express the warmth and generosity of his personality.

Sullivan's music is infused with the qualities of openness, sincerity and simplicity which were so prominent in his own psychological and spiritual make-up. As a person and as composer, he was without deviousness, contrivance or pretence. His own openness naturally led him to emphasize in his sacred works the themes of God's grace, forgiveness and loving mercy over those of judgement, divine wrath and punishment for sin. There was a fundamental innocence in his character, and it is not surprising that in a striking passage in his Birmingham address he identified innocence as one of the chief attributes that makes music divine:

Herein lies one of the divine attributes of music, in that it is absolutely free from the power of suggesting anything immoral. Its countless moods and richly varied forms suit it to every organisation, and it can convey every meaning except one – an impure one. Music can suggest no improper thought, and herein may be claimed a superiority over painting and sculpture, both of which may, and indeed do at times depict and suggest impurity. This blemish, however, does not enter into music; sounds alone (apart from articulate words, spectacle, or descriptive programme) must, from their indefinite nature, be innocent. Let us thank God that we have one elevating and ennobling influence in the world which can never, never lose its purity and beauty.[16]

In its clean, uncomplicated simplicity and lyricism Sullivan's own music has considerable purity and beauty. George Grove reflected that it had that same 'divine quality which made Mozart, Beethoven and Schubert couch their thoughts in the most beautiful forms they could find'. Grove saw Sullivan, indeed, as the last representative of 'the old school' in contrast to the modern composers who 'worship ugliness and have no affection, no love for their music'.[17] His point was well made. Critics persistently chided Sullivan for not being more contemporary and forward-looking in style, more discordant and atonal in his harmonies. The fact was that he was happier to remain in the conservative classical tradition of Mozart, Schubert and Mendelssohn, because he prized beauty and purity above innovation and novelty.

If there is one quality that Sullivan's music exhibits above all others, it is surely accessibility. Its appeal is instant, its style wonderfully limpid and clear. Critics decried it as the kind of music that people came out of the concert hall whistling and therefore as being banal, shallow and vulgar. Not requiring degree-level study or repeated exposure to appreciate, it was consigned to the dreaded category of 'easy listening'. Those of a less snobbish disposition, like Henry Lytton, the D'Oyly Carte patter man, on the other hand, rightly extolled this feature as especially worthy of praise:

Sullivan's greatest virtue was that he wrote music that was 'understanded of the people' ... His music is never in the problem style – the problem of intricate chords and modern progressions – and just as certainly does it avoid the strident atrocities of the modern ragtime type. It is transparent and simple.[18]

For Lytton this accessibility and simplicity was 'perfectly and typically British'. Perhaps it was and is a particularly British quality. In the so-called 'land without music' Sullivan's infectiously lyrical melodies have appealed especially to the unmusical, as demonstrated by the confession of the early twentieth-century Liberal prime minister, H. H. Asquith, that the Savoy operas were 'almost the only form of music that has ever given me any real pleasure'.[19] The British prefer their music, like their food, to be straightforward, uncomplicated, simple and satisfying. Maybe there is more to it than this – a particularly British, or more precisely English, quality in Sullivan's music, and especially in his sacred pieces, which reflects the *via media* of moderate Anglicanism and the post-Reformation liberal Protestantism of the Cambridge Platonists and the Caroline divines with its emphasis on gentleness and moderation and its lack of stridency.

It is worth repeating Sullivan's commendation of the English church musicians of early Tudor times in the 1888 Birmingham address (page 50). The sweet reasonableness, human feeling and attention to words that he found in their work are very English and very Anglican qualities that perhaps found their fullest expression in the Authorized Version of the Bible and the Book of Common Prayer. They are also the theological and spiritual hallmarks of moderate, liberal Protestantism. These qualities very clearly characterize Sullivan's compositions, both sacred and secular. Analysing the acclamation which greeted his early works, Percy Young writes that 'Sullivan's immediate contribution to English music was recognized as the quality of gracefulness' and notes how this term was used by the *Musical Times* to describe several of his compositions of the late 1860s.[20] Gracefulness, understood both in its technical theological sense as well as in a more general way, remained an abiding characteristic of his work. *The Times* critic hit the nail on the head when he wrote about the performance of *The Golden Legend* in the Albert Hall in November 1886: 'Sir Arthur Sullivan has the rare gift of placing the cynical mind at rest.'[21]

This ability to put the cynical mind at rest points to the spiritual quality at the heart of Sullivan's music, which is nothing less than redemptive in the true sense of the word. Sullivan wrote his hymn tunes, sacred songs, anthems and oratorios to encourage, console and reassure, not to promote angst-ridden conscience searching. It is no coincidence that his tunes predominate in those sections of early twentieth-century hymn books entitled 'Witness and Encouragement'. There is a feel good factor in nearly all his music which is ultimately impossible to define. It simply makes one feel better for listening to it. I have written elsewhere about how for me and for many others that I know, Gilbert and Sullivan is 'a balm, a tonic, and a stimulant. When I am down, it picks me up. When I am tired, it restores me. When I am feeling on top of the world, it lets me express my joy.'[22] There is room for several doctoral theses on the special therapeutic magic that the Savoy operas work on those who are depressed, lonely and anxious.

In the case of Sullivan's sacred music, which has been the particular subject of this book, it is perhaps the pervasive note of reassurance which provides this element of balm and healing. I have identified it as the key motif in his first published work, 'O Israel' (pages 46–7), in his 1869 anthem 'Sing, O Heavens' (page 147) and in his final work, the *Boer War Te Deum* (pages 158–62). In many ways it has a softening effect, rather as Sullivan's music so often does with respect to Gilbert's words in the Savoy operas. Hugh Haweis could have had Sullivan in mind when he wrote in his best-selling *Music and Morals* that 'music has the subtle power to soften melancholy by presenting it with its fine emotional counterpart'.[23] So, indeed, could John Bacchus Dykes when he wrote that 'music should be beautiful, that it may be a more fitting offering for Him, and better calculated to impress, soften, humanise and win'.[24]

It is important not to over-spiritualise Sullivan. He was not a saint or a mystic, but neither was he the shallow, worldly, hedonistic gambler and womaniser that he has so often been portrayed. If I have emphasized his spiritual qualities in this book it is partly because they have been almost wholly neglected by his biographers. The truth is that Sullivan's character was one in which the sacred and the secular jostled together and his life one where personal spirituality co-existed with utter exuberance. This juxtaposition is nicely summed up in one of his many letters to his beloved mother who acted as his confidante, personal assistant and general factotum, constantly forwarding on mail and other requested items when he was away on one of his many foreign jaunts. Writing from Baden-Baden in 1867, he upbraids her: 'You remembered my Prayer Book but forgot my collars which in this world are almost as necessary as the Prayer Book. I shall have to buy one or two over here and charge them to you.'[25] Prayer Book and collars were both important to Sullivan. If the latter epitomised his sociability and love of house parties and aristocratic society, the former testified to his abiding attachment to the liturgy and the faith of the church in which he had been brought up.

In many respects the softening, emollient quality at the heart of Sullivan's sacred music is very Victorian. It would be a mistake, however, to regard it simply as a product or reflection of the sentimentality of the age or the composer. Although he shared many of the characteristic values of his time, Sullivan was not a maudlin sentimentalist. This is indicated in another revealing comment in one of his letters to his mother, written in the aftermath of the death of his beloved brother, Fred: 'It is of no use grieving and repining. Those who are left behind have cares and responsibilities and must brace themselves up and face them courageously.'[26] This stoical attitude is reflected in his music which is first and foremost a natural and spontaneous expression of his own character and spiritual sensitivity. The note of reassurance that is at the heart of Sullivan's sacred music is there without artifice or contrivance. It came from the soul of the composer, just like the lost chord that came from the soul of the organ in his most famous song. It sprang from a simple trusting faith in a God of love who is endlessly gracious, forgiving and merciful. It can, indeed, be hailed as Divine Emollient.

Appendix 1

List of Hymn Tunes

Sullivan's congregational hymn and carol tunes listed chronologically by date of first publication. Harmonizations, adaptations and arrangements are in italics, original compositions in Roman type.

Date	Tune title	Words to which first set	Publication
1858	*Quando noctis medium*	When in silence and in shadow	HN
	Magnae Deus Potentiae	Almighty God, who from the flood	HN
	Iam Christus	Now Christ, ascending whence he came	HN
	Haec rite mundi gaudia	The world and all its boasted good	HN
1867	Hymn of the homeland	The homeland, the homeland	Good Words
	Mount Zion	Rock of Ages	P & H
	St Luke, later St Nathaniel	God moves in a mysterious way	P & H
	Formosa, or Falfield	Love Divine, all loves excelling	P & H
	Thou God of love	Thou God of love	A Hymnal
	Of thy love, or St Lucian	Of thy love, some gracious token	A Hymnal
1869	Heber, later Gennesareth[1]	When through the torn sail	Sarum

1 Although these tunes have the same name, they should not be confused. The first is an original tune by Sullivan and the second an arrangement by him of a tune attributed to Reginald Heber.

Date	Tune title	Words to which first set	Publication
	St Ann, or *St Anne*[2]	The son of God goes forth to war	STB
1871	*All This Night*	All this night bright angels sing	Christmas
	St Gertrude	Onward, Christian soldiers	Musical Times
1872	Lux in tenebris[3]	Lead, kindly Light	Sacred Songs
	Courage, brother	Courage brother, do not stumble	Good Words
	Angel Voices	Angel voices, ever singing	Hymnary
	Rest, later Venite ad me	Art thou weary, art thou languid	Hymnary
	St Kevin	Come ye faithful, raise the strain	Hymnary
	Lacrymae	Lord, in this, Thy mercy's day	Hymnary
	Propior Deo, or Aspiration	Nearer, my God, to Thee	Hymnary
	Lux mundi	O Jesu, Thou art standing	Hymnary
	Safe home	Safe home, safe home in port	Hymnary
	The long home, Gentle Shepherd or Tender Shepherd	Tender Shepherd, Thou hast still'd	Hymnary

---

2 Although this tune is usually spelled as ST ANNE, Sullivan always used the form ST ANN, and I have kept to his preferred spelling throughout the text of this book.

3 Sullivan's setting of J. H. Newman's 'Lead, Kindly Light' first appeared as one of his *Five Sacred Part Songs* published in 1871. There it was set in the key of G and given an optional 'Amen' at the end 'for use in church'. It is, strictly speaking, more of a part-song than a hymn tune, but it was incorporated in *Church Hymns with Tunes* in 1874, where it was set in F and with the Amen included as part of the text. It has appeared in several subsequent hymnals, usually in the Anthem section, and although it is more clearly a choir rather than a congregational item, it takes its place alongside other settings of Newman's classic text and is perhaps best treated as a hymn tune rather than a sacred part-song.

Date	Tune title	Words to which first set	Publication
1872	Fatherland, or St Edmund	We are but strangers here	Hymnary
	Welcome, happy morning, or Fortunatus	Welcome, happy morning	Hymnary
	St Mary Magdalene	Saviour, when in dust to Thee	Hymnary
1874	Audite audientes Me	I heard the voice of Jesus say	NCTB
	Promissio Patris	Our Blest Redeemer	NCTB
	Ecclesia	O where shall rest be found	NCTB
	Constance	Who trusts in God, a strong abode	NCTB
	Leominster	A few more years shall roll	Church Hymns
	Dulce sonans	At Thine altar, Lord, we gather	Church Hymns
	Leonburg	Before the ending of the day	Church Hymns
	Te Lucis	Before the ending of the day	Church Hymns
	Lucerne	Bow down Thine ear, Almighty Lord	Church Hymns
	St Theresa	Brightly gleams our banner	Church Hymns
	Resurrexit	Christ is risen!	Church Hymns
	Leipzig	Christ, whose glory fills the skies	Church Hymns
	Conway	Christians, awake	Church Hymns
	Stockport	Christians, awake	Church Hymns
	St Hilary	Church of Christ, whose glorious warfare	Church Hymns

Date	Tune title	Words to which first set	Publication
1874	Veni, Creator	Come, Holy Ghost, our souls inspire	Church Hymns
	Come Unto Me	Come unto me, ye weary	Church Hymns
	Munich	Come, ye faithful, raise the anthem	Church Hymns
	Coronae	Crown Him with many crowns	Church Hymns
	St Sylvester	Days and moments quickly flying	Church Hymns
	Old 104th	Disposer Supreme	Church Hymns
	Coena Domini	Draw nigh, and take the body of the Lord	Church Hymns
	Congleton	Draw nigh to thy Jerusalem	Church Hymns
	St Francis	Father of heaven, who hast created all	Church Hymns
	Chesterfield	Father, Son and Holy Ghost	Church Hymns
	Springtime	For all Thy love and goodness	Church Hymns
	Nearer Home	For ever with the Lord	Church Hymns
	Hernlein	Forty days and forty nights	Church Hymns
	Pilgrimage	From Egypt's bondage come	Church Hymns
	Heber[4]	From Greenland's icy mountains	Church Hymns
	Ultor Omnipotens	God the all-terrible	Church Hymns
	Luther's Hymn	Great God, what do I see and hear	Church Hymns

---

4 See note 1 on page 188.

Date	Tune title	Words to which first set	Publication
1874	*Old 137th*	Father, before Thy throne of light	Church Hymns
	Stuttgart	Hail! Thou source of ever blessing	Church Hymns
	Lux Eoi	Hark! A thrilling voice is sounding	Church Hymns
	St Patrick	He is gone – a cloud of light	Church Hymns
	Light	Holy Spirit, come in might	Church Hymns
	Hezekiah	House of our God	Church Hymns
	Hushed was the evening Hymn, later Samuel	Hushed was the evening hymn	Church Hymns
	Evelyn	In the hour of my distress	Church Hymns
	Bohemia	In the hour of trial	Church Hymns
	Noel	It came upon the midnight clear	Church Hymns
	Submission	Jerusalem, my happy home	Church Hymns
	Litany, No.1	Jesu, we are far away	Church Hymns
	Litany, No.2	Jesu, Life of those who die	Church Hymns
	Litany, No.3[5] (later *Lebbaeus*)	Jesu, in thy dying woes	Church Hymns
	Chemnitz	I see the crowd in Pilate's hall	Church Hymns
	Hanford	Jesu, my Saviour, look on me	Church Hymns

5 Litany, No. 3 appears in the 1902 Novello collection of Sullivan's hymn tunes as an original tune by him, set to 'Be Thou with us every day' and with *Hymns Ancient and Modern* given as its source. It does appear as the second tune to No. 466 in *Hymns Ancient and Modern* (1889 edition) set to a Litany of Penitence, where it is described as arranged by Sullivan, but it also makes an earlier appearance in *Church Hymns with Tunes* (1874), where it is set to 'Jesu, in thy dying woes' (No. 123) and attributed to Anon. but arranged by Sullivan. The attribution in the Novello collection seems to be wrong.

Date	Tune title	Words to which first set	Publication
1874	*Altenburg*	Joy, because the circling year	Church Hymns
	St Alban	Let me be with Thee	Church Hymns
	St Millicent	Let no tears today be shed	Church Hymns
	Ever faithful, ever sure	Let us with a gladsome mind	Church Hymns
	Ein' feste Burg	Lift up your heads, eternal gates	Church Hymns
	Oriel	Lo, he comes with clouds descending	Church Hymns
	Brunswick	Lord God, we worship Thee	Church Hymns
	Nun Danket	Now thank we all our God	Church Hymns
	Jam Lucis	Now that the daylight fills the sky	Church Hymns
	Adeste Fidelis	O, Come, all ye faithful	Church Hymns
	Daughters of Galilee	O Daughters blest of Galilee	Church Hymns
	Sunrise	O God, who canst not change nor fail	Church Hymns
	Winchester Old	O Jesu, our redeeming Lord	Church Hymns
	Crefeld	O Love, who formedst me	Church Hymns
	Saxony	O Merciful Creator, hear	Church Hymns
	Paradise	O Paradise! O Paradise!	Church Hymns
	Marlborough	O Strength and Stay	Church Hymns
	Corde Natus	Of the Father's love begotten	Church Hymns
	Babylon	Oh come, and mourn	Church Hymns
	Wearmouth	Oh sight for Angels to adore	Church Hymns

Date	Tune title	Words to which first set	Publication
1874	*Bavaria*	On this day when days began	Church Hymns
	Nurnberg	One with God the Father	Church Hymns
	Salzburg	Pleasant are Thy courts above	Church Hymns
	Praise, my soul	Praise my soul, the King of Heaven	Church Hymns
	Hilderstone	Praise to our God, whose bounteous hand	Church Hymns
	Vesper Hymn	Round the Lord in glory seated	Church Hymns
	Adoro Te	Saviour, again to Thy dear name	Church Hymns
	Pastor Bonus	Saviour, who Thy flock art feeding	Church Hymns
	Bevan	Servants of God awake	Church Hymns
	Christus	Show me not only Jesus dying	Church Hymns
	St Basil	Sing to the Lord a joyful song	Church Hymns
	Holy City	Sing Alleluia forth in duteous praise	Church Hymns
	Valete	Sweet Saviour! Bless us ere we go	Church Hymns
	Magdeburg	The dawn of God's new Sabbath	Church Hymns
	Rising	The Lord ascendeth up on high	Church Hymns
	Saints of God	The Saints of God, their conflict past	Church Hymns
	St James	The splendours of Thy glory, Lord	Church Hymns
	Kreuznach	The strain of joy and gladness	Church Hymns

Date	Tune title	Words to which first set	Publication
1874	*Zwingle*	This is the day the light was made	Church Hymns
	Golden Sheaves	To Thee, O Lord, our hearts we raise	Church Hymns
	St Gregory	Up to the throne of God is borne	Church Hymns
	St Charles	We come to Thee, dear Saviour	Church Hymns
	Missionary	We sing the glorious conquest	Church Hymns
	Verona	What our Father does is well	Church Hymns
	Bethlehem, also *Gabriel*	While shepherds watched their flocks	Church Hymns
	Caersalem	Who are these, like stars appearing	Church Hymns
	Clarence	Winter reigneth o'er the land	Church Hymns
	Parting	With the sweet word of peace	Church Hymns
	Ancient Litany	Yesterday with worship blest	Church Hymns
1875	Carrow	My God, I thank Thee who hast made	CP
1876	Upon the snow clad earth[6]	Upon the snow clad earth	Metzler
1880	Dominion Hymn	God bless our wide Dominion	Chappell

---

6 'Upon the snow clad earth' was published as a 'carol for Christmas-tide' by Metzler in 1876. It is included in this list rather than alongside other carol tunes listed as sacred part-songs because of its clearly hymnodic style and structure. It was, indeed, later taken up for William Walsham How's hymn, 'The joyous life that year by year'.

Date	Tune title	Words to which first set	Publication
1888	Unnamed[7]	Another sun shines bright	Children
	Unnamed	Palmy isles, like jewels	Children
	Unnamed	When dark grey clouds come rolling	Children
	Unnamed	The service due to God	Children
1897	Bishopgarth	O King of kings, whose reign of old	Jubilee Hymns
1902	Chapel Royal	O Love that wilt not let me go	Hymn Tunes
	Victoria	To mourn our dead we gather here	Hymn Tunes
	The roseate hues	The roseate hues of early dawn	Hymn Tunes
	Bolwell	Thou, to Whom the sick and dying	Hymn Tunes

(These last four tunes appear to have existed during Sullivan's life only in manuscript form and were first published after his death in the 1902 Novello edition of his hymn tunes. BOLWELL was used for a hymn to celebrate Edward VII's coronation in 1902 (pages 161–2) and appears in the 1910 *Primitive Methodist Hymnal Supplement* set to 'O God our Father, throned on high' by G. T. Coster.)

Total number of Sullivan hymn tunes: 61 original tunes and 75 arrangements.

---

7 The first edition of Sarah Wilson's *Hymns for Children* (1888) has printed on the title page 'Music by Sir Arthur Sullivan'. In the second edition, this is changed to 'Music by Sir Arthur Sullivan and Other Composers', which is a more accurate reflection of the provenance of the tunes. It also notes that the music is adapted from tunes in *Church Hymns with Tunes*. In fact, I cannot trace all the tunes which appear in *Hymns for Children* to this source. It does include several Sullivan tunes (ST LUKE, LUX MUNDI, ST KEVIN, CORONAE and ANGEL VOICES), set to newly written children's hymns as well as melodies attributed to Samuel Webbe and Mayer Lutz. There are four uncredited tunes, however, which do not seem to appear in *Church Hymns with Tunes*. I have listed them here as they appear to be original Sullivan compositions.

Observations

In several cases, more than one hymn text was set to the same tune on its first appearance in print – this was especially the case in *Church Hymns with Tunes*, where the same melody was used for as many as four different hymns. In these cases, I have only given the opening phrase of one of these hymns. I have not attempted to list the many other hymn texts subsequently set and widely sung to Sullivan tunes (such as 'Alleluia, Alleluia, hearts to heaven and voices raise' to LUX EOI), only those which they accompanied when first published.

The above list only includes tunes specifically written or arranged for a hymn or carol. It does not include melodies by Sullivan originally written for other purposes (e.g. secular songs and orchestral works) to which hymns and carols were later set, usually after the composer's death, such as the theme from the overture *In Memoriam* and King Henry's Song from his incidental music to Shakespeare's Henry VIII. Nor does it include sacred part-songs, anthems, liturgical settings and choruses which appeared in hymn books.

A harmonization of the tune BENEDICTION, later known as ELLERS, by E. J. Hopkins, which appeared in *Church Hymns with Tunes* set to the evening hymn 'Saviour, again to Thy dear name we raise', is credited to Sullivan in many modern hymn books. This seems to be a mistake. Hopkins's tune was first published as a unison tune in Robert Brown-Borthwick's *Supplemental Tune Book* in 1869. A harmonized version by Hopkins was published in the appendix to the *Bradford Tune Book* in 1872. The arrangement found in *Church Hymns with Tunes*, and subsequently adopted in many hymnals, is not credited to Sullivan in any edition of *Church Hymns with Tunes*, and it seems likely that it was the work of Hopkins. The false attribution to Sullivan may well have arisen because of confusion with the other tune to which 'Saviour, again' was set in *Church Hymns with Tunes*, ADORO TE, which was, indeed, harmonized by him.

Sources in Chronological Order

HN	*Accompanying Harmonies to the Hymnal Noted*, Part II, ed. T. Helmore (Novello, 1858).
P & H	*Psalms and Hymns for Divine Worship*, collection for Presbyterian Church of England (James Nisbet, 1867).
A Hymnal	*A Hymnal, chiefly from the Book of Praise*, ed. John Hullah (Macmillan, 1867).

Sarum	*The Sarum Hymnal*, ed. H. Nelson (Brown & Aylward, Salisbury, 1869).
STB	*Supplemental Hymn and Tune Book*, ed. R. Brown-Borthwick, 1869.
Christmas	*Christmas Carols New and Old*, Second Series, ed. H. R. Bramley & J. Stainer (London: Novello, Ewer & Co., 1871).
Sacred Songs	*Five Sacred Part Songs* (Boosey, 1871).
Hymnary	*The Hymnary: A Book of Church Song*, ed. W. Cooke & B. Webb, music editor J. Barnby (Novello, 1872).
NCTB	*New Church Tune Book* (Shaw, 1874).
Church Hymns	*Church Hymns with Tunes*, ed. A. Sullivan (SPCK, 1874).
CP	*The Congregational Psalmist*, ed. H. Allen (Hodder & Stoughton, 1875).
Children	*Hymns for Children by Sarah Wilson, music by Arthur Sullivan* (Eyre and Spottiswoode, 1888).
Jubilee Hymns	*Jubilee Hymns for Queen Victoria* (Eyre & Spottiswoode, 1897).
Hymn Tunes	*Hymn Tunes Composed by Arthur Sullivan* (Novello, 1902).

Appendix 2

Alternative Lyrics for 'Onward, Christian Soldiers'

Keen not to lose a good tune, those offended by the perceived militarism of Sabine Baring Gould's words have been supplying alternative words to go with ST GERTRUDE for a long time. Among the first was the American Unitarian minister, Frederick Hosmer, who in 1908 came up with:

> Forward through the ages,
> In unbroken line,
> Move the faithful spirits
> At the call divine.

More recent attempts have included David Wright's well-intentioned 'Onward, Christian pilgrims, Working hard for peace' and Derek Rawcliffe's 'Battle hymn of the gay community' written for a festival of the Lesbian and Gay Christian Movement at Southwark Cathedral in 1996:

> Onward, Christian homos,
> Marching out with pride.
> Queers and fags and drag queens
> Walking side by side.

Gilbert and Sullivan scholar Harry Benford noted down this version sung as part of a pitch to promote overseas missionary work in a church in the United States in 1999:

> Mission opportunity
> Is our song today.
> Bring to Christ your chequebook,
> So you, too, can pay.
> If you cannot go abroad,
> Send your cash instead.

This through countless ages
Helps to lift the load.
Mission opportunity
Is our song today.
Bring to Christ your chequebook,
Please do not delay.[1]

A parody whose provenance I have been unable to trace expresses the frustrations of those who seek to reform the Church:

Like a mighty tortoise,
Moves the Church of God;
Brothers we are treading
Where we've always trod.
We are all divided,
Not one body we,
We are long in doctrine,
Short in charity.

Perhaps most satisfying of all the words written with ST GERTRUDE in mind comes from the pen of Gordon Reynolds, who was organist and master of the choristers at the Chapel Royal, Hampton Court, from 1967 until his death in 1995. It provides a splendid exposition of just how Sullivan achieves such a compelling tune:

Arthur Seymour Sullivan
Worked out in his head
How to keep us marching
With a steady tread.
Tonic first, then Dominant,
That's the way it's done,
Wrapped up in a chorus
Sung by everyone (two, three, four):
Onward, Christian soldiers!
Hear the organ roar –
Lest the congregation
Reach the end before.[2]

---

1 *SASS Magazine* No.48 (Summer 1999), p. 11.
2 G. Reynolds, *Cassock Pocket Book*, Croydon: Royal School of Church Music, 1979.

Appendix 3

Sullivan's Possible Involvement in

ST CLEMENT

ST CLEMENT, inseparably associated with John Ellerton's 'The day, Thou Gavest, Lord, is ended' remains one of the most popular hymn tunes in Britain. It first appeared as the second tune for Ellerton's hymn in *Church Hymns with Tunes*, the book that Sullivan edited in 1874. It was attributed there to Clement Scholefield (1839–1904), an Anglican clergyman, who served curacies at Hove and Chelsea and went on to become chaplain at Eton and vicar of Holy Trinity, Knightsbridge. This attribution has been followed in all subsequent hymnals. Could it be, however, that this extraordinarily popular melody may at least in part have been composed by Sullivan?

The suggestion that 'Sullivan had a larger hand in ST CLEMENT than has been, or can ever definitively be, credited to him' was first made by the composer and editor, Mervyn Horder, in an article in the Hymn Society Bulletin in 1994.[1] He pointed out that Scholefield, who was an entirely self-taught musician, was curate at St Peter's, Cranley Gardens, when Sullivan was organist there. The two men became close friends and six of Scholefield's tunes appeared in *Church Hymns with Tunes*, all apparently commissioned by Sullivan and written expressly for this book. Aside from ST CLEMENT, they are undistinguished and unmemorable, as indeed are the 35 other hymn tunes, which Scholefield wrote in the course of his life. Not one of them has the triple time signature, which makes ST CLEMENT so lilting and memorable. Horder gently posed the question as to whether on the evidence of these other tunes it was likely that Scholefield had come up with ST CLEMENT unaided. He also invited hymnologists to 'take a dozen of Sullivan's own tunes, and play them in succession with ST CLEMENT somewhere in the middle of them, and see what a close fit it is musically'.

---

1 M. Horder, 'A Note on St Clement', *Bulletin of The Hymn Society of Great Britain and Ireland* 200 (July 1994), pp. 67–8.

Reading Horder's article set me thinking about other respects in which
ST CLEMENT is Sullivanesque. Its reception at the hands of the ecclesiastical and musical establishment was certainly similar to that of several
of Sullivan's tunes. When the editors of *Hymns Ancient and Modern*,
contemplating a major revision of the hymnal in the 1890s, proposed
dropping ST CLEMENT, Sullivan's great friend and defender, William
Walsham How, Bishop of Wakefield, strongly protested. He doubtless felt
about it what he wrote concerning another popular tune that they wished
to drop, ALSTONE, indissolubly linked with Mrs Alexander's children's
hymn 'We are but little children weak', that 'it may not be high class
music but it has entered into the whole church life of the land'.[2] The editor of *Hymns Ancient and Modern,* W. H. Frere, retorted in respect of ST
CLEMENT, 'It is quite true that people like waltz-tunes but does the Bishop
seriously hold that that is a reason for providing them?'[3] Ralph Vaughan
Williams consigned ST CLEMENT to his 'Chamber of Horrors' appendix
in the 1906 *English Hymnal* along with Sullivan's GOLDEN SHEAVES and
other examples of the high Victorian hymn tune. In its place, he paired
'The day, Thou Gavest' with LES COMMANDMENTS DE DIEU, based on
a melody in the 1543 Genevan Psalter. ST CLEMENT suffered further cen-
sure in 1932 when the Archbishop of Canterbury, Cosmo Gordon Lang,
suggested in a letter to *The Times* that it was high time that this 'feeble
waltz tune' was dismissed from service.

Somewhat provocatively, I included ST CLEMENT in the compilation
of Sullivan hymn tunes that I put together for the Hymn Makers CD in
2000. I wrote in the sleeve notes: 'It seems quite likely that the amateur
and inexperienced Scholefield was helped over ST CLEMENT by Sullivan,
who with characteristic generosity probably allowed the young curate to
take all the credit for a melody that would become one of the all-time
favourite Victorian hymn tunes.'[4] I made a similar claim in my sermon
in the BBC Radio 4 Sunday Worship service broadcast from the Buxton
Gilbert and Sullivan Festival, prompting *The Times* to run a news story
with the heading 'Is this the hymn thou gavest, Sullivan?' My thesis was
strongly challenged by John Harper, director-general of the Royal School
of Church Music, who was quoted as saying:

I cannot believe that a priest would name a tune after his place of birth
– St Clement's Church, Edgbaston – nor that he would continue to

2 Hymns Ancient and Modern Archives, Norwich. Letter from How, 12 June 1897.
3 Hymns Ancient and Modern Archives, Letter from Frere, 21 June 1897.
4 *The Hymn Makers: Arthur Seymour Sullivan*, Eastbourne: Kingsway Music, 2000,
CD booklet.

exercise his personal copyright, unless he had actually composed it. Admittedly, no other tune by him was such a success but that is not an unknown occurrence with others. If Sullivan had a hand, it may have been to improve the harmony. But my overriding feeling is that Scholefield would not have named his 'newborn' tune after his own place of birth had it been 'adopted'.[5]

In fact, I am not sure that Professor Harper is right in suggesting that the name ST CLEMENT derives from Scholefield's place of birth. The only church dedicated to St Clement that I can identify in the vicinity of Edgbaston, where Scholefield was born in 1839, is one in Nechells Park Road, which was not built until 1859. I think it more likely that, as with ST GERTRUDE, the name was, in the words of Richard Watson, 'a little joke by Arthur Sullivan'.[6] More recently, my suggestion that Sullivan may have been involved in the tune has found some support from the *Daily Telegraph* music critic, Rupert Christiansen:

> The waltzing tune, 'St Clement', is usually credited to the Revd. Clement Scholefield, commissioned by Arthur Sullivan for a collection of new hymn tunes. Ian Bradley plausibly argues that Scholefield's other compositions are so feeble that Sullivan might have acted as more than editor, pointing out that its 'highly sentimental streak and triple time signature' suggests the musical idiom of the Savoy Operettas.[7]

Perhaps the most persuasive argument in favour of the idea that Sullivan may have been responsible for suggesting the melodic outline of ST CLEMENT comes from David Owen Norris, who emphatically rejects the description of it as a waltz tune. He has recently pointed out that only three Victorian hymn tunes begin with a rising sixth from the dominant to the mediant and then rise further up to the dominant before falling back to the tonic – they are CRIMOND, GOLDEN SHEAVES and ST CLEMENT. In his words, 'This is a shape deeply embedded in Sullivan's mind – it is found in the phrase "But it struck one chord of music" in *The Lost Chord* and in the refrain to his song *Sweethearts*.'[8]

---

5 *The Times*, 25 November 2000.

6 R. Cronin, A. Chapman & A.Harrison (eds), *A Companion to Victorian Poetry*, Oxford, Blackwell, 2002, p. 144.

7 *Daily Telegraph*, 22 September 2007.

8 Talk to SASS Festival, Cirencester, September 2011, expanded in emails to the author, November 2011.

We shall never know what role if any Sullivan played in the composing or arranging of ST CLEMENT. What we can be certain of is that he was responsible for its first appearance in print and for introducing it to the British hymn-singing public who have continued to love it, despite the best efforts of elitist clergy and musicians to take it away from them. There is one further curious fact that I feel I should add before resting my case. Browsing in the library of Iona Abbey in May 2011, I came across a book on Scottish church music published in 1891. It notes that in the first edition of the 1885 *Scottish Hymnal* a tune by Sullivan, his Litany No. 2, was wrongly attributed to Clement Scholefield. Could a similar misattribution have occurred when ST CLEMENT first appeared in *Church Hymns with Tunes*? It seems highly unlikely but stranger things have been known.

Appendix 4

Sullivan's Sacred Songs

Part-Songs

I sing the birth	Ben Jonson	Boosey, 1868
The long day closes	Henry Chorley	Boosey, 1871
It came upon the midnight clear	Edmund Sears	Boosey, 1871
Lead, kindly light[1]	John Henry Newman	Boosey, 1871
Say watchman, what of the night?	Isaiah 21.11	Boosey, 1871
The way is long and dreary	Adelaide Procter	Boosey, 1871
Through sorrow's path	H. Kirk-Whyte	Boosey, 1871
Hark, what mean those holy voices	John Cawood	Patey & Willis, 1883

Solo Songs

O Israel	Hosea 14.1–2	Novello, 1855
Sweet day	George Herbert	Metzler, 1864
Thou art lost to me	Anonymous	Boosey, 1865
Will he come?	Adelaide Procter	Boosey, 1865
Give (See the rivers flowing)	Adelaide Procter	Boosey, 1867
The mother's dream	Revd William Barnes	Boosey, 1868
The village chimes	C. J. Rowe	Boosey, 1870
The sailor's grave	Henry Lyte	Cramer, 1872

---

1 This is the same setting listed in Appendix 1 as a hymn tune.

The First Departure[2]	Edward Monro	Cramer, 1874
Thou Art Weary	Adelaide Procter	Chappell, 1874
We've ploughed our land	Anonymous	Novello, 1875
The Distant Shore	W. S. Gilbert	Chappell, 1875
Christmas Bells at sea	C. L. Kenney	Novello, 1875
Thou'rt Passing Hence	Felicia Hemans	Chappell, 1875
The Lost Chord	Adelaide Procter	Boosey, 1877
St Agnes' Eve	Alfred Tennyson	Boosey, 1879
Ever	Clara Bloomfield Moore	Chappell, 1887
Longing for Home	Jean Ingelow	Novello, 1904

---

2 Frederic Weatherly wrote 'The Chorister' for this tune. It was published by Metzler in 1876.

Appendix 5

The Prodigal Son: Musical Numbers and Biblical Sources

1 Introduction

2 Chorus   There is joy in the presence of the
                                   angels of God (Luke 15.10;
                                   Psalm 103.13; Rev. 7.16, 17).

3 Solo (Tenor)   A certain man had two sons
                                   (Luke 15.11, 12; Eccles. 3.12, 13).

4 Recitative and Aria (Bass)   My son, attend to my words
                                   (Prov. 4.18, 20; 3.6, 9).

5 Recitative (Soprano)   And the younger son gathered all
                                   together (Luke 15.13).

6 Solo (Tenor) and Chorus   THE REVEL – Let us eat and drink
                                   (Isa. 22.13; 56.12).

7 Recitative (Contralto) and   Woe unto them that rise up early in
   Chorus   the morning (Isa. 5.11, 12; 24.8).

8 Song (Contralto)   Love not the world (1 John 2.17).

9 Recitative (Soprano)   And when he had spent all, there
                                   arose a mighty famine
                                   (Luke 15.14–16).

10 Aria (Soprano)   O that thou hadst hearkened to my
                                   commandments (Isa. 48.18).

11 Solo (Tenor)   How many hired servants of my
                                   father's (Luke 15.17–19).

12 Chorus   There is joy in the presence of the
                                   angels of God (Luke 15.10;
                                   Psalm 51.17).

13	Recitative (Soprano) and Duet (Tenor and Bass)	And he arose and came to his father (Luke 15.20, 21; Gen. 45.28; 46.30).
14	Recitative and Aria (Bass)	Bring forth the best robe and put it on him (Luke 15.2; Psalm 103.13; 66.20).
15	Chorus	O that men would praise the Lord for His goodness (Psalm 107.4–6, 8).
16	Recitative and Aria (Tenor)	No chastening for the present seemeth too joyous (Heb. 12.11, 6; Psalm 39.6, 11).
17	Quartet *(unaccompanied)*	The Lord is nigh unto them that are of contrite heart (Psalm 34.18; Isa. 57.18).
18	Chorus	Thou, O Lord art our Father, our Redeemer (Isa. 63.16).

.

Appendix 6

The Light of the World:
Musical Numbers and Biblical Sources

The First Part

1	Prologue (Chorus)	There shall come forth a rod (Isa. 11.1–2; 61.15; 25.8).

Bethlehem

2	Introduction and Recitative	There were shepherds (Luke 2.8–12).
3	Chorus of Angels	Glory to God (Luke 2.14).
4	Chorus of Shepherds	Let us now go even into Bethlehem (Luke 2.15).
5	Solo (Bass)	Blessed art thou (Luke 1.42, 32).
6	Air (Soprano)	My soul doth magnify the Lord (Luke 1.46–49).
7*		
8	Chorus of Shepherds	The whole earth is at rest (Isa. 14.7; 25.9).
9	Solo (Contralto)	Arise and take the young child (Matt. 2.13).
10	Solo (Soprano) and Chorus	In Rama was there a voice heard (Jer. 31.15).
11	Air (Tenor)	Refrain thy voice from weeping (Jer. 31.16).
12	Solo (Contralto)	Arise and take the young child (Matt. 2.20; Isa. 65.19)
13	Chorus	I will pour my spirit (Isa. 44.3; Micah 5.4).

Nazareth – In the Synagogue

14	Solo (Baritone) and Chorus	The spirit of the Lord (Luke 4.18–19, 21; Matt. 13.54–55; Luke 4.22–29; John 12.38–40, 44).
15	Quintet	Doubtless thou art our Father (Isa. 63.16).
16	Solo (Baritone)	Blessed are they that are persecuted (Matt. 5.10; Luke 7.37).
17	Chorus	He maketh the sun to rise (Matt. 5.45).

Lazarus

18	Duet (Tenor and Baritone)	Lord, behold he whom thou lovest (John 11.3–16).
19	Solo (Contralto) and Chorus	Weep ye not for the dead (Jer. 22.10; 31.13).
20	Scena (Soprano)	Lord, if thou had'st been here (John 11.21–26, 34).
21	Chorus	Behold how He loved him (John 11.36–37).
22	Solo (Baritone)	Said I not unto thee (John 11.40; Isa. 26.19).
23	Chorus	The grave cannot praise thee (Isa. 38.18–19).

The Way to Jerusalem

24	Solos (Bass, Tenor, Baritone)	Perceive ye how we prevail nothing (John 12.19; 11.48, 50; Luke 13.33; 18.31).
25	Chorus of Children	Hosanna to the Son of David (Matt. 21.9).
26	Air (Soprano)	Tell ye the daughter of Zion (Matt. 21.5; Isa. 62.11, Luke 19.39–40).
27	Chorus of Disciples	Blessed be the Kingdom (Mark 11.10; Luke 19.42).
28	Trio and Chorus	Hosanna to the Son of David (Mark 11.9–10; Luke 19.38).

The Second Part

Jerusalem

29	Overture	
30	Solo (Baritone)	When the Son of man shall come (Matt. 25.31–46).
31	Solos (Tenor and Bass) and Chorus	Is not this He whom they seek to kill (John 7.25–27, 31, 41–42, 46–52).
32	Chorus of Women	The hour is come (Matt. 26.45; Psalm 59.3; Jer. 26.11; Lam. 5.17).
33	Solo (Baritone)	Daughters of Jerusalem (Luke 23.28; Matt. 24.21; Luke 21.28; John 16.33).
34	Quartet	Yea, though I walk through the valley (Psalm 23.4).
35	Chorus	Men and brethren (Acts 13.26; 2.22–23; 13.29; Isa. 53.9, 12).

At the Sepulchre

36	Recitative (Soprano)	Where have they laid Him (Mark 16.3; 2 Sam. 12.23; Jer. 45.3).
37	Aria (Soprano)	Lord, why hidest thou thy face (Psalm 88.14, 18; Gen. 25.32; Psalm 44.23).
38	Recitative (Contralto)	Why weepest thou (John 20.13; Eph. 5.14; Luke 24.5–6).
39	Aria (Contralto)	The Lord is risen (Luke 24.34; Rev. 21.3–4).
40	Chorus	The Lord is risen (Acts 2.32; 2 Cor. 5.17; 2 Cor. 4.6).
41	Solo (Tenor)	If ye be risen with Christ (Col. 3.1; 1 Tim. 6.12; Heb. 12.2).
42	Finale (Chorus)	Him hath God exalted (Acts 5.31; Rev. 12.10; Gal. 1.4–5).

7* is omitted from the score

Appendix 7

Sullivan's Anthems and Liturgical Pieces

Anthems in Order of Composition with Source of Text

By the Waters of Babylon (Psalm 137), 1850, unpublished.

Sing unto the Lord (Psalm 96), 1855, unpublished.

Bless the Lord, O my soul (Psalm 103), 1856, unpublished.

We have heard with our ears (Psalm 44), 1860, revised version published
by Novello 1865.

O Love the Lord (Psalm 31), published by Novello 1864.

O taste and see (Psalm 34), published by Novello 1867.

O God, Thou art worthy (Psalm 20), 1867, published by Novello 1871.

I will lay me down in peace (Psalm 4), 1868, published by Novello 1910.

Rejoice in the Lord (Psalm 33), published by Boosey 1868.

The Strain Upraise in Joy and Praise (Balbulus Notker, translated by J. M.
Neale), published by Novello 1869.[1]

Sing, O Heavens (Isaiah chapters 49 and 25, Psalms 85 and 45), published
by Novello 1869.

I will worship towards thy holy temple (Psalm 138), published by Boosey,
1871.

I will mention the loving-kindnesses of the Lord (Isaiah 63), published by
Novello 1875.

I will sing of Thy power (Psalm 59), published by Novello 1877.

Hearken unto me, my people (Isaiah 51), published by Novello 1877.

Turn Thy face from my sins (Psalm 51), published by Novello 1878.

---

1 'The strain upraise' is usually listed among Sullivan's hymn tunes (as in A. Jacobs,
Arthur Sullivan: A Victorian Musician, 2nd edn, Aldershot: Scolar Press, 1992, p. 461).
However, it is much more appropriately placed among his anthems, being a complex set-
ting of words by the ninth-century Benedictine monk, Balbulus Notker, translated by J.
M. Neale, clearly designed to be sung by choirs rather than congregations and involving
lengthy passages of plainchant. It was commissioned for and first published in Brown-
Borthwick's *Supplemental Hymn and Tune Book*, but its subsequent appearances in print
have largely been in anthem books.

There is none like unto the God of Jeshurun (Deuteronomy 33.26), published by Novello 1882.[2]

Who is like unto Thee? (Exodus 15), published by Novello 1883.

Wreaths for our graves (Mrs L. Massey), 1898.[3]

Liturgical Settings in Order of Composition

Jubilate, Kyrie and Te Deum in D, published by Novello in 1866.

Festival Te Deum, published by Novello 1872.

Mercy and truth are met together – arrangement of Russian church chant, published by Novello 1874.

Turn Thee again, O Lord – arrangement of Russian church chant, published by Novello 1874.

Chant for Psalm 150, unpublished, 1887.

Te Deum Laudamus (A Thanksgiving for Victory), 1900, published by Novello 1902.

---

2 'There is none like unto the God of Jeshurun' is usually described as an unfinished anthem by John Goss, which Sullivan completed. In fact, only a small part of the opening section was set by Goss, who left few intentions of what he intended for the rest of the work. The anthem as set is substantially the original work of Sullivan.

3 'Wreaths for our graves' is usually listed as a part-song (as in Jacobs, *Arthur Sullivan*, p. 462), but it was written as an anthem and is better treated as such. It is listed as an anthem in the article on Sullivan as a church musician which appeared in the *Musical Times* on 1 January 1901.

Notes

Abbreviations used in notes

SASS   Sir Arthur Sullivan Society
PML   Pierpont Morgan Library, New York, Gilbert and Sullivan Collection

Preface and Acknowledgements

1 E. Walker, *A History of Music in England*, Oxford: Clarendon Press, 1907, p. 283.

1 Things Are Seldom What They Seem: Changing Views of Sullivan's Sacred Music

1 A. Jacobs, *Arthur Sullivan: A Victorian Musician*, 2nd edn, Aldershot: Scolar Press, 1992, p. 223.
2 H. Orel, *Gilbert and Sullivan: Interviews and Recollections*, Iowa City: University of Iowa Press, 1994, p. 118.
3 *The Times*, 29 November 1900.
4 *Musical Times*, 1 December 1900, p. 787.
5 *Musical Times*, 1 January 1901, p. 21.
6 H. Sullivan & N. Flower, *Sir Arthur Sullivan*, London: Cassell, 1927, p. 39.
7 E. Smyth, *Impressions that Remained: Memoirs*, London: Longmans, Green, 1920, II, p. 232.
8 A. H. Godwin, *Gilbert & Sullivan: A Critical Appreciation of the Savoy Operas*, London: Dent, 1926, p. 50.
9 D. Scott, *The Singing Bourgeois: Songs of the Victorian Drawing Room and Parlour*, 2nd edn, Aldershot: Ashgate, 2001, p. 211.
10 J. Bennett, *Forty Years of Music, 1865–1905*, London: Methuen, 1908, p. 65.
11 H. Pearson, *Gilbert and Sullivan*, Harmondsworth: Penguin Books, 1950, pp. 64, 65.
12 J. Dibble, *C. Hubert Parry: His Life and Music*, Oxford: Clarendon Press, 1992, p. 161.
13 C. V. Stanford, *Studies and Memories*, London: Archibald Constable, 1908, pp. 162, 168–9.

14 This process is described in some detail in B. W. Findon, *Sir Arthur Sullivan: His Life and Music*, London: James Nisbet, 1904, pp. 157–69.

15 *Cornhill Magazine*, March 1901, pp. 300–9.

16 J. N. Moore, *Edward Elgar: A Creative Life*, Oxford: Oxford University Press, 1984, p. 479.

17 E. Walker, *A History of Music in England*, Oxford: Clarendon Press, 1907, pp. 293–4.

18 *Hymn Society Bulletin* 2:7 (April 1949), p. 105.

19 *Hymn Society Bulletin*, 20 (July 1942), p. 7.

20 *Hymn Society Bulletin* 2:7 (April 1949), p. 109.

21 *Hymn Society Bulletin* 2:7 (April 1949), p. 110.

22 G. Hughes, *The Music of Arthur Sullivan*, London: Macmillan, 1960, pp. 13, 16, 66, 82, 162 & 166.

23 A. Hutchings, *Church Music in the Nineteenth Century*, London: Herbert Jenkins, 1967, pp. 151, 18, 109.

24 K. Long, *The Music of the English Church*, London: Hodder & Stoughton, 1972, p. 366.

25 *SASS Magazine* 41 (Autumn 1995), p. 23.

26 M. Saremba (ed.), *Sullivan Perspektiven*, Essen: Odlib Verlag, 2012, p. 132.

27 Jacobs, *Arthur Sullivan*, p. 410.

28 Jacobs, *Arthur Sullivan*, p. 281; radio interview quoted in M. Saremba, 'Edward Elgar and Arthur Sullivan', *Elgar Society Journal* 17:4 (April 2012), p. 13.

29 *Hymn Society Bulletin* 193 (October 1992), p. 175.

30 *SASS Magazine* 41 (Autumn 1995), p. 25.

31 Sullivan & Flower, *Sir Arthur Sullivan*, p. 18.

32 Jacobs, *Arthur Sullivan*, p. 44; H. Saxe Wyndham, *Arthur Seymour Sullivan*, London: Kegan Paul, 1926, p. 88.

33 P. Young, *Sir Arthur Sullivan*, London: J. M. Dent, 1971, p. 52.

34 Young, *Sir Arthur Sullivan*, p. 52.

35 Letter, 31 January 1885. Ms copy in possession of Mrs Katie Trehrene.

36 Jacobs, *Arthur Sullivan*, p. 221; Sullivan & Flower, *Sir Arthur Sullivan*, pp. 218, 219.

37 *SASS Journal* 41 (Autumn 1995), p. 26.

38 *New York Herald*, 23 October 1879.

39 *SASS Journal* 41 (Autumn 1995), p. 26.

40 E. Dicey, 'Recollections of Arthur Sullivan', *Fortnightly Review* 77 (January 1905), p. 80.

41 S. Hayes, *Uncle Arthur: The California Connection*, 2nd edn, SASS, 2008.

42 H. Lytton, *The Secrets of a Savoyard*, London: Jarrolds, n.d., p. 62.

43 C. V. Stanford, *Pages From an Unwritten Diary*, London: Edward Arnold, 1914, p. 247.

44 Jacobs, *Arthur Sullivan*, p. 40.

45 K. Jackson, *Beyond the Craft*, London: Lewis Masonic, 2005, p. 12.

46 Jackson, *Beyond the Craft*, p. 3.

47 M. Saremba, 'Brother Sir Arthur Sullivan – Sullivan and Freemasonry', *SASS Magazine* 61 (Winter 2005), p. 14. Sullivan's Freemasonry is also discussed by Yasha Beresiner in 'Gilbert and Sullivan Musical Masons', *Review of Freemasonry*, 13 January 2011, at <http://www.freemasons-freemasonry.com/beresiner12.html.>

48 *Masonic Illustrated* (January 1901), p. 69.
49 Saremba, 'Brother Sir Arthur Sullivan', p. 14.
50 PML: Letter to his mother simply dated Sunday 1875, PML.

2 Are You in Sentimental Mood? The Religious, Cultural and Musical Context

1 O. Chadwick, *The Victorian Church*, London: A & C Black, 1972, Part 2, pp. 218–38.
2 G. St Aubyn, *Souls in Torment: The Victorian Crisis of Faith*, London: Sinclair-Stevenson, 2011, p. 231.
3 T. Larsen, *A People of One Book: The Bible and the Victorians*, Oxford University Press, 2011.
4 See Aubyn, *Souls in Torment* and J. C. Livingston, *Religious Thought in the Victorian Age: Challenges and Reconception*, London: Continuum, 2007; for a riposte, see T. Larsen, *Crisis of Doubt: Honest Faith in Nineteenth Century England*, Oxford: Oxford University Press, 2006.
5 F. Kaplan, *Sacred Tears: Sentimentality in Victorian Literature*, Princeton: Princeton University Press, 1987, p. 6. See also M. Bell, *Sentimentalism, Ethics and the Culture of Feeling*, Basingstoke: Palgrave Macmillan, 2000; J. Howard, 'What is Sentimentality?', *American Literary History* Vol. 11 (1999); P. Schlike, 'Sentiment', in *Oxford Reader's Companion to Dickens*, Oxford: Oxford University Press, 1999.
6 M. W. Driver, *Victorian Song: From Dive to Drawing Room*, London: Phoenix House, 1955, p. 140.
7 H. N. Fairchild, *Religious Trends in English Poetry*, Vol. IV, 1830–1880, New York: Columbia University Press, 1957, p. viii.
8 W. E. Houghton, *The Victorian Frame of Mind*, New Haven: Yale University Press, 1957, p. 96.
9 Houghton, *The Victorian Frame of Mind*, p. 97.
10 Houghton, *The Victorian Frame of Mind*, p.277
11 Houghton, *The Victorian Frame of Mind*, p.276.
12 A. Jacobs, *Arthur Sullivan: A Victorian Musician*, 2nd edn, Aldershot: Scolar Press, 1992, p. 410.
13 Fairchild, *Religious Trends*, p. 17.
14 R. L. Todd, *Mendelssohn: A Life in Music*, Oxford: Oxford University Press, 2005, p. xxvii.
15 C. Eatock, *Mendelssohn and Victorian England*, Aldershot: Ashgate, 2001, p. 137.
16 W. Mellers, *Romanticism and the Twentieth Century*, London: Salisbury Square, 1957, p. 31; S. Banfield, 'The Artist and Society', in N. Temperley (ed.), *Music in Britain: The Romantic Age 1800–1914*, London: Athlone Press, 1981, p. 23.
17 Eatock, *Mendelssohn*, p. 128.
18 M. Hughes, *The English Musical Renaissance*, 2nd edn, Manchester: Manchester University Press, 2001, p. 9.
19 D. Burrows, 'Victorian England: An Age of Expansion', in J. Samson (ed.), *Man and Music: The Late Romantic Era*, London: Macmillan, 1991, p. 281.

20 Eatock, *Mendelssohn*, p. 128.

21 Jacobs, *Arthur Sullivan*, p. 3.

22 For a discussion of tonic sol-fa and its impact, see C. E. McGuire, *Music and Victorian Philanthropy: The Tonic Sol Fa Movement*, Cambridge: Cambridge University Press, 2009. For the spread of singing in Victorian Britain, see I. Bradley, *Abide With Me: The World of Victorian Hymns*, London: SCM Press, 1997, pp. 30–7.

23 P. Drummond, *The Provincial Music Festival in England, 1784–1914*, Aldershot: Ashgate, 2011, p. 1.

24 Bradley, *Abide With Me*, p. 30.

25 On the choral revival and its impact on church music, see Bradley, *Abide With Me*, Chapter 2; B. Rainbow, *The Choral Revival in the Anglican Church*, London: Barrie & Jenkins, 1970 and N. Temperley, *The Music of the English Parish Church*, Vol. 1, Cambridge: Cambridge University Press, 1979.

26 Hughes, *English Musical Renaissance*, p. 7.

27 H. R. Haweis, *Music and Morals*, 14th edn, London: W. H. Allen, n.d., p. 526.

28 Haweis, *Music and Morals*, p. 111.

29 Haweis, *Music and Morals*, p. 117.

30 Haweis, *Music and Morals*, p. 118.

31 Haweis, *Music and Morals*, pp. 113–14; H. R. Haweis, *My Musical Life*, London: 1898, p. 208.

32 Haweis, *Music and Morals*, p. 112.

33 Haweis, *Music and Morals*, p. 506.

34 Haweis, *Music and Morals*, pp. 111–12.

35 Haweis, *Music and Morals*, p. 507.

36 Haweis, *Music and Morals*, p. 498.

3 When I First Put this Uniform On: Sullivan's Upbringing and Formative Years

1 A. Lawrence, *Sir Arthur Sullivan: Life Story, Letters & Reminiscences*, London: James Bowden, 1899, pp. 9–10.

2 *Gazetteer and New Daily Advertiser*, 6 March 1772. I owe this reference to David Eden, who discusses Sullivan's antecedents in 'From York Town to Bolwell', *SASS Magazine* 79 (Summer 2012), pp. 21–5.

3 R. E. Francillon, *Mid-Victorian Memories*, London: Hodder & Stoughton, 1914, p. 194.

4 A. Jacobs, *Arthur Sullivan: A Victorian Musician*, 2nd edn, Aldershot: Scolar Press, 1992, pp. 454–5. *The Jewish Chronicle* confidently asserted Sullivan's Jewish ancestry in its review of his opera *Ivanhoe*, 6 February 1891. Jacobs's is not the most recent biography of Sullivan – that accolade goes to Meinhard Saremba's *Arthur Sullivan: Ein Komponistenleben im viktorianischen England*, Wilhelmshaven: F. Noetzel, 1993.

5 P. Young, *Sir Arthur Sullivan*, London: J. M. Dent, 1971, p. 54.

6 6 October 1856, quoted Lawrence, *Sir Arthur Sullivan*, p. 11.

7 Lawrence, *Sir Arthur Sullivan*, pp. 236–7.

8 Lawrence, *Sir Arthur Sullivan*, p. 6.

9 F. Helmore, *Memoir of the Rev Thomas Helmore*, London: J. Masters, 1891, p. 73. See also B. Rainbow, *The Choral Revival in the Anglican Church*, London: Barrie & Jenkins, 1970, p. 77.

10 Helmore, *Memoir*, 1891, p. 73.

11 D. Eden, *Gilbert and Sullivan: Creative Conflict*, Madison: Farleigh Dickinson University Press, 1986, p. 175.

12 For the history of the institution, see D. Baldwin, *The Chapel Royal*, London: Duckworth, 1990.

13 Rainbow, *Choral Revival*, p. 76.

14 'The Chapel Royal Days of Arthur Sullivan', *Musical Times*, 1 March 1901, p. 167.

15 *Musical Times*, 1 December 1900, p. 785.

16 *St Michael's College Magazine* (December 1918), reprinted *SASS Magazine*, 72 (Summer 2009), p. 22 and in D. Bland, *Ouseley and His Angels: The Life of St Michael's College, Tenbury and Its Founder*, Eton: David Bland, 2000, p. 89, where the name of the anthem in which Sullivan sang the solo is wrongly given as 'O Praise the Lord of Heaven' by Elvey.

17 H. Sullivan & N. Flower, *Sir Arthur Sullivan*, London: Cassell, 1927, p. 12.

18 Sullivan & Flower, *Sir Arthur Sullivan*, p. 13.

19 *Jackson's Oxford Journal*, 16 December 1854.

20 Quoted in Jacobs, *Arthur Sullivan*, p. 16.

21 Sullivan & Flower, *Sir Arthur Sullivan*, p. 28.

22 *Musical Times*, 1 March 1901, p. 167.

23 *Musical Times*, 1 March 1901, p. 167.

24 Jacobs, *Arthur Sullivan*, p. 12

25 B. W. Findon, *Sir Arthur Sullivan: His Life and Music*, London: James Nisbet, 1904, p. 14. For the significance of Helmore's work in promoting the revival of plainchant, see B. Zon, *The English Plainchant Revival*, Oxford: Oxford University Press, 1999, pp. 254 & 280–91 and Rainbow, *Choral Revival*, pp. 58–94.

26 Jacobs, *Arthur Sullivan*, p. 15.

27 Sullivan & Flower, *Sir Arthur Sullivan*, p. 13.

28 Lawrence, *Sir Arthur Sullivan*, p. 269.

29 Findon, *Sir Arthur Sullivan*, p. 15.

30 PML: Letter to Helmore, 9 April 1882.

31 PML: Letter to Mary Sullivan, November 1875; letter to Helmore, 26 December 1889.

32 W. A. Barrett, *English Church Composers*, London: Sampson, Low, Marston 1882, p. 173.

33 *Musical Times*, 1 December 1900, p. 785.

34 On this friendship, see J. Dibble, *John Stainer: A Life in Music*, Woodbridge: Boydell Press, 2007, pp.15, 35–6, 86, 247, 308.

35 M. Saremba (ed.), *Sullivan Perspektiven*, Essen: Odlib Verlag, 2012, p. 146.

36 Saxe Wyndham, *Arthur Seymour Sullivan*, p. 49.

37 Sullivan & Flower, *Sir Arthur Sullivan*, p. 10.

38 Young, *Sir Arthur Sullivan*, p. 176.

39 *Musical Times*, 1 January 1901, p. 21.

40 Jacobs, *Arthur Sullivan*, p. 21.

41 Lawrence, *Sir Arthur Sullivan*, p. 27.
42 *Musical Times*, 1 February 1901, p. 101.
43 *Musical Times*, 1 January 1901, pp. 22–3.
44 *Musical Times*, 1 February 1901, p. 101.
45 Sullivan & Flower, *Sir Arthur Sullivan*, p. 39.
46 *Musical Times*, 1 February 1901, p. 101.
47 Letter to Mrs Lehmann, 9 January 1863, quoted in Saxe Wyndham, *Arthur Seymour Sullivan*, p. 66.
48 *Daily Telegraph*, 26 November 1900.
49 *Musical Times*, 1 February 1901, p. 101.
50 Lawrence, *Sir Arthur Sullivan*, pp. 57–8.
51 *Musical Times*, 1 January 1901, p. 22.
52 Lawrence, *Sir Arthur Sullivan*, p. 58. According to Byng's recollections, quoted in Young, *Sir Arthur Sullivan*, p. 52, it was he who suggested that Sullivan play 'Will he come?'
53 *Musical Times*, 1 January 1901, p. 23. This contains a misprint of 'first' instead of 'finest' – Saxe Wyndham, *Arthur Seymour Sullivan*, p. 99 prints it correctly.
54 Young, *Sir Arthur Sullivan*, p. 52.
55 *Musical Times*, 1 January 1901, p. 23.
56 *Musical Times*, 1 January 1901, p. 23.
57 C. L. Graves, *Life of Sir George Grove*, London: Macmillan, 1903, p. 127.
58 Saxe Wyndham, *Arthur Seymour Sullivan*, pp. 60–1.
59 Lawrence, *Sir Arthur Sullivan*, p. 98.
60 Jacobs, *Arthur Sullivan*, p. 100.
61 PML: Letter to Mary Sullivan, 27 June 1881.
62 PML: Letter to Mary Sullivan, 25 December 1877.
63 PML: Letter to Mary Sullivan, 23 January 1882,
64 PML: Letter to Mary Sullivan, 5 January 1878.

4 They Only Suffer Dr Watts' Hymns: Hymn Tunes and Arrangements

1 The booklet containing Sullivan's hymn tunes is available from Richard Cockaday, Handel House, 78 Brian Avenue, Norwich, Norfolk, NR1 2PD. Email: richardmusic@hotmail.co.uk.
2 N. Temperley, *The Music of the English Parish Church*, Vol. 1, Cambridge: Cambridge University Press, 1979, p. 314.
3 A. Lawrence, *Sir Arthur Sullivan: Life Story, Letters & Reminiscences*, London: James Bowden, 1899, p. 20.
4 *SASS Journal* 41 (Autumn 1995), p. 23.
5 Temperley, *Music of the English Parish Church*, p. 296.
6 *Musical Times*, July 1902. Percy Young erroneously locates the Clay Ker Seymers' house in Hanford, Staffordshire (P. Young, *Sir Arthur Sullivan*, London: J. M. Dent, 1971, p. 99). Speaking on BBC Radio 4's *Desert Island Discs* on 29 July 2012, Mary Berry, the cookery book editor, claimed that ST GERTRUDE had been written in the summer house in the garden of Sir George Grove's coun-

try house near Bath where she herself was subsequently brought up. I can find nothing to substantiate this claim.

7 *Hymn Tunes Composed by John Stainer*, London: Novello, 1900, p. iv.

8 *Hymn Tunes Composed by John Stainer*, p. iii.

9 G. Roe & A. Hutchings, *J. B. Dykes, Priest and Musician*, Durham: St Oswald's Church, 1976, p. 4; J. T. Fowler, *The Life and Letters of John Bacchus Dykes*, London: John Murray, 1897, p. 199.

10 J. Balls, 'Sullivan's Music and the *Titanic*', *SASS Magazine* 78 (Spring 2012), pp. 11–14.

11 J. B. Dykes, *Hymn Tunes*, London: Novello, n.d., p. vii.

12 Letter to the author, 13 January 1992.

13 A. Jacobs, *Arthur Sullivan: A Victorian Musician*, 2nd edn, Aldershot: Scolar Press, 1992, pp. 74–5.

14 A. S. Sullivan (ed.), *Church Hymns With Tunes*, London: SPCK, 1881, p. iv. On the different churchmanship of the main Victorian hymnals, see L. Benson, *The English Hymn: Its Development and Use in Worship*, Philadelphia: The Presbyterian Board of Publication, 1915, p. 507 and Temperley, *Music*, p.300.

15 Sullivan, *Church Hymns With Tunes*, p. iv.

16 J. Heywood, *Our Church Hymnody*, London: Simpkin, Marshall & Co., 1881, pp. 22–4.

17 I. Bradley, *Abide With Me: The World of Victorian Hymns*, London: SCM Press, 1997, p. 202.

18 Hymns Ancient and Modern Archives, Norwich: Letter from Francis Pott, November 1887.

19 Hymns Ancient and Modern Archives: Letter from John Ellerton, 8 June 1874.

20 PML: Letters from Kipling to Sullivan, 14 May 1898 and 27 May 1900.

21 J. T. Lightwood, *Hymn Tunes and Their Story*, London: Charles Kelly, 1905, p. 207.

22 Bradley, *Abide With Me*, p. 98.

23 *English Hymnal*, London: Oxford University Press, 1906, p. ix. See I. Bradley, 'Vaughan Williams' Chamber of Horrors', in A. Luff (ed.), *Strengthen for Service: 100 Years of the English Hymnal 1906–2006*, Norwich: Canterbury Press, 2005, pp. 231–41.

24 *Guardian*, 31 October 1900, p. 1531.

25 *English Hymnal*, pp. viii & ix.

26 E. Walker, *A History of Music in England*, Oxford: Clarendon Press, 1907, p. 308.

27 C. V. Stanford, *Pages from an Unwritten Diary*, London: Edward Arnold 1914, p. 310.

28 *Bulletin of the Hymn Society of Great Britain and Ireland* (July 1942), p. 6.

29 E. Routley, 'Victorian Hymn-Tune Composers – IV: Arthur Seymour Sullivan', *Bulletin of the Hymn Society of Great Britain and Ireland* 2:7 (July 1949), pp. 104, 105, 106.

30 E. Routley, *The Music of Christian Hymnody*, London: Independent Press, 1957), p. 124.

31 E. Routley, *The Musical Wesleys*, London: Herbert Jenkins, 1968, p. 200.

32 Letter to the author, 3 November 1992.

33 Routley, *Musical Wesleys*, p. 199.

34 Roe & Hutchings, *Dykes*, p. 21.
35 K. Long, *The Music of the English Church*, London: Hodder & Stoughton, 1972, pp. 360, 366.
36 S. Rogal, 'The Hymn Tunes of Arthur Seymour Sullivan', in J. Helyar (ed.), *Gilbert and Sullivan. Papers Presented at the International Conference held at the University of Kansas in May 1970*, Lawrence, KS: University Press of Kansas, 1971, p. 179.
37 Temperley, *Music of the English Parish Church*, p. 303.
38 Temperley, *Music of the English Parish Church*, p. 300.
39 N. Temperley, 'The Music of Dissent', in I. Rivers & D. L. Wykes (eds), *Dissenting Praise: Religious Dissent and the Hymn in England and Wales*, Oxford: Oxford University Press, 2011, p. 225.
40 <http://nethymnal.biz/htm/c/o/s/cospirit.htm>. Accessed November 2011.
41 B. Braley (ed.), *The Hymns and Ballads of Fred Pratt Green*, London: Stainer & Bell, 1982, p. 145.
42 G. E. Buckle (ed.), *Letters of Queen Victoria*, 3rd Series, Vol. III, London: John Murray, 1932, p. 147.
43 Buckle, *Letters of Queen Victoria*, p. 148.
44 PML: Letter from How to Sullivan, Easter Day 1897.
45 PML: Letter from Bigge to Sullivan, 24 April 1897.
46 F. D. How, *Bishop Walsham How: A Memoir*, London: Isbister, 1898, p. 352.
47 How, *Bishop Walsham How*, p. 359.
48 PML: Letter from Sullivan to How, 27 May 1897.
49 J. Richards, *Imperialism and Music, Britain 1876–1953*, Manchester: Manchester University Press, 2001, p. 137.
50 Jacobs, *Arthur Sullivan*, p. 377.
51 Lightwood, *Hymn Tunes and their Story*, p. 311.

5 Ballads, Songs and Snatches: Sacred Ballads and Part-Songs

1 N. Temperley (ed.), *Music in Britain: The Romantic Age 1800–1914*, London: Athlone Press, 1981, p. 131.
2 D. Scott, *The Singing Bourgeois: Songs of the Victorian Drawing Room and Parlour*, 2nd edn, Aldershot: Ashgate, 2001, pp. 141, 142.
3 Maurice Wilson Disher, *Victorian Song: from Dive to Drawing Room*, London: Phoenix House, 1955, p. 141.
4 J. Caldwell, *The Oxford History of Music*, Vol. II, Oxford: Oxford University Press, 1999, p. 271.
5 P. Young, *A History of British Music*, London: Ernest Benn, 1967, p. 72.
6 *SASS Magazine* 47 (Autumn 1998), p. 7.
7 Harold Simpson, *A Century of Ballads 1810–1910: Their Composers and Singers*, London: Mills & Boon, 1911, p. 149.
8 SASS Magazine 41 (Autumn 1995), pp. 25–6.
9 H. N. Fairchild, Religious Trends in English Poetry, Vol. IV, 1830–1880, New York: Columbia University Press, 1957, p. 265.
10 C. Willeby, Masters of English Music, London: James Osgood, 1893, pp. 41–2.
11 A. Lawrence, Sir Arthur Sullivan: Life Story, Letters & Reminiscences, London:

James Bowden, 1899, pp. 116–17; H. Sullivan & N. Flower, Sir Arthur Sullivan, London: Cassell, 1927, p. 82.

12 A. S. Sullivan, *Amy's Book*, ed. J. L. Smith, Escondido, CA: C. D. Smith, 1998, pp. 31–2.

13 Sullivan & Flower, *Sir Arthur Sullivan*, p. 85.

14 Sullivan & Flower, *Sir Arthur Sullivan*, p. 84, assert that 'the first phonograph record ever played in England was that of Mrs Ronalds singing this song, and it was first performed in Sullivan's drawing room'. I have not been able to corroborate this. Certainly, the recording of 'The Lost Chord' played by cornet and piano seems to be the oldest surviving phonographic recording in existence.

15 Sullivan & Flower, *Sir Arthur Sullivan*, p. 83.

16 E. F. Benson, *As We Were*, London: Hogarth Press, 1985, p. 20.

17 *Hymn Society Bulletin* Vol.2, No.7 (July 1949), p. 108.

18 Caldwell, *Oxford History of Music*, p. 276.

19 Temperley, *Music in Britain*, pp. 129, 130.

20 *Elgar Society Journal* 17:4 (April 2012), p. 11.

21 Disher, *Victorian Song*, p. 141.

22 A. Jacobs, *Arthur Sullivan: A Victorian Musician*, 2nd edn, Aldershot: Scolar Press, 1992, pp. 110–11.

23 Sullivan Song Day, Gresham College, London, 24 September 2011.

24 Scott, *Singing Bourgeois*, p. 147.

6 They Sing Choruses in Public: Oratorios and Cantatas

1 N. Burton, 'Oratorios and Cantatas', in N. Temperley (ed.), *Music in Britain: The Romantic Age 1800–1914*, London: Athlone Press, 1981, p. 214.

2 F. Spark & J. Bennett, *History of the Leeds Musical Festivals 1858–1889*, Leeds: Fred Spark & Son, 1892, p. 319; A. Lawrence, *Sir Arthur Sullivan: Life Story, Letters & Reminiscences*, London: James Bowden, 1899, p. 252.

3 R. Silverman, 'Zur Musik von The Prodigal Son', *Deutsche Sullivan Gesellschaft Magazin* Nr.7 (June 2012), p. 9.

4 L. Baily, *The Gilbert and Sullivan Book*, London: Cassell & Company, 1956, p. 94.

5 J. T. Fowler, *Life and Letters of John Bacchus Dykes*, London: John Murray, 1897, p. 125; H. Sullivan & N. Flower, *Sir Arthur Sullivan*, London: Cassell, 1927, p. 62.

6 J. Dibble, *John Stainer: A Life in Music*, Woodbridge: Boydell Press, 2007, p. 114.

7 *Musical Times*, 1 October 1869.

8 Quoted in sleeve notes to *The Prodigal Son* CD, Hyperion, 2003.

9 Temperley, *Music in Britain*, p. 228; *SASS Magazine* 33 (Autumn 1991), p. 3.

10 D. Brown, 'From *Elijah* to *The Kingdom*', in M. Clarke (ed.), *Music and Theology in Nineteenth Century Britain*, Aldershot: Ashgate, 2012, pp. 187–8.

11 R. Silverman, 'Zur Musik von The Prodigal Son', p. 28.

12 Sullivan & Flower, *Sir Arthur Sullivan*, p. 72.

13 M. Ainger, *Gilbert and Sullivan: A Dual Biography*, Oxford: Oxford University Press, 2002, p. 102.

14 J. Maas, *Holman Hunt and the Light of the World*, London: Scolar Press, 1984.
15 *The Times*, 3 September 1873; A. Jacobs, *Arthur Sullivan: A Victorian Musician*, 2nd edn, Aldershot: Scolar Press,1992, p. 78; letter to Davidson, 16 May 1873.
16 I. Bradley, *You've Got to Have a Dream: The Message of the Musical*, London: SCM Press, 2004, p. 126.
17 G. Upton, *The Standard Oratorios*, Chicago: McClurg, 1886, p. 299.
18 P. Young, *Sir Arthur Sullivan*, London: J. M. Dent, 1971, p. 96.
19 *Observer*, 31 August 1873; *Standard* review quoted by A. Lawrence, *Sir Arthur Sullivan: Life Story, Letters & Reminiscences*, London: James Bowden, 1899, p. 101.
20 *The Times*, 3 September 1873.
21 *The Times*, 29 May 1878.
22 H. Orel, *Gilbert and Sullivan: Interviews and Recollections*, Iowa City: University of Iowa Press, 1994, p. 73.
23 Baily, *The Gilbert and Sullivan Book*, p. 117; E. Walker, *A History of Music in England*, Oxford: Clarendon Press, 1907, p. 294.
24 Unpublished typescript, 'The Light of the World – Breaking the Critical Silence (n.d.).
25 <http://gasdisc.oakapplepress.com/sullvocal-lotw2001.htm> (accessed August 2012).
26 Spark & Bennett, *History of the Leeds Musical Festivals*, p. 146.
27 Spark & Bennett, *History of the Leeds Musical Festivals*, p. 146–7.
28 Spark & Bennett, *History of the Leeds Musical Festivals*, p.147.
29 B. Whitworth, 'Literary Re-Appropriations of Latin Liturgical Hymns', Unpublished D. Phil. thesis, University of Oxford, 2010, pp. 101–5.
30 Jacobs, *Arthur Sullivan*, p. 146.
31 Spark & Bennett, *History of the Leeds Musical Festivals*, pp. 199–200.
32 Quoted in S. Tillett, *The Martyr of Antioch*, SASS, 1983.
33 *Daily Telegraph,* 18 October 1880.
34 Young, *Sir Arthur Sullivan*, pp. 218, 221.
35 H. H. Milman, *The Martyr of Antioch: A Dramatic Poem*, London: John Murray, 1822, p. vii.
36 Spark & Bennett, *History of the Leeds Musical Festivals*, p. 200.
37 *Scotsman*, 26 February 1898.
38 Caldwell, *Oxford History of Music*, p. 260.
39 Jacobs, *Arthur Sullivan*, pp. 151–2.
40 Jacobs, *Arthur Sullivan*, p. 151.
41 *Punch*, 23 October 1880.
42 Spark & Bennett, *History of the Leeds Musical Festivals*, p. 216.
43 Spark & Bennett, *History of the Leeds Musical Festivals*, p. 257.
44 Spark & Bennett, *History of the Leeds Musical Festivals*, pp. 292 & 293.
45 Spark & Bennett, *History of the Leeds Musical Festivals*, p. 284.
46 J. Bennett, *Forty Years of Music*, London: Methuen, 1908, p. 78.
47 Jacobs, *Arthur Sullivan*, p. 232.
48 G. Hughes, *The Music of Arthur Sullivan*, London: Macmillan, 1960, p. 66.
49 Spark & Bennett, *History of the Leeds Musical Festivals*, p. 309.
50 Temperley, *Music in Britain*, p. 229.

51 Spark & Bennett, *History of the Leeds Musical Festivals*, p. 309.
52 Orel, *Gilbert and Sullivan*, p. 117.
53 Bennett, *Fifty Years of Music*, p. 86.
54 Jacobs, *Arthur Sullivan*, p. 385.
55 Jacobs, *Arthur Sullivan*, p. 395.
56 *Musical Times*, 1 February 1901, p. 101.
57 J. Dibble, *C. Hubert Parry: His Life and Music*, Oxford: Clarendon Press, 1992, p. 264.
58 Dibble, *Hubert Parry*, p. 265.
59 E. Fenby, *Delius as I Knew Him*, London: George Bell, 1936, p. 124; R. J. Buckley, *Sir Edward Elgar*, London: Bodley Head, 1904, p. 31.
60 Spark & Bennett, *History of the Leeds Musical Festivals*, p. 154.
61 Young, *Sir Arthur Sullivan*, pp. 217–18.
62 D. Russell Hulme, sleeve notes to *Golden Legend* CD, Hyperion, 2001; M. Saremba, ' "… Unconnected with the schools" – Edward Elgar and Arthur Sullivan', *Elgar Society Journal* 17:4 (April 2012), pp. 9–10; Burton, 'Oratorios and Cantatas', pp. 229–30.

7 For All Our Faults, We Love Our Queen: Anthems and Other Liturgical Pieces

1 N. Temperley, *The Music of the English Parish Church*, Vol. 1, Cambridge: Cambridge University Press, 1979, p. 287.
2 P. Horton, 'Beyond the Psalms: The Metamorphosis of the Anthem Text during the Nineteenth Century' in M. Clarke (ed.), *Music and Theology in Nineteenth Century Britain*, Aldershot: Ashgate, 2012, pp. 133–80. It is from this source that I have extrapolated the number of anthems by other composers.
3 *Musical Times*, 1 December 1867, p. 220.
4 J. Dibble, *John Stainer: A Life in Music*, Woodbridge: Boydell Press, 2007, p. 186; P. Young, *Sir Arthur Sullivan*, London: J. M. Dent, 1971, p. 77; N. Temperley (ed.), *Music in Britain: The Romantic Age 1800–1914*, London: Athlone Press, 1981, p. 203.
5 Young, *Sir Arthur Sullivan*, p. 76.
6 Temperley (ed.), *Music in Britain*, p. 203
7 Temperley, *Music of the English Parish Church*, p. 288.
8 A. Jacobs, *Arthur Sullivan: A Victorian Musician*, 2nd edn, Aldershot: Scolar Press, 1992, pp. 164–5.
9 *SASS Magazine* 76 (Summer 2011), p. 21.
10 PML: Letters to Stainer, 4 May 1887.
11 CD issued with *BBC Music Magazine*, Vol. 9, No. 7 (March 2001).
12 *Musical Times*, 1 June 1872, p. 23.
13 B. Taylor, 'Features of Sullivan's Religious Style Found in the Festival Te Deum', *SASS Magazine* 58 (Summer 2004), p. 13.
14 Taylor, 'Features of Sullivan's Religious Style', p. 15.
15 Taylor, 'Features of Sullivan's Religious Style', p. 13.
16 Young, *Sir Arthur Sullivan*, pp. 90–1.
17 K. Long, *The Music of the English Church*, London: Hodder & Stoughton,

1972, p. 366; J. Richards, *Imperialism and Music, Britain 1876–1953*, Manchester: Manchester University Press, 2001, p. 23.

18 Young, *Sir Arthur Sullivan*, p. 91.

19 K. Young, *Chapel,* London: Eyre Methuen, 1972, p. 93.

20 *The Times*, 29 November 1900.

21 *The Times*, 9 June 1902.

22 Quoted in Novello advertisement, *Musical Times*, 1 July 1902, p. 497.

23 R. Silverman, 'The Singularity of the Boer War Te Deum', *SASS Magazine* 50 (Summer 2000), pp. 6–8.

24 B. Taylor, 'Musical Aspects of Sullivan's Boer War Te Deum', *SASS Magazine* 66 (Winter 2007), p. 15.

25 Richards, *Imperialism and Music*, p. 38.

26 Sir Arthur Sullivan: Boer War Te Deum. Full Score and Background Notes, SASS, 2002, p. 4.

27 *Musical Times*, 1 September 1902, p. 598.

8 I Hear the Soft Note: Spiritual Echoes in Sullivan's Secular Works

1 Obituary in the *Birmingham Post* quoted in P. Young, *Sir Arthur Sullivan*, London: J. M. Dent, 1971, pp. 42–3.

2 H. Sullivan & N. Flower, *Sir Arthur Sullivan*, London: Cassell, 1927, p. 51.

3 G. Hughes, *The Music of Arthur Sullivan*, London: Macmillan, 1960, p. 12.

4 S. Tillett, *On Shore and Sea*, SASS pamphlet, n.d., p. 13.

5 J. Richards, *Imperialism and Music, Britain 1876–1953*, Manchester: Manchester University Press, 2001, p. 28.

6 H. Klein, *Thirty Years of Musical Life in London*, London: 1903, p. 336.

7 *Jewish Chronicle*, 6 February 1891.

8 A. Lawrence, *Sir Arthur Sullivan: Life Story, Letters & Reminiscences*, London: James Bowden, 1899, pp. 299–300.

9 Notes for *Ivanhoe* CD, Chandos, 2010, p. 32.

10 'The Book of the Beauty Stone', *SASS Magazine* No. 28 (Spring 1989), p. 15.

11 *The Times*, 30 May 1898.

12 Young, *Sir Arthur Sullivan*, p. 185.

13 A. Jacobs, *Arthur Sullivan: A Victorian Musician*, 2nd edn, Aldershot: Scolar Press,1992, p. 16; Sullivan & Flower, *Sir Arthur Sullivan*, p. 187.

14 B. Taylor, 'Features of Sullivan's Religious Style Found in the Festival Te Deum', *SASS Magazine* 58 (Summer 2004), p. 12.

15 Sullivan & Flower, *Sir Arthur Sullivan*, p. 117.

16 Jacobs, *Arthur Sullivan*, p. 140.

17 Hughes, *Music*, pp. 86–7.

18 I. Bradley, *You've Got to Have a Dream: The Message of the Musical*, London: SCM Press, 2004, p. 46.

19 R. B. Oost, *Gilbert and Sullivan: Class and the Savoy Tradition, 1875–1896*, Farnham: Ashgate, 2009, p. 28; *American Review*, 19 May 1879. On the continuing appeal of G & S to churchgoers see I. Bradley, *Oh Joy! Oh Rapture! The Enduring Phenomenon of Gilbert and Sullivan*, New York: Oxford University Press, 2005, Chapters 5 & 6.

20 Bradley, *You've Got to Have a Dream*, p. 43.

21 For these and other observations on Gilbert's character see my article 'He was an Englishman', *History Today* 61:3 (May 2011), p. 44.

22 Hughes, *Music*, p. 151; Jacobs, *Arthur Sullivan*, pp. 110–11.

23 I develop this argument in my annotation to this song in I. Bradley (ed.) *The Complete Annotated Gilbert and Sullivan*, Oxford: Oxford University Press, 1996, p. 440.

24 N. Burton, 'Opera 1865–1914', in N. Temperley (ed.), *Music in Britain: The Romantic Age 1800–1914*, London: Athlone Press, 1981, p. 339.

9 Conclusion: All Hail, All Hail, Divine Emollient

1 *Daily Telegraph*, 28 November 1900, p. 10.

2 *The Times*, 23 November 1900, p. 8.

3 *The Times*, 24 November 1900, p. 10.

4 H. Sullivan & N. Flower, *Sir Arthur Sullivan*, London: Cassell, 1927, p. 210.

5 A. Lawrence, *Sir Arthur Sullivan: Life Story, Letters & Reminiscences*, London: James Bowden, 1899, p. 299.

6 See I. Bradley 'The Theology of the Victorian Hymn Tune' in M. Clarke (ed.), *Music and Theology in Nineteenth Century Britain*, Aldershot: Ashgate, 2012, pp. 8–11.

7 G. Hughes, *The Music of Arthur Sullivan*, London: Macmillan, 1960, p. 163.

8 H. Orel, *Gilbert and Sullivan: Interviews and Recollections*, Iowa City: University of Iowa Press, 1994, p. 78.

9 Lawrence, *Sir Arthur Sullivan*, p. 261.

10 PML: Letter to O. Goldschidt, 7 November 1887.

11 Lawrence, *Sir Arthur Sullivan*, p. 276.

12 Lawrence, *Sir Arthur Sullivan*, p. 279.

13 M. Coveney, *Cats on a Chandelier*, London: Hutchinson, 1999, p. 261.

14 *Musical Times*, 1 February 1901, p. 100.

15 W McQueen-Pope and D. L Murray, *Fortune's Favourite: the Life and Times of Franz Lehár*, London: Hutchinson, 1953, p. 52.

16 Lawrence, *Sir Arthur Sullivan*, p. 285.

17 C. L. Graves, *Life of Sir George Grove*, London: Macmillan, 1903, p. 434.

18 H. Lytton, *The Secrets of a Savoyard*, London: Jarrolds, n.d., p. 123.

19 H. H. Asquith, *H. H. A.: Letters of the Earl of Oxford and Asquith to a Friend*, Vol. 1, London: Geoffrey Bles, 1933, p. 10.

20 P. Young, *Sir Arthur Sullivan*, London: J. M. Dent, 1971, p. 74.

21 *The Times*, 16 November 1886.

22 I. Bradley, *Oh Joy! Oh Rapture! The Enduring Phenomenon of Gilbert and Sullivan*, New York: Oxford University Press, 2005, p. ix.

23 H. R. Haweis, *Music and Morals*, 14th edn, London: W. H. Allen, n.d., p. 21.

24 G. Roe & A. Hutchings, *J. B. Dykes, Priest and Musician*, Durham: St Oswald's Church, 1976, p. 4.

25 PML: Letter to Mary Sullivan, 1 October 1867.

26 PML: Letter to Mary Sullivan, Christmas Day 1877.

Select Bibliography

M. Ainger, *Gilbert and Sullivan: A Dual Biography*, Oxford: Oxford University Press, 2002.

L. Baily, *The Gilbert and Sullivan Book*, London: Cassell & Company, 1956.

I. Bradley, *Abide With Me: The World of Victorian Hymns*, London: SCM Press, 1997.

I. Bradley, *You've Got to Have a Dream: The Message of the Musical*, London: SCM Press, 2004.

J. Caldwell, *The Oxford History of Music*, Vol. II, Oxford: Oxford University Press, 1999.

M. Clarke (ed.), *Music and Theology in Nineteenth Century Britain*, Aldershot: Ashgate, 2012.

J. Dibble, *C. Hubert Parry: His Life and Music*, Oxford: Clarendon Press, 1992.

J. Dibble, *John Stainer: A Life in Music*, Woodbridge: Boydell Press, 2007.

Maurice Wilson Disher, *Victorian Song: from Dive to Drawing Room*, London: Phoenix House, 1955.

P. Drummond, *The Provincial Music Festival in England, 1784–1914*, Aldershot: Ashgate, 2011.

C. Eatock, *Mendelssohn and Victorian England*, Aldershot: Ashgate, 2001.

D. Eden, *Gilbert and Sullivan: Creative Conflict*, Madison: Farleigh Dickinson University Press, 1986.

H. N. Fairchild, *Religious Trends in English Poetry*, Vol. IV, 1830–1880, New York: Columbia University Press, 1957.

B. W. Findon, *Sir Arthur Sullivan: His Life and Music*, London: James Nisbet, 1904.

R. Gordon-Powell, *Sullivan's Golden Legend*, Retford: SASS, 2012.

C. L. Graves, *Life of Sir George Grove*, London: Macmillan, 1903.

H. R. Haweis, *Music and Morals*, 14th edn, London: W. H. Allen, n.d.

F. Helmore, *Memoir of the Rev Thomas Helmore*, London: J. Masters, 1891.

W. E. Houghton, *The Victorian Frame of Mind*, New Haven: Yale University Press, 1957.

G. Hughes, *The Music of Arthur Sullivan*, London: Macmillan, 1960.

M. Hughes, *The English Musical Renaissance*, 2nd edn, Manchester: Manchester University Press, 2001.

A. Hutchings, *Church Music in the Nineteenth Century*, London: Herbert Jenkins, 1967.

A. Jacobs, *Arthur Sullivan: A Victorian Musician*, 2nd edn, Aldershot: Scolar Press, 1992.

A. Lawrence, *Sir Arthur Sullivan: Life Story, Letters & Reminiscences*, London: James Bowden, 1899.

K. Long, *The Music of the English Church*, London: Hodder & Stoughton, 1972.

H. Orel, *Gilbert and Sullivan: Interviews and Recollections*, Iowa City: University of Iowa Press, 1994.

B. Rainbow, *The Choral Revival in the Anglican Church*, London: Barrie & Jenkins, 1970.

J. Richards, *Imperialism and Music, Britain 1876–1953*, Manchester: Manchester University Press, 2001.

M. Saremba (ed.), *Sullivan Perspektiven*, Essen: Odlib Verlag, 2012.

H. Saxe Wyndham, *Arthur Seymour Sullivan*, London: Kegan Paul, 1926.

F. Spark & J. Bennett, *History of the Leeds Musical Festivals 1858–1889*, Leeds: Fred Spark & Son, 1892.

D. Scott, *The Singing Bourgeois: Songs of the Victorian Drawing Room and Parlour*, 2nd edn, Aldershot: Ashgate, 2001.

H. Sullivan & N. Flower, *Sir Arthur Sullivan*, London: Cassell, 1927.

N. Temperley, *The Music of the English Parish Church*, Vol. 1, Cambridge: Cambridge University Press, 1979.

N. Temperley (ed.), *Music in Britain: The Romantic Age 1800–1914*, London: Athlone Press, 1981.

R. L. Todd, *Mendelssohn: A Life in Music*, Oxford: Oxford University Press, 2005.

E. Walker, *A History of Music in England*, Oxford: Clarendon Press, 1907.

P. Young, *A History of British Music*, London: Ernest Benn, 1967.

P. Young, *Sir Arthur Sullivan*, London: J. M. Dent, 1971.

Select Discography

The Hymn Makers: Arthur Seymour Sullivan – Nearer My God To Thee (Kingsway Music, 2000) includes 13 Sullivan hymn tunes plus ST CLEMENT.

The British Music Collection – Arthur Sullivan (Decca, 2001) includes 'The Lost Chord' and 'Onward, Christian Soldiers'.

20 *Gramophone All-Time Greats* (Academy Sound and Vision, 1993) includes 'The Lost Chord' sung by Dame Clara Butt.

Arthur Sullivan: The Prodigal Son and The Boer War Te Deum (Hyperion, 2003).

Arthur Sullivan: The Light of the World (2000, available from Raymond Walker, 6 Lindow Fold, Wilmslow, Cheshire, SK9 6DT).

Arthur Sullivan: The Martyr of Antioch (Symposium, 2000).

Arthur Sullivan: The Golden Legend (Hyperion, 2001).

Arthur Sullivan: The Masque at Kenilworth (Symposium, 1999) includes the *Boer War Te Deum* and 'The Long Day Closes'.

That Glorious Song of Old (Cantoris, 1992) includes anthems, hymns and items from the *Festival Te Deum* and from oratorios and cantatas sung by the choir of Ely Cathedral.

The Church Music of Arthur Sullivan (Priory, 2000) includes anthems and liturgical items sung by the choir of Keble College, Oxford.

Index